THE LOGIC OF ANALOGY

THE LOGIC OF ANALOGY
AN INTERPRETATION OF ST THOMAS

by

RALPH M. McINERNY

University of Notre Dame

THE HAGUE

MARTINUS NIJHOFF

1961

PRINTED IN THE NETHERLANDS

PREFACE

The need for another study on the doctrine of analogy in the writings of St Thomas may not be obvious, since a complete bibliography in this area would doubtless assume depressing proportions. The present work is felt to be justified because it attempts a full-fledged alternative to the interpretation given in Cajetan's *De nominum analogia*, an interpretation which has provided the framework for subsequent discussions of the question. Recently, it is true, there has been growing dissatisfaction with Cajetan's approach; indeed there have been wholesale attacks on the great commentator who is alleged to have missed the *clef de voûte* of the metaphysics of his master. Applied to our problem, this criticism leads to the view that Cajetan was not metaphysical enough, or that he was metaphysical in the wrong way, in his discussion of the analogy of names. As its title indicates, the present study is not in agreement with Cajetan's contention that the analogy of names is a metaphysical doctrine. It is precisely a logical doctrine in the sense that "logical" has for St Thomas. We have no desire to be associated with attacks on Cajetan, the metaphysician, attacks we feel are quite wrongheaded. If Cajetan must be criticized for his interpretation of the analogy of names, it is imperative that he be criticized for the right reasons. Moreover, criticism of Cajetan in the present study is limited to his views on the analogy of names.

Some readers may be surprised to find the writings of St Thomas treated as a whole in which a consistent doctrine is sought, particularly when some of the knottiest textual problems seemingly could be, if not solved, at least dispelled by chronological considerations. For example, the commentary on the *Sentences* and the *Quaestio disputata de veritate*, early works, contain remarks on the analogy of names difficult to reconcile with the *Summa theologiae*. Given this, one might wish to opt for an evolution of thought and the need for reconciliation would thereby vanish. But the problem cannot be handled in this way. Late writings of St Thomas present essentially the same problems as those found in earlier works. Furthermore, these problems can be solved and the consistency of St Thomas' thought on the analogy of names is not so much an assumption as a conclusion of the research whose fruits are set forth in this study. It should be added that the author has learned not to be surprised by such a conclusion. As has been pointed out by others, the genetic approach lends itself all to easily to the dismissal of difficulties and the avoidance of the philosophical task. St Thomas did change his mind on several points and thought this important enough to bring to his reader's attention. In the matter of the analogy of names, there is no such warning nor is there any evidence that his thought underwent any significant change.

No attempt is made in the chapters which follow to take into account the vast literature on analogy in St Thomas, although a good portion of it has been consulted over the years. As is pointed out at the end of the first chapter, that literature is fundamentally defined by the interpretation of Cajetan; consequently, a questioning of the very source of that literature enables us to postpone the assessment of later modifications, additions and nuances. This is by no means to suggest that the author has come away from his reading of post-Cajetanian writings on analogy unenlightened; far from it. But it seemed preferable, after an initial statement of dissatisfaction with Cajetan on analogy, to make the sequel as pure a textual analysis as possible, with periodic applications of the results to the schema of Cajetan.

One of the more serious contentions of the present work is that St Thomas used the Latin *analogia* in a decidedly different way than Aristotle did the Greek ἀναλογία. Cajetan's failure to take this into account had much to do with his view on what is truly an analogous name. Let it be noted, however, that the difference between St Thomas and Aristotle is a verbal one. The present study is not intended as an indirect contribution to the belief that the philosophy of St Thomas is radically different from that of Aristotle. The observation that St Thomas wrote Latin and Aristotle Greek does not lead to the conclusion that they taught different things, even on the signification of words. But, as we shall see, the attempt to hold Latin authors to the proprieties of Greek usage leads to grave misunderstanding.

The present interpretation was first suggested by M. l'abbé Maurice Dionne, now *doyen* of the *Faculté de philosophie*, Laval University. In developing that suggestion, the author does not wish to share the deficiencies of his efforts with that learned priest, but to indicate one in many ways responsible for whatever merits this book may have. Thanks must also be expressed to Professor Charles DeKoninck, who has a special knack for making students disciples, not of himself, but of St Thomas; to Professors John Oesterle and Joseph Bobik of the University of Notre Dame. To my other colleagues, both at Creighton University and at Notre Dame, and to those students who have endured my enthusiasm for the subject of this book over several years, my sincere gratitude; though they are too many to be named here, I wish them entry in the Book of Life, a somewhat more important volume. This study was completed on a Fulbright Research Fellowship for the year 1959–1960. I dedicate the book to my wife, Constance, who has always lived up to her name both with respect to its *id a quo* and *id ad quod*.

Louvain
March, 1960

TABLE OF CONTENTS

CHAPTER I

THE PROBLEM OF ANALOGY

"Let us start with a review of the theories of other thinkers;
for the proofs of a theory are difficulties for the contrary
theory. Besides, those who have first heard the pleas of our
adversaries will be more likely to credit the assertions we
are going to make."[1]

One does not have to be a student of the writings of St Thomas for very
long before being struck by the importance that analogy seems to have
for his thought. In the commentaries on Aristotle, in the two *Summae*,
in the disputed questions, the matter of analogy comes up soon and in
an obviously important way. Analogy is appealed to to explain our knowledge of prime matter, the unity of the subject of metaphysics and the
way in which names are common to God and creature. But despite
the fact that it seems to pervade his thought, one does not find any
work of St Thomas devoted to analogy. It does not provide the subject of a question, a *lectio* or a *distinctio*. Indeed, one becomes increasingly aware of the fact that when analogy is mentioned, it is most often
the case that knowledge of what it is is assumed, that we are being
presented with an example of it rather than an *ex professo* treatment
of analogy itself.

The thought occurs that, by amassing the texts where analogy is
mentioned and by separating the doctrine on analogy from the example
of analogy under consideration, an intricate and perhaps consistent
treatise could be constructed. It is at this point that thomists for centuries have breathed a sigh of relief. The painstaking work has already been
done, the treatise has been written. One of the most influential works
by a follower of St Thomas is the *De nominum analogia* by Thomas De
Vio Cardinal Cajetan (1468–1534). This treatise, completed on the
first day of September, 1498, when its author was thirty years of age,
is not a long one. In eleven brief chapters, Cajetan, drawn by the difficulty of, as well as by the superficiality of current writings on, the
subject, attempts to give the basic points necessary for an understanding
of the analogy of names. Father Alverez-Menendez, in his preface to
a recent Latin edition of the work, gives some indication of the approval

[1] Aristotle, *On the Heavens*, trans. J. L. Stocks, I, 10. 279b5–9.

with which the opusculum of Cajetan has been met in the thomistic school down to our own times.[2] This is not to say, of course, that no dissenting voices have been heard. In a moment we will see that Sylvester of Ferrara opens the way to disagreement with Cajetan on several points. But it is still true that the majority of dissenters adopts the basic *point d'appui* of Cajetan's work. Suarezians and Scotists have contributed important and illuminating criticisms of the work of Cajetan, questioning that it faithfully reflects the thought of Aristotle and St Thomas. In recent times, there has been a remarkable revival of interest in St Thomas' doctrine on analogy. This revival has involved a fairly general agreement with Cajetan, although some have expanded the criticisms implicit in Sylvester of Ferrara. Presently, Cajetan's opusculum is being treated quite critically. In function of a new and influential interpretation of the metaphysics of St Thomas, Cajetan's authority in general is being questioned. At first proposed as an hypothesis,[3] but now assumed as somehow evident, it is said that Cajetan failed to grasp the very key to thomistic metaphysics. And, although it was Cajetan who insisted that analogy is metaphysical, the Cardinal's inadequate understanding of the metaphysics of his master is said to weaken if not vitiate his interpretation of analogy.

Nevertheless, agreeing or disagreeing, discussions of analogy forever go back to the *De nominum analogia*. One who has studied Cajetan and found him wanting cannot abstract from his opusculum in presenting another interpretation of the texts of St Thomas. And, of course, disagreement with such a one as Cajetan is always accompanied by some measure of agreement. Any interpretation of St Thomas on analogy must profit from Cajetan's work. This is not to say that our own departure from the great commentator is a minor one; indeed, we feel it is most fundamental. One does not take on the drudgery of writing a book to list minor disagreements, or relatively unimportant emendations to a substantially helpful existent work.

What we want to do is outline the basic doctrine of the *De nominum analogia*, considered as a résumé of the thought of St Thomas, and then observe what happens when Cajetan, as commentator, encounters texts of St Thomas which do not seem to coincide with the doctrine of his opusculum. The result of this, we feel, will indicate a serious problem for the student who wants to accept the *De nominum analogia* as a faithful

[2] Cajetan, *Scripta Philosophica: De Analogia Nominum; De Conceptu Entis*, ed. P. N. Zammit, O.P., (revised, P. M. Hering, O.P.; Romae, 1952), pp. xv–xvi.

[3] Cf. Etienne Gilson, "Cajetan et l'existence," *Tijdschrift voor Philosophie*, (June, 1953).

and accurate statement of St Thomas' teaching on analogy. The net effect should be the elucidation of a problem which is, first of all, a textual one, but as well and more importantly, a philosophical problem not restricted to the school in which it is discussed and of such magnitude that it cannot be ignored.

1. CAJETAN ON ANALOGY

(a) De nominum analogia
The term, "analogy," Cajetan begins, as we have received it from the Greeks, means a proportion or a proportionality. From meaning this, the word has been extended so that we now call many names analogous. This extension has led to such an abuse of the term that impossible confusion has resulted, something that can be discovered by attempting to reduce the many meanings of "analogy" to any kind of unity. Cajetan himself proposes a trimembered division which will comprise every use of "analogy" and which will enable him to discuss each type by moving from what is least properly analogy to what is truly analogy. The three-fold division of analogy proposed by Cajetan is: analogy of inequality, analogy of attribution and analogy of proportionality. If we take the term "analogy" in its proper and true sense, only the last type can be called analogy; that such is the case, moreover, is clear from the usage of Aristotle. The first member of the division is said to be totally alien to analogy. Cajetan turns immediately to an analysis of the three kinds of analogy.

Cajetan's procedure is noteworthy. We must not overlook his insistence on the meaning of "analogy" *ut a Graecis accepimus*.[4] This will be a reiterated theme of the book, dictating what is properly analogy. The initial statement that proportionality alone is truly and properly analogy is based on Aristotle's use of the Greek term. Moreover, it is curious that Cajetan should elect to proceed "a minus proprie analogis ad vere analoga."[5] Surely something can be shown to be *minus proprie* only when that which is *vere et proprie* is known. It could be replied to this that Cajetan is simply trying to embrace in one division what *de facto* have been called analogous names. After doing this, he will show what St Thomas really meant by the analogy of names. There are two difficulties with this suggestion. First, it is to St Thomas that appeal will be made to exemplify each member of the division given, that is, three

---

[4] Cajetan, *op. cit.*, n. 2.
[5] *Ibid.*

presumably different uses of "analogy" in the texts of St Thomas are referred to. And one of these, again, is "alienus ab analogia omnino."[6] This leads to the second difficulty. If the *De nominum analogia* is a précis of the doctrine of St Thomas on the analogy of names, and if one of his uses of "analogy" is utterly alien to what the term means, it is more important than ever that we know at the outset what the analogy of names properly is. Once more, what is less properly or utterly alien to analogy can be shown to be such only when we know what analogy is. One is reminded of the Socrates of the *Theaetetus* who, when he asks what knowledge is, does not want to be told its kinds, or to be given examples of it, but wants to be told what it is of which these are kinds or examples. To this it might be said: you have to realize that "analogy" is not a univocal term. Analogy is analogous. Perhaps, but such a remark only increases the difficulty – unless one already knows what analogy is. For to be told that analogy is analogous when one has asked what analogy is, is – to heighten the mystery – analogous to the unfruitful infinity created by barbershop mirrors. This may seem mere cavilling. Read on, it might be urged. Perhaps the procedure is not the best, but its seeming deficiencies will be excused when more is seen of the difficulties of the subject. A good beginning may be half the journey, but one is a better judge of the route taken after the destination has been reached.

(1) Analogy of Inequality
The definition Cajetan gives of this type of analogy imitates the definitions with which the *Categories* of Aristotle begins. Indeed, it was when he was commenting on the definition of equivocals given by Aristotle that Cajetan promised to write the work under consideration.[7] "Analoga secundum inaequalitatem vocantur quorum nomen est commune, et ratio secundum illud nomen est omnino eadem, inaequaliter tamen participata."[8] The example given, together with the phrase used to describe this type, is taken from St Thomas (*I Sent.*, d. 19, q. 5, a. 2, ad 1). The term "body" is common to celestial and terrestial bodies and the notion signified by the name is the same when applied to either insofar as they are bodies. Things named in this way are said, by the logician, to be named univocally, although the philosopher would say that they are named equivocally. The reason for the disagreement is

---

[6] *Ibid.*, n. 3.
[7] Cajetan, *Scripta Philosophica: Commentaria in Praedicamenta Aristotelis*, ed. M. H. Laurent, O.P., (Romae, 1939), pp. 8–14.
[8] *De analogia nominum, ed. cit.*, n. 4.

that the former considers the intentions of the names, the latter considers natures.[9] Thus Aristotle can say (*Metaphysics*, Book Ten, chapter
ten) that there is nothing univocally common to the corruptible and
incorruptible, because he is ignoring the unity of the notion or concept.
So too he will warn that the genus conceals a multitude of equivocations
(*Physics*, Book Seven, chapter four), since the generic concept is not of
a nature absolutely one. Thanks to this, every genus can be called analogous,[10] although we usually reserve the designation for those which are
supreme genera or nearly so.

In calling this analogy "secundum esse tantum," St Thomas points
out that the analogates are made equal *(parificantur)* in the notion signified by the common name, but not in the "esse illius rationis."[11] The
generic notion always exists more perfectly in one species than in the
other, which is why Averroes can say that there is priority and posteriority among things which fall under the same genus. Cajetan adds this
enigmatic observation:

Haec pro tanto analoga vocantur, quia considerata inaequali perfectione inferiorum,
per prius et posterius ordine perfectionis de illis dicitur illud nomen commune. Et
iam in usum venit, ut quasi synonyme dicamus aliquid dici analogice et dici per
prius et posterius. Abusio tamen vocabulorum haec est; quoniam dici per prius et
posterius superius est ad dici analogice.[12]

The reason that analogy of inequality is called analogy is the inequality
of the *esse* of the common notion signified by a univocal name, an order
per prius et posterius. It has become a matter of usage to take as synonymous
what is said unequally *per prius et posterius* and what is said analogously.
Although a matter of usage, even on the part of St Thomas, apparently,
this is really an abuse of terms, that is, contrary to usage. What is true
is that *dici per prius et posterius* is more common than *dici analogice*.

Notice that this constitutes Cajetan's first statement on analogous
names: such names are instances of *dici per prius et posterius*. A generic name
is only abusively an analogous name. Why? Though it may appear to
be an instance of *dici per prius et posterius*, the logician will deny that it
is really so. For him, it is a univocal name. This leads us to expect that
it is for some logical reason that the generic name is a univocal one and
that if it were really an analogous name, the logician could tell us why.
We will see that this is a suggestion Cajetan seemingly does not wish to
make. Thus far one thing seems quite clear. A treatise on the analogy

[9] *Ibid.*, n. 5.
[10] *Ibid.*
[11] *Ibid.*, n. 6.
[12] *Ibid.*, n. 7.

of names, presumably as St Thomas understood and taught this doctrine, is ill begun by discussing a name that is univocal and yet somehow is said to involve an analogy if "analogy" is taken abusively. It must be remembered that it is St Thomas who has used the phrase *analogia secundum esse* – the context in which it is found presents many problems, but the problems cannot even be meaningfully formulated by beginning in the way Cajetan has.

(2) Analogy of Attribution

Again Cajetan begins with a definition imitating those of the *Categories*. "Analoga autem secundum attributionem sunt quorum nomen commune est, ratio autem secundum illud nomen est eadem secundum terminum, et diversa secundum habitudines ad illum."[13] The example given is one often used by Aristotle and St Thomas. "Healthy" is a name common to medicine, urine and animal. The notion signified by "healthy" as applied to each of them implies different relations to one term: "...ratio omnium in quantum sana sunt, ad unum terminum (sanitatem scilicet), diversas dicit habitudines."[14] If one asks what is meant by calling an animal healthy, the reply is: he is the subject of health; so too, urine is a sign of health, medicine is a cause of health. "Ubi clare patet, rationem sani esse nec omnino eamdem, nec omnino diversam, sed eamdem secundum quid, et diversam secundum quid. Est enim diversitas habitudinum, et identitas termini illarum habitudinum."[15]

This analogy can come about in four ways according to the four species of cause. Things can be related diversely according to a denomination from or attribution to one end, one efficient cause, one exemplar or one subject. Cajetan's references are to the Fourth Book of the *Metaphysics*, chapter one; the Third Book of the same work, chapter two; and the First Book of the *Nicomachean Ethics*, chapter seven. There follow four conditions of this type of analogy.

First, it is according to extrinsic denomination alone. The first analogate formally is what the name signifies and the others are denominated such extrinsically: "ita quod primum analogatorum tantum est tale formaliter, caetera autem denominantur talia extrinsice."[16] The animal is healthy formally, whereas urine, medicine and the rest are denominated healthy, not from any health inherent in them, but extrinsically from

---

[13] *Ibid.*, n. 8.
[14] *Ibid.*
[15] *Ibid.*
[16] *Ibid.*, n. 10.

the health of the animal insofar as they signify it, cause it, etc. So too with "medical" and with "good." Cajetan adds a cautionary note.

Sed diligenter advertendum est, quod haec huiusmodi analogiae conditio, scilicet quod non sit secundum genus causae formalis inhaerentis, sed semper secundum aliquid extrinsecum, est formaliter intelligenda et non materialiter: idest non est intelligendum per hoc, quod omne nomen quod est analogum per attributionem, sit commune analogatis sic, quod primo tantum conveniat formaliter, caeteris autem extrinseca denominatione, ut de sano et medicinali accidit; ista enim universalis est falsa, ut patet de ente et bono, nec potest haberi ex dictis, nisi materialiter intellectis. Sed est ex hoc intelligendum, quod omne nomen per attributionem ut sic, vel in quantum sic analogum, commune est analogatis sic, quod primo convenit formaliter, reliquis autem extrinseca denominatione.[17]

This is an extremely puzzling addendum. We have been given to understand that only the first analogate of many formally is what the name signifies; the others are named such by extrinsic denomination and not because they formally are what the name signifies. We are then told that this must be understood formally and not materially. A material understanding of the rule would be that in analogy of attribution what is common "primo tantum conveniat formaliter, caeteris autem extrinseca denominatione." But this is simply a reiteration of the rule. The rule, we are reminded, was exemplified by "healthy" and "medical" and it is true of them, but only accidentally *(accidit)*. Cajetan does not want us to believe that what "being" or "good" signify exists only in that of which these words are primarily said, that only the primary analogate of these words has the perfection *formaliter*. So the rule must be understood formally if it is to apply to "being" and "good," but what is the formal understanding of the rule? Strangely enough, it appears to be identical with the material understanding which, in turn, is identical with the rule. "Sed est ex hoc intelligendum, quod omne nomen per attributionem, ut sic, vel in quantum sic analogum, commune est analogatis sic, quod primo convenit formaliter, reliquis autem extrinseca denominatione." The additions of *sic, ut sic* lead to the following understanding. As named by an analogy of attribution, the secondary analogates are not signified as possessing by an inherent form what the name signifies, but we cannot infer from this that they could not receive the same name and be denominated from an inherent form. It is in terms of the latter possibility that Cajetan wants to distinguish "good" and "being" from "healthy" and "medical." Let us consider Cajetan's discussion of the first two words.

Being, we are told, belongs formally *(formaliter)* to all substances, accidents, etc.; however, insofar as they are beings they are all said to

[17] *Ibid.*, n. 11.

be such with reference to what is being *subiective* and thus only substance is being *formaliter*. Other things are said to be being because they are "entis passiones vel generationes, etc. licet entia formaliter alia ratione dici possint."[18] Far from clarifying the issue, this obscures it more. Accidents are being *formaliter*. Obviously this will be indicated by applying the term "being" to them. But, insofar as accidents are named "being" they are referred to substance and only substance is being *formaliter*. Nevertheless, accidents can be said to be beings *formaliter alia ratione*. Does *alia ratione* mean for another reason, or according to another notion signified by "being" thanks to which accidents are not referred to substance? If the first, it is difficult to imagine what the reason would be. Actually, it is not unlikely that Cajetan thinks "being" can signify a common notion in which accidents can participate without reference to substance.[19] But for an accident to be, *formaliter*, is for it to be in substance; only in this way is it named "being"; only in this way can it be.

Cajetan's discussion of "good" gets him on more solid ground in the texts of St Thomas, as we will see later.

Licet enim omnia entia bona sint, bonitatibus sibi formaliter inhaerentibus, in quantum tamen bona dicuntur, bonitate prima effective aut finaliter aut exemplariter, omnia alia nonnisi extrinseca denominatione bona dicuntur: illamet bonitate, qua Deus ipse bonus formaliter in se est.[20]

Things are good, and formally so, by a goodness inherent in them, but when they share the name "good" with God, it is not the goodness formally in them that is named, but they are named by an extrinsic denomination from God who is formally good in Himself. Something can be called good without knowledge that God exists; when God is known to exist and to be good and to be the cause of goodness in creatures, creatures can be denominated good from God. This appeal to something outside themselves to name them good does not mean that they cannot be named good from something intrinsic to them.

The more one considers this rule and Cajetan's discussion of it, the more one thing becomes clear, namely that the rule is irrelevant to the analogy of names. Several things receive a common name in such a way that some of them are denominated such-and-such by reference to one of the things so named. That from which they are denominated is the primary analogate; they themselves are secondary analogates. Now it sometimes happens (Cajetan's word) that the secondary analo-

---

[18] *Ibid.*
[19] Cf. *ibid.*, nn. 40, 77.
[20] *Ibid.*, n. 11.

gates cannot receive the name because of an inherent form; but it also happens that secondary analogates do receive the name thanks to an inherent form. Therefore, simply by taking Cajetan's words for it, we can conclude that remarks about inherent forms and intrinsic possession are accidental to what he presumably is talking about. We will see later that Cajetan is led up this byway by two things: first, by certain remarks of St Thomas on the divine names; secondly, by his own misinterpretation of *Ia*, q. 16, a. 6.

The second rule of the analogy of attribution is that the one in which the diverse relations terminate is *unum numero*. Cajetan makes a distinction between "numerically one" considered universally and particularly. When we are speaking universally of animal, diet and urine, the phrase should be understood negatively. "Non enim numeratur sanitas in animali, urina et diaeta, quoniam non est alia sanitas in urina, et alia in animali, et alia in diaeta."[21] Cajetan obviously has in mind the text of *In IV Metaphys.*, lect. 1, n. 536. He explicates "...non quidem quod sit solum ratione unum, sed quod est unum sicut una quaedam natura" with reference to univocation, as St Thomas himself does. Here is Cajetan's understanding of the comparison of things named univocally and things named analogically. "Et sequitur ista conditio ex praecedenti: quoniam commune secundum denominationem extrinsecam non numerat id a quo denominatio sumitur in suis analogatis, sicut univocum multiplicatur in suis univocatis; et propter hoc dicitur unum ratione tantum, et non unum numero in suis univocatis. Alia est enim animalitas hominis, et alia equi, et alia bovis, *animalis* nomine adunatae in una ratione."[22]

The third condition of analogy of attribution follows from the others. It is this: the first analogate from which the others are denominated must be placed in the definition of the others insofar as they are signified by the common name: quoniam caetera non suscipiunt illud nomen, nisi per attributionem ad primum in quo formaliter salvatur eius ratio."[23]

The fourth condition is that there is neither an objective nor formal concept which can be abstracted from the concepts of the analogates: "sed sola vox cum identitate termini diversimode respecti communis est: vox scilicet, terminus et respectus diversi ad illum; nomen analogum terminum quidem distincte significat, ut sanum sanitatem; respectus autem diversos ita indeterminate et confuse importat, ut primum dis-

---

[21] *Ibid.*, n. 12.
[22] *Ibid.*, n. 13.
[23] *Ibid.*, n. 14.

tincte vel quasi distincte ostendat, caeteros autem confuse, et per reduc-
tionem ad primum."[14] A name common by analogy of attribution distinctly signifies that from which the name is imposed to signify (e.g.
health); it signifies distinctly or quasi distinctly the primary analogate
(e.g. healthy animal) and only confusedly the secondary analogates.
There is nothing superior to all the analogates which could be signified
by the name. This is indicated by the fact that, if used alone, it stands
for the primary analogate.[25]

Cajetan says that St Thomas divided analogy of attribution into
analogia duorum ad tertium and *analogia unius ad alterum*.[26] It doesn't matter
in which species of cause the primary analogate may fall; this division
of analogy of attribution can be had in any case.[27]

The logician calls this kind of analogy equivocation, something clear
from the opening of the *Categories*. The example of *animal verum* and
animal pictum given there is an analogy of attribution. The Greek philosophers call analogy of attribution names which are *ex uno, ad unum*
or *in uno* and say that they are midway between pure equivocation and
univocation. However, as is evident from the First Book of the *Ethics*,
such names are distinguished from analogous names. Latin writers call
such names analogous or *aequivoca a consilio*.[28] With respect to St Thomas,
it can be said that he designates analogy of attribution by the phrase
"secundum intentionem et non secundum esse." He does this "eo quod
nomen analogum non sit hic commune secundum esse, idest formaliter;
sed secundum intentionem, idest secundum denominationem." *Formaliter* here seems clearly to mean "exists in" which according to the first
rule is and is not what is meant by analogy of attribution. Should this
kind of name be called analogous? "Haec ideo apud Latinos analoga
dicuntur: quia proportiones diversae ad unum dicunt, extenso proportionis nomine ad omnem habitudinem. Abusiva tamen locutio haec
est, quamvis longe minor quam prima."[29] One can see that it is to Greek
usage that appeal is made to determine correct usage in Latin. The
Greek term was said at the outset[30] to signify a proportion or proportionality. Since it is by an extension of the term, abuse though it be,
that attribution is called an analogy, it is less improperly so called than
is analogy of inequality. Aside from holding Latin authors to Greek

[24] *Ibid.*, n. 15.
[25] *Ibid.*, n. 16.
[26] *Ibid.*, n. 17.
[27] *Ibid.*, n. 18.
[28] *Ibid.*, n. 20.
[29] *Ibid.*, n. 21.
[30] *Ibid.*, n. 2.

usage, Cajetan's procedure is curious on the level of Greek alone. In the latter language, it is only by an extension of its meaning that ἀναλογία can be used in other than mathematical discussions. Why is not such usage abusive? Doubtless because it became a matter of usage. Apart then from other considerations, it seems odd to berate Latin authors for abuse of terminology while at the same time admitting that the Greek term had been extended to include non-mathematical relations. This is not our main point of contention, however. That will turn on the way Cajetan's division of the analogy of names, and the restriction of what is given in rules two and three to what he calls analogy of attribution, relate to the texts of St Thomas. But let us turn to what Cajetan feels is truly and properly analogy.

(3) Analogy of Proportionality

"Dicimus analoga secundum proportionalitatem dici, quorum nomen est commune et ratio secundum illud nomen est proportionaliter eadem. Vel sic: analoga secundum proportionalitatem dicuntur, quorum nomen commune est, et ratio secundum illud nomen est similis secundum proportionem."[31] For example, to see by corporeal vision and to see intellectually are two uses of "to see"; they share the common name because, as understanding presents something to the mind, so seeing presents something to the animal. "Proportion" signifies a determinate relation of one quantity to another: the proportion of 4 to 2 is double. Proportionality is the similarity of two proportions: 8 to 4 and 6 to 3 are similar in that both are doubles. "Transtulerunt tamen Philosophi proportionis nomen ad omnem habitudinem conformitatis, commensurationis, capacitatis, etc."[32] Thus, "proportionality" has been extended to signify any similarity of relations and it is in this extended meaning of the term that Cajetan wants us to understand his use of it in discussing analogy of proportionality.

This analogy can be of two kinds, metaphorical and proper. *Metaphorical analogy* is had "quando nomen illud commune absolute unam habet rationem formalem, quae in uno analogatorum salvatur, et per metaphoram de alio dicitur."[33] Metaphorical proportionality sounds a good deal like Cajetan's analogy of attribution. The difference, for the moment, can be said to lie in a similarity of proportions, on the part of metaphor, as opposed to a proportion of one thing to another. "Ut

---

[31] *Ibid.*, n. 23.
[32] *Ibid.*, n. 24.
[33] *Ibid.*, n. 25.

ridere unam secundum se rationem habet, analogum tamen metaphorice est vero risui, et prato virenti aut fortunae successui; sic enim
significamus haec se habere, quemadmodum homo ridens."[34]

Proper proportionality is had "quando nomen illud commune in utroque
analogatorum absque metaphoris dicitur: ut principium in corde respectu animalis, et in fundamento respectu domus salvatur."[35] This is
analogy *par excellence* for two reasons. First, "quia haec fit secundum
genus causae formalis inhaerentis: quoniam praedicat ea, quae singulis
inhaerent."[36] Secondly, from the point of view of the word "analogy":
"quia analoga nomina apud Graecos (a quibus vocabulum habuimus)
haec tantum dicuntur."[37] Aristotle's use of the Greek term is cited. "Et
quod plus est, in I *Ethic.*, cap. 7 distinguit nomina *ad unum* aut *ex uno*
contra analoga; dum, loquens de communitate boni ad ea quae bona
dicuntur, ait: 'Non assimilantur a casu aequivocis, sed certe ei quod
est ab uno esse, vel ad unum omnia contendere, vel magis secundum
analogiam.' Et subdens exemplum analogiae dicit: 'Sicut enim in corpore visus, in anima intellectus.' In quibus verbis diligenti lectori, non
solum nomen analogiae hoc, quod diximus, sonare docuit; sed prae-
ferendum esse in praedicationibus metaphysicis hanc insinuavit analogiam (in ly *magis*) ut S Thomas ibidem propter supra dictam rationem
optime exponit."[38] By means of the analogy of proper proportionality
we can know the intrinsic being, truth and goodness of things, something
the other types of analogy cannot enable us to do. "Unde sine huius
analogiae notitia, processus metaphysicales absque arte dicuntur."[39] Ignorance of it is compared with ignorance of logic. It is the analogy of
proper proportionality, Cajetan states,[40] that St Thomas designates by
the phrase "secundum intentionem et secundum esse" since things
named analogously in this way are not made equal *(parificantur)* in a
common notion nor in the *esse illius rationis*. Moreover, they participate
both in the common notion and in the being of this notion.

Analogy of proper proportionality, then, is what is truly and properly
analogy. This is said to be true, not only on the basis of Greek usage,
but as well on the basis of the practise of St Thomas. What is more,
this analogy is metaphysical.

The task of the present study is not to determine how faithfully

---

[34] *Ibid.*
[35] *Ibid.*, n. 26.
[36] *Ibid.*, n. 27.
[37] *Ibid.*, n. 28.
[38] *Ibid.*
[39] *Ibid.*, n. 29.
[40] *Ibid.*, n. 30.

Cajetan may be following Aristotle's usage of the Greek equivalent of "analogy." Rather, we want to ask how his division of the analogy ot names and his statements about the members of this division enable him to interpret the texts of St Thomas. Cajetan refers his reader to a number of texts in the writings of St Thomas; one text in particular suggested to him the threefold division of analogy. But there are many texts which treat the analogy of names in a way that calls into question Cajetan's opusculum considered as a statement of St Thomas' doctrine on the subject. As it happens, in the *Summa theologiae*, on which Cajetan is justly considered *the* commentator, there are several important statements concerning the analogy of names. Let us look at the way in which Cajetan deals with them.

(b) The Commentary on 'Summa Theologiae'

As has been mentioned before, Cajetan wrote the *De nominum analogia* while yet a young man. It was somewhat later that he wrote his commentary on the *Summa*. Now the nature of the opusculum is such that it introduces an alien factor into Cajetan's commentary. In reading Cajetan the commentator, one becomes increasingly aware that the neat division of his opusculum intrudes itself between him and the text. Indeed, as will be shown in a moment, Cajetan becomes, on the matter of analogy, not so much a commentator who wants to understand the text before him, as an author who sees the text in the light of his own independent work.

In question thirteen of the *Prima pars*, St Thomas is discussing the divine names. It is one of the most important sources for his views on the analogy of names, since it is a prolonged and profound discussion of names which are necessarily analogous. In the course of the question, St Thomas makes some universal statements about analogous names. Thus, in article five, which asks whether names common to God and creature are said univocally of both, St Thomas, having pointed out that such names can be neither univocal nor purely equivocal, concludes that they must be analogous, that is, said according to a proportion. He then adds this about names which are said *secundum analogiam, idest proportionem*.

Quod quidem dupliciter contingit in nominibus: vel quia multa habent proportionem ad unum, sicut *sanum* dicitur de medicina et urina, inquantum utrumque habent proportionem ad sanitatem animalis. Cuius hoc quidem signum est, illud vero causa; vel ex eo quod unum habet proportionem ad alterum, sicut *sanum* dicitur de medicina et animali, inquantum medicina est causa sanitatis quae est in animali.[41]

[41] *Ia*, q. 13, a. 5. For our mode of reference to the texts of St Thomas, see below, Appendix.

It is in the second way that names are said analogously of God and creature. For centuries this passage has been read as if St Thomas were speaking about Cajetan's "analogy of attribution." It is not surprising that Cajetan himself reads it this way. In number XIV of his commentary, he observes that "being" and "healthy" are analogous in different ways, one by extrinsic denomination, the other not.

Sed in hoc tenet similitudo, quod utrobique est analogia ratione ordinis duorum inter se, quamvis dissimiliter hic et ibi. Nam inter Deum et creaturam est similitudo formalis imitativa (quae etiam in littera tangitur, dum creaturas ordinari in Deum dicitur ut causam, in qua praeexistunt perfectiones omnes) : inter animal vero sanum et urina non est similitudo, sed relatio significationis. Et propterea ibi est analogica communitas secundum praedicationem formalem: hic autem proprie est communitas attributionis ad unum secundum praedicationem quamcumque, sive extrinsece sive intrinsece, etc.[42]

Cajetan refers his reader (for the third time in this article) to the *De nominum analogia*. It seems that the reference is to the chapter on analogy of attribution. It will be recalled that the division into *multa ad unum* and *unius ad alterum* was there given as a division of the analogy of attribution. And this is the beginning of the difficulty. According to Cajetan, analogy of attribution is not truly and properly the analogy of names. But in the fifth article of question thirteen, *Prima pars*, St Thomas is clearly talking about the analogy of names. Moreover, as Cajetan observes at the outset of his commentary, before discussing the analogy of names St Thomas discusses univocity and equivocity precisely as these are treated in the *Categories*. "In titulo, ly *univoce* sumitur ut in *Praedicamentis* definiuntur univoca: nec oportet addere aut minuere, ut etiam in fine huius articuli dicitur."[43] If then St Thomas is speaking *proprie et formaliter* of equivocation and univocation, we should expect him to speak in the same way of the analogy of names and to give rules of it which pertain to it *formaliter et ut sic*. But Cajetan has assigned the division in the text to an analogy described in his opsuculum as *minus proprie*.

In the sixth article of the same question, St Thomas asks whether names common to God and creature are said first of God or first of creatures. He begins by saying that "...in omnibus nominibus quae de pluribus analogice dicuntur, necesse est quod omnia dicantur per respectum ad unum: et ideo illud unum oportet quod ponatur in definitione omnium."[44] In commenting on this, Cajetan raises a twofold doubt.

---

[42] Cajetan, *In Iam*, q. 13, a. 5, n. XIV.
[43] *Ibid.*, n. I.
[44] *Ia*, q. 13, a. 6.

The first difficulty is textual, since elsewhere[45] St Thomas seems to indicate that the second part of the rule, with respect to definition, is not universal. Indeed, he appears to exclude it from the divine names which are just what is under consideration in the text before us. The second difficulty has to do with the first part of the rule, reference to one. It would seem that creatures are not called wise with reference to God, nor God called wise with reference to creatures. Moreover, divine wisdom is not included in the *ratio* of human wisdom, nor vice versa.[46] Here is Cajetan's solution.

Ad hoc breviter dicitur, quod analoga inveniuntur duobus modis. Quaedam enim significant *ipsos respectus* ad primum analogatum, ut patet de *sano*. Quaedam vero significant *fundamenta* tantum illorum respectuum; ut communiter invenitur in omnibus vere analogis, proprie et formaliter salvatis in omnibus analogatis. Propositio ergo illa universalis in antecedente assumpta, intelligenda est universaliter in primo modo analogiae: ita quod sensus est, quod in omnibus nominibus quae de pluribus analogice, idest secundum diversos respectus, dicuntur, oportet poni unum. In quaestione autem *de Veritate*, de secundo modo analogiae dixit oppositum. Et haec responsio est universalior ea quam alibi assignavimus, ex *Qu. de Ver.*, quia ista responsio habet locum etiam in analogis secundum proportionalitatem, metaphorice tamen dictis: in his etiam unum ponitur in ratione alterius, propter praedictam causam.[47]

The text from the *De veritate* does propose, as Cajetan puts it, "dubium non dissimulandum,"[48] but it is questionable whether Cajetan has adequately resolved it. It is clear that he is invoking here his distinction between analogy of attribution and analogy of proper proportionality. By distinguishing between relations *(respectus)* and the foundations of relations,[49] he finds himself able to interpret the rule of the text as universal, not to the analogy of names but to a kind of analogous name which is not really and truly an analogous name. Moreover, in correction of the stand of his opusculum, he sees the rule as applicable to both attribution and metaphor.

It is curious that Cajetan rejects the rule of the text as applicable to what he feels is properly the analogy of names. St Thomas is speaking precisely of names as Cajetan himself has pointed out: "Adverte hic quod quaestio praesentis litterae non est de rebus, sed de nominibus."[50] Would it be fair to wonder if Cajetan's insistence on *fundamenta* is a matter of things rather than names? It is surely not a consummation devoutly to be wished that St Thomas in speaking generally of the

---

[45] *Q.D. de ver.*, q. 2, a. 11, ad 6.
[46] Cajetan, *In Iam*, q. 13, a. 6, n. III.
[47] *Ibid.*, n. IV.
[48] *Ibid.*, n. III.
[49] Cajetan doubtless has in mind *Q.D. de ver.*, q. 21, a. 4, ad 2.
[50] Cajetan, *In Iam*, q. 13, a. 4, n. IV.

divine names, of modes of signification, should be read as setting forth rules that do not properly pertain, truly and formally pertain, to what he is talking about. Cajetan has, as he could hardly avoid doing, linked the discussion of question thirteen to the logical doctrine of the *Categories*. Without trying to diminish the difficulties raised by the other texts to which Cajetan refers, it can be suggested that a judgment of what is formally and properly and truly of the analogy of names can be decided only with reference to what is proper and formal to the context of that doctrine. This is but a hint at the direction our own interpretation of St Thomas will take. That another direction than Cajetan's is desirable is clear from the way the remarks of St Thomas must be interpreted when the *De nominum analogia* is taken as the measure. For then we must say that when St Thomas is speaking quite formally of things named analogously, as he is in question thirteen, he is not speaking as formally and properly as he might.

There are two other points of interest in Cajetan's commentary on article six. The first has to do with his discussion of the way names common to God and creatures are said *per prius* of God. This cannot be solely because God is the cause of the perfection in creatures, since medicine is the cause of health in the animal and medicine is not the *per prius* of the name "healthy."

Adverte quod, cum dicitur nomina huiusmodi communia prius dici de Deo quantum ad rem significatam, non intelligas hoc materialiter, sed formaliter; ita quod hoc verificari oportet de re formaliter significata. Et ratio assignata in littera complectitur utrumque necessarium ad hoc: scilicet et quod nomen salvatur formaliter; et quod illa ratio formalis est prior secundum rem caeteris: quod probatur, quia est causa caeterarum. Neutrum enim horum seorsus sufficeret ad concludendum nomina prius dici de illo, ut patet inductive: ratio enim *sani* in causa, licet sit prior secundum rem ratione sani in animali, quia tamen ratio sani non formaliter in causa est, posterius de causa dicitur; ratio quoque *boni*, licet sit formaliter in homini, non tamen prius dicitur de eo quam de aliis.[51]

In article six, St Thomas argues that, in names common to God and creature, God is the *per prius* of the name from the point of view of the *res significata* because he is not only the cause of the perfection in creatures but also that of which the perfection can be predicated *essentialiter* or *substantialiter*. For example, God *is* goodness, justice, being, etc. Cajetan finds this most congenial because it seems to agree with his own insistence on *formaliter*. Both God and creature are named good *formaliter;* therefore "good" in this case is more properly an analogous name. Where the perfection is not possessed *formaliter* by the various analogates, the name is less properly analogous and is, it would appear, indistin-

[51] *Ibid.*, a. 6, n. X.

guishable from metaphor. We want to suggest that Cajetan is being misled here because of a special problem which arises in the divine names, misled into making into a distinct type of analogous name what is in fact only a difficult instance of analogy. One sign of this is the impression created that the possession of the perfection *formaliter* constitutes the analogy of names. And yet St Thomas leaves no doubt that a name could be analogously common to God and creature even if it was intended to signify God only *causaliter*. The difference would be that the creature would be the *per prius* of the name in a way he is not when God is intended to be named *substantialiter*. "De aliis autem nominibus, quae non metaphorice dicuntur de Deo, esset etiam eadem ratio, si dicerentur de Deo causaliter..."[52] Notice that on this hypothesis these names do not revert to metaphors. Cajetan, as we have seen, has a tendency to identify what he calls attribution with metaphor. It will be appreciated that if discussions about whether or not the analogates intrinsically possess the perfection signified by the name are incidental to the analogy of names as such, and not merely to what Cajetan calls attribution, the major basis for a distinction between attribution and proportionality will disappear.

Secondly, Cajetan returns to the question as to whether the perfection of the creature is included in the name signifying a divine perfection. The difficulty arises from a remark in article two of question thirteen concerning the meaning of "good" in the statement, "God is good." St Thomas has said this: "id quod bonitatem in creaturis dicimus, emenentius in Deo praeexistit."[53] This would seem to indicate that created goodness enters into the notion signified by "good" as said of God, something which seems to go contrary to another text.[54] Yet another text[55] would seem to suggest that the reverse is true, since the names are said of creatures *in ordine ad Deum*. Cajetan suggests the following resolution.

Ad hoc breviter dicitur quod secundum veritatem, haec nomina dicuntur analogice, idest proportionaliter, et prius de Deo quam aliis: quia, cum in utrisque dicantur formaliter, formalitas tamen in Deo prior est, secundum rem, formalitate illa in aliis. Non tamen est sic prior, ut scilicet definiens est prius definito: sed est prior ut causa exemplaris saltem est prior exemplato. Et propterea, sicut omnia exemplata sunt talia in ordine ad exemplar, sic omnes creaturae dicuntur tales, puta bonae, in ordine ad divinam bonitatem. Et sicut non oportet exemplata significari cum ordine ad exemplar, quamvis illud habeant, ita non oportet bonitatem creaturae significari in ordine ad bonitatem divinam, quamvis, secundum esse, illam semper respeciat ut

[52] *Ia*, q. 13, a. 6.
[53] *Ibid.*, a. 2.
[54] *Q.D. de ver.*, q. 2, a. 11, ad 6.
[55] *Ia*, q. 13, a. 5.

exemplar. – Verba igitur 5 art., et similia, hic non sunt confutata, sed exposita: quod scilicet intelliguntur secundum *esse*, et non secundum *significari*, nisi fundamentaliter, pro quanto rationes formales per ea significatae in creaturis, fundant ordinem ad Deum ut causam.[56]

Cajetan here touches on a problem which occupied Sylvester of Ferrarra at some length and with which we ourselves will have to come to grips later on. If God is the *per prius* of names common to God and creatures, creatures should be denominated from God. And yet we know creatures first and we first apply to them names which later are seen to be applicable to God. Thus, God is named from creatures and in some sense creatures are named from God. But, just as creatures are first named without reference to God, it would seem that God can be named without reference to creatures. The problems, then, are obvious, but we shall insist that they are problems of the *applicability* of a doctrine of the analogy of names previously elaborated and do not call for the constitution of a new type of analogous name.

Before leaving question thirteen, we want to call attention to article ten of that question, an article which does not arrest Cajetan's attention. There St Thomas maintains that the name "God" is analogous as applied to the true God, what is thought to be God and what is called God through participation. "Et sic manifestum est quod alia et alia est significatio nominis, sed una illarum significationum clauditur in significationibus aliis. Unde manifestum est quod analogice dicitur."[57] We can surmise that Cajetan would allow that this is an analogy of attribution, but not properly and truly an analogous name. His reason would be that divine nature is not possessed by the secondary analogates. This whole approach of Cajetan's, that of extrinsic denomination, is based on his understanding of the contention that, in analogous names, the "ratio propria non invenitur nisi in uno," the equivalent of which is found in article six, question sixteen, *Prima pars*.

In the article mentioned, St Thomas asks whether there is but one truth in terms of which everything is true. His reply is that in one way there is but one truth, in another way there are many truths.

Ad cuius evidentiam, sciendum est quod, quando aliquid praedicatur univoce de multis, illud in quolibet eorum secundum propriam rationem invenitur, sicut *animal* in qualibet specie animalis. Sed quando aliquid dicitur analogice de multis, illud invenitur secundum propriam rationem in uno eorum tantum, a quo alia denominantur. Sicut *sanum* dicitur de animali et urina et medicina, non quod sanitas sit nisi in animali tantum, sed a sanitate animalis denominatur medicina sana, inquantum

---

[56] *In Iam*, q. 13, a. 6, n. XII.
[57] *Ia*, q. 13, a. 10.

est illius sanitatis effectiva, et urina, inquantum est illius sanitatis significativa. Et quamvis sanitas non sit in medicina, neque in urina, tamen in utroque est aliquid per quod hoc quidem facit, illud autem significat sanitatem.[58]

St Thomas, on the basis of these remarks, is going on to speak of "true." The *per prius* of the word, that which saves its *ratio propria*, is intellect; the *per posterius* of the word is any thing *in ordine ad Deum*. If we speak of truth as it is in the intellect, *secundum propriam rationem nominis*, there are many truths in many intellects and indeed in the same intellect. If we are speaking of the truth in things, then they are all true by the first truth to which each is similar in its very being. Thus, though there are many forms or essences of things, there is one truth of the divine intellect in terms of which they are all denominated true.

Cajetan raises three difficulties, two with respect to the *per prius*, one with respect to the *per posterius*, of the name "true."

(1) What does it mean to say that the truth in the intellect is many?[59] Either this is not proved, or truth is found univocally in all intellects, at least in all created intellects. But this is false. The proof in the text is in terms of the differences between univocal and analogous names, and multiplicity is shown on the part of univocation, not analogy. Thus, either the point is not proved, or it is proved from univocity and not from analogy, from which it would follow that truth is found univocally in created intellects. Cajetan feels that it is clear from the text that the proof of multiplicity of truths must be from analogy. It cannot be proved from univocity because of the difference of truth in angelic and human intellects.

(2) The second difficulty is this: "Quoniam si analogum in uno tantum secundum propriam rationem salvatur; et ex qu. 13 constat omnia nomina communia Deo et aliis analoga, et consequenter veritatem analogice inveniri in intellectu divino et aliis intellectibus, sequitur quod in multis intellectibus non sunt multae veritates, sed omnes intellectus sunt veri una sola veritate, scilicet intellectus divini. Et e converso, si veritas multiplicatur ad multiplicationem intellectuum verorum, ergo non per prius et posterius dicitur de eis: quia quod per prius et posterius dicitur, in uno tantum formaliter invenitur, ut littera sonat."[60]

(3) With respect to the truth in things *in ordine ad Deum*: either they are named true by intrinsic or extrinsic denomination. "Et si sic, ergo

---

[58] *Ia*, q. 16, a. 6.
[59] *In Iam*, q. 16, a. 6, n. II.
[60] *Ibid.*, n. III.

res aut non sunt verae formaliter, quod est inconveniens, quia una-
quaeque res habet in se propriam veritatem rei, qua dicitur vera, ut
patet de sensu respectu proprii sensibilis. Aut sunt verae utroque modo;
sicut in Qu. *de bono* dictum est quod omnia sunt bona bonitate divina
exemplariter, finaliter et effective et tamen, cum hoc, sunt bonitatibus
propriis formaliter bonae. Et si sic, ergo non sunt verae sola veritate
divina."[61]

That these objections arise out of his own understanding of the analogy of names will be immediately evident. It is also clear that the resolution of these doubts, particularly the second, is dictated by the doctrine of the *De nominum analogia*.

Ad 1; Cajetan distinguishes two aspects of univocal predication: (a)
to be predicated formally of its inferiors, and (b) to be predicated of
them according to a formal *ratio* in every way the same. Its multipli-
cation according to its subjects does not belong to it because of (b) but
because of (a). But (a) is something which can be had in common by
univocals and non-univocals. Thus, the multiplicity is due not to the
fact that a name is univocal, but to the more general truth that "praedicatum formaliter (multiplicatur ad) multiplicationem subiectorum."
And, since truth is formally predicated of all intellects, Cajetan can
allow that truth is multiplied as intellects are, or in one intellect, without
agreeing that "true" is univocal. "Meminit autem littera potius *univoci*
quam *praedicati formaliter*, ut a notioribus traderetur disciplina."[4] We
will reserve comment on this, since its full import emerges in the solution
of the second difficulty.

Ad 2; In replying to the second difficulty, Cajetan must, given the
De nominum analogia, reject the rule stated in the text. This rejection is
far more emphatic here than in the commentary on question thirteen.

Ad secundam vero dubitationem dicitur, quod illa regula de analoga tradita in littera,
non est universalis de omni analogiae modo: imo, proprie loquendo ut patet I Ethic.
nulli analogo convenit, sed convenit nominibus *ad unum vel in uno aut ab uno*, quae nos
abusive vocamus analoga. Veritas autem, si comparetur ad res et intellectus, est nomen
ab uno: quoniam in intellectu solo est veritas, a qua res dicuntur verae. Si vero comparetur ad intellectus inter se, est nomen analogum: nam proportionaliter salvatur,
formaliter tamen, in quolibet intellectu cognoscente verum. Esse ergo nomen aliquod
secundum propriam rationem in uno tantum, est conditio nominum quae sunt *ad unum*,
aut *ab uno*, etc. et non nomen proportionaliter dictorum. Veritas autem, respectu
intellectu divini et aliorum, proportionale nomen est. *Et ideo non sequitur quod in solo
Deo sit.* Iam enim dictum est in solutione primi dubii, quod omni praedicato formaliter
de pluribus convenit plurificari ad plurificationem subiectorum, sive illud sit univo-

[61] *Ibid.*, n. IV.
[62] *Ibid.*, n. V.

cum, ut animal, sive proportionale, ut ens, etc. De huiusmodi autem differentia nominum plene scriptum invenies in tractatu de Analogia nominum.[63]

From this solution, it is abundantly clear that, despite the hesitancy and confusion which attended the first condition of his "analogy of attribution," Cajetan feels that to say that the *ratio propria* of an analogously common name is saved in only one of the things to which it is common is to say that the others can only be denominated such extrinsically. That is why he must say that "true" is not really said analogously of intellect and things. Moreover, Cajetan must then say that the truly analogous name is such that the perfection signified by it is found according to its *ratio propria* in each of the analogates. But this, according to the text before us, is to make analogous names univocal. The distinction Cajetan offers in the answer to the first difficulty has the unintended effect of indicating that his problems are illusory. Everything stems from his understanding of *ratio propria*.[64] He takes the phrase "praedicari secundum rationem propriam" to say something which is not peculiar to univocal names, but common to univocal and truly analogous names. What he takes it to mean is "praedicari formaliter," i.e. to be predicated as intrinsic to that of which it is said. Thus there must be something intrinsic to the secondary analogates in virtue of which they receive the common name. And if this intrinsic base is thought to found the name *formaliter* so that they too save the *ratio propria*, we arrive at Cajetan's position. His position, moreover, is intended to enable him to distinguish between such names as "healthy," on the one hand, and "true" said of the human and divine intellects, on the other. But, as St Thomas says explicitly in the text before us, there is something in medicine and urine thanks to which they are named "healthy" with reference to the healthy animal. So too there is something in things whereby they are named true with reference to God. The point is that "healthy" will not signify the same *ratio* as applied to animal and medicine, nor will "true" applied to things and God, nor will "true" as applied to human and divine intellects. In every one of these examples it is the case that the *ratio propria* of the name is saved in only one of those things of which the common name is said. Despite the difficulties which attend the divine names, their solution does not lead to the position that the *ratio propria* of the common name is saved in God and creatures, for that would make the name univocally common. A good indication that Cajetan is going wrong is had in the necessity he feels to reject clear-cut

[63] *Ibid.*, n. VI.
[64] For another treatment of *ratio propria*, see Cajetan, *In Iam*, q. 13, a. 9, n. VII.

statements about the analogy of names in the text of St Thomas. When St Thomas says something about analogous names, Cajetan tells us the saint is abusing terms. Surely what a commentator should do is determine how an author uses his terms. There is no justification whatsoever in the texts of St Thomas for saying that "healthy" and "true" (said of intellect and things) are only abusively called analogous names. What must be found is an interpretation of St Thomas' doctrine on the analogy of names which does not entail the dismissal of most of what he has to say on the subject. It is not of minor importance that elsewhere St Thomas faces an objection which sounds very much like the solution Cajetan offers in his commentary on article six, question sixteen, *Prima pars*.[65]

Ad 3: This is in function of "licet plures sunt essentiae vel formae rerum, tamen una est veritas, etc." in the text. Things may be called "good" both intrinsically and extrinsically, but they are called "true" only extrinsically. "...verae autem dicuntur extrinseca tantum denominatione, ita quod nulla est in rebus formaliter veritas: sed imitative seu adimpletive respectu intellectus divini et causaliter respectu nostri intellectus speculativi."[66] What Cajetan means by saying that there is no truth in things is that they do not save the *ratio propria* of the word.

In this section, we have tried both to indicate what Cajetan has taught about the analogy of names and to suggest certain difficulties involved in accepting his interpretation of St Thomas. First of all, there is a difficulty involved in accepting his distinction between analogy of attribution and analogy of proper proportionality. This follows from the confusion generated by any attempt to deny the universality of the dictum that "quando aliquid dicitur analogice de multis, illud invenitur secundum propriam rationem in uno eorum tantum, a quo alia denominatur."[67] To deny this is to deny that the name is said *per prius et posterius*: it is not enough to say that God who saves the *ratio propria* of the name is cause of the creature who also saves the *ratio propria*, since this is the case with univocal causes. What is more, Cajetan seems to have no way of distinguishing analogous names from metaphors. The most important difficulty, one which involves the others, is that Cajetan far too readily rejects what to all appearances are formal statements by St Thomas on the analogy of names. Doubtless he felt this was called

---

[65] Cf. *I Sent.*, d. 19, q. 5, a. 2, obj. 1.
[66] *In Iam*, q. 16, a. 6, n..
[67] *Ia*, q. 16, a. 6.

for by other texts, but it is surely evident that the systematization of the *De nominum analogia* is exerting an overwhelming influence on Cajetan when he comments on the *Summa*.

We shall turn now to the examination of another commentator on St Thomas, Sylvester of Ferrara. While at all times feeling the influence of Cajetan, Sylvester continues to let the text before him speak for itself and this leads to a number of statements which paved the way for some measure of disagreement with Cajetan.

2. SYLVESTER OF FERRARA

In commenting on the First Book of the *Summa Contra Gentiles*, chapter thirty-four, which sets out to show that things said of God and creatures are said analogously, Sylvester takes into account other texts of St Thomas as well as the interpretation made of them by Cajetan. Before examining Sylvester's comments, we will first outline the chapter itself.

In the two preceding chapters, St Thomas has argued that nothing can be said univocally of God and creature and that not all names said of God and creature are purely equivocal. There remains the possibility that some things are said of God and creature analogically, and this is what St Thomas wishes to show to be true. He does two things in chapter thirty-four: he proposes a division of things named analogically, and distinguishes the order of priority and posteriority based on the *ratio nominis* from that based on the *res* named. First, the division of things said "analogice: hoc est, secundum ordinem vel respectum ad aliquid unum."

Quod quidem dupliciter contingit. Uno modo, secundum quod multa habent respectum ad aliquid unum: sicut secundum respectum ad unam sanitatem animal dicitur *sanum* ut eius subiectum, medicina ut eius effectivum, cibus ut conservativum, urina ut signum. Alio modo, secundum quod duorum attenditur ordo vel respectus, non ad aliquid tertium, sed ad unum ipsorum: sicut ens de substantia et accidente dicitur secundum quod accidens ad substantiam respectum habet, non secundum quod substantia et accidens ad aliquid tertium referantur.[68]

These two modes of analogous name are presented as exhaustive; consequently, names said analogically of God and creature must represent one of these modes. They are in fact analogous in the second mode, since if they were instances of the first, it would be necessary to posit something prior to God.

Secondly, St Thomas observes that in analogical predication it is

[68] *Summa Contra Gentiles*, I, 34.

sometimes the case that there is the same order according to the name and in reality, although at other times this is not the case. There can be a difference because the order of the name follows the order of knowledge, the name being a sign of what we know. Thus, if what is primary in reality is also what we first know, the same thing can be primary *secundum nominis rationem et secundum rei naturam*. This is the case with things named being: substance is prior to accident in reality, for it is the cause of the latter; it is also prior in knowledge since substance enters into the definition of accident. "Et ideo ens dicitur prius de substantia quam de accidente et secundum rei naturam et secundum nominis rationem."[69] Of course, when what is prior in reality is posterior so far as our knowledge is concerned, the order of the name will not reflect the real order of priority and posteriority: "sicut virtus sanandi quae est in sanativis, prior est naturaliter sanitate quae est in animali, sicut causa effectu; sed quia hanc virtutem per effectum cognoscimus, ideo etiam ex effectu nominamus. Et inde est quod *sanativum* est prius ordine rei, sed animal dicitur per prius *sanum* secundum nominis rationem."[70] Since we name as we know and must move from the things around us as effects to God as their cause, the extension of names originally imposed to signify created perfections to God brings it about that the order of the name is just the reverse of the real order. In reality, God is first, but since he is not first known by us, he cannot be primary in the notion signified by the name.

Sylvester raises three difficulties in commenting on this chapter. (1) First, with respect to St Thomas' denial that the first mode of analogy is applicable to the case in point because this would necessitate positing something prior to God: what kind of priority is envisaged? If priority in reality, the conclusion would not follow, since health, in the example of things called healthy, is not prior in reality; rather it is medicine which is prior in the real order. If priority in the notion signified by the name is meant, it is surely not absurd that in this way something be prior to God. (2) Secondly, the mode here assigned to the divine names seems incompatible with article eleven, question two of the *De veritate* where it is denied that something is said of God and creature because of a similarity or proportion of one to the other. (3) Finally, article five, question three, *Prima pars*, seems to deny that something can be prior to God according to the notion of a name: "Deo nihil est prius nec secundum rem nec secundum intellectum."

[69] *Ibid.*
[70] *Ibid.*

We shall be concerned only with the first two difficulties. Sylvester briefly dismisses the third by pointing out that the meaning of the remark is not that we cannot know something prior to God but that we cannot understand that something is prior to God.

Ad 1: St Thomas is speaking of priority in the real order. Sylvester would have us realize that, in the first mode of analogy, it sometimes happens that, with respect to what is formally and per se signified by the name, only one of the things is denominated intrinsically, whereas the others are denominated extrinsically, thanks only to their reference to it. Sometimes, however, what is formally signified by the name is had by the secondary analogates too, and then there is an intrinsic denomination of them as well. An example of the first is "healthy": health *(sanitas)* is found only in the animal, and he is denominated healthy *(sanum)* intrinsically; medicine and food, on the other hand, are denominated healthy extrinsically, with reference to the health of the animal. The second possibility is exemplified by "being," since what is formally signified by the name formally is in substance, quality and quantity. "In utroque ergo modo verum est quod aliquid est prius secundum rem utroque eorum quae analogice dicuntur in ordine ad tertium."[71] The two modes of which Sylvester speaks are not, of course, the two modes mentioned by St Thomas, but rather a subdivision of the first mode of the text. The upshot of his remarks is that, whatever else might be said of things named analogously in the first mode, it is true that this mode implies that something is prior in reality to the many which are named with reference to another. That is, the statement of St Thomas is true of the first mode whatever examples be adduced with whatever attendant differences *secundum rem*.

Yet Sylvester remains in difficulty with respect to what St Thomas has said of "healthy." His analysis[72] has led to the conclusion that in things named healthy, animal is the *per prius* of the name and is prior *secundum rem*. But, in exemplifying the difference between the order of a name and the order of reality, St Thomas points out that medicine, as cause of the health of the animal, is really prior though named only secondarily by "healthy."[73]

Dicitur quod non loquitur Sanctus Thomas de formali et primo significato *sani*, de quo locuti sumus, sed de materiali, et fundamento respectus ad sanitatem; virtus enim sanativa non significatur formaliter nomine *sani*, sed materialiter. Unde voluit dicere

[71] Sylvester of Ferrara, *In I Contra Gentiles*, cap. 34, n. III.
[72] *Ibid.*, n. IV.
[73] Cf. *ibid.*, n. V.

quod *sanum*, secundum quod dicitur de sanativo, dicitur de re naturaliter priori: virtus enim sanativa est prior sanitate. Sed tamen, quia illa res non significatur formaliter, sed tantum materialiter, tanquam fundamentum respectus ad sanitatem animalis; ideo sanum dictum de animali et sanativo, quantum ad fundamentum unde habet sanativum ut significetur nomine sani per habitudinem ad sanitatem animalis, prius dicitur secundum rem de sanativo quam de animali; quia videlicet virtus sanativa est naturaliter prior sanitate, sicut causa effectu.[74]

With respect to what is formally signified by the name, however, animal is prior *in the real order*, not medicine.

This resolution of Sylvester's is a curious one, and he himself is dissatisfied by it, for he comes at the same problem once more.[75] "Healthy" can be considered analogous in either of two ways, by one of which animal is *per prius secundum rem*, by the other, medicine. (Again the reader must be warned against confusing Sylvester's two modes with the two modes of the chapter he is supposedly commenting.) We can consider "healthy" from the point of view of what is properly and formally signified by the term and thus "non tantum secundum nominis rationem et impositionem, sed etiam secundum rem significatum prius convenit animali quam aliis."[76] What is the second way of considering the example?

Si autem accipiatur tanquam plura primo significans ex parte rei, scilicet et ipsam humorum debitam proportionem, quod est proprium significatum, a qua medicina extrinsice dicitur sana, et sanativum virtutem, secundum quod intrinsice et formaliter, licet improprie, medicina dicitur sana; sic ad secundum analogiae modum pertinet, et prius secundum rem dicitur de medicina quam de animali; licet secundum nominis rationem sit e converso, inquantum prius formavimus conceptum sub quo humorum proportionem significat, quam conceptum sub quo virtutem significat sanativam.[77]

It is quite clear from this that the two modes of analogy Sylvester is speaking of are not those distinguished in the text of St Thomas. "Healthy" could be used to exemplify either the analogy of many things to one, or of one thing to another, and in both cases, medicine would be prior in reality. St Thomas is quite unconcerned with the difficulties Sylvester is raising and has no hesitation in saying that medicine, and not the animal, is prior in the order of reality to animal with respect to "healthy." Sylvester is encountering difficulties precisely because he wants to speak of the *ordo rerum* in terms of the *ordo rationis nominis* while weighting the latter in terms of intrinsic denomination. He wants animal to be first in the real order because it is denominated healthy from an inherent form; the only way he can grudgingly admit that medicine

[74] *Ibid.*
[75] *Ibid.*, n. V, 2.
[76] *Ibid.*
[77] *Ibid.*

is first in the real order is by saying that it too is denominated from an inherent form. What St Thomas is getting at is that the health of the animal, as effect of medicine, is thereby posterior even though medicine is denominated healthy with reference to a quality of the animal, namely a balance of the humors. It takes no scholarly sleuth to see the influence of Cajetan in the difficulties Sylvester is raising.

But Sylvester is not yet done. Obviously aware of the source of his difficulties, he proposes to compare his contention that the "formale et per se significatum nominis analogi aliquando inveniri in uno tantum, aliquando vero in omnibus"[78] with St Thomas' assertion that, in things named analogously, "nomen secundum propriam rationem invenitur in uno tantum, a quo alia denominantur."[79] Reconciliation is to be had by noting that "ratio propria" can be understood in two ways.

Nam per propriam rationem duo possumus intelligere: scilicet rationem sive naturam primo et principaliter importatum, per comparationem ad quam alia dicuntur talia, – haec enim dicitur propria ratio nominis, quod primo et principaliter importatur, et nomen analogum, absolute prolatum, accipitur pro illo significato, ut dicitur I Perihermeneias, lect. 5, sicut nomen entis absolute dictum, accipitur pro substantia aut rationem omnem formaliter per nomen importatum.[80]

St Thomas, Sylvester points out, is using "ratio propria" in the first way in the *Summa Theologiae* and thus his statement is true. Sylvester himself has been using it in the second way, a way he feels is justified by another text of St Thomas[81] according to which formal and proper signification means "exists in" that which is named. The echo of Cajetan becomes even more audible. St Thomas, in the text from the *Prima pars*, is not speaking of analogy "in tota sua communitate et universaliter" but only of those things said *ab uno aut ad unum*, this being sufficient for his purposes there. "Nos autem locuti sumus universaliter de analogo. Si enim universaliter accipiatur, constat quod aliquod invenitur in uno tantum secundum suum formale significatum, aliquod vero in omnibus invenitur."[82]

Thus, although Sylvester's first interpretation of "ratio propria" – which happens to be the correct one – enables St Thomas' statement to be universal and indifferent to "exists in" and "does not exist in," Sylvester ends by preferring the second, incorrect meaning, rendering

[78] *Ibid.*, n. VI.
[79] Either Sylvester is quoting from memory or the editors have put quotation marks around an accurate paraphrase.
[80] *Loc. cit.*, n. VI.
[81] *I Sent.*, d. 19, q. 5, a. 2, ad 1.
[82] Sylvester, *loc. cit.*, n. VI.

St Thomas' statement a partial one. For to call his own disjunctive view the more universal implies, of course, that the second way of understanding "ratio propria" is the correct one.

Ad 2: Sylvester prepares for the statement of his solution by pointing out that much confusion is generated in discussions of analogy because the Greeks use the term in a more narrow way than do the Latins. The Greek use is the *vera analogiae ratio*, however, and St Thomas is said to have it in mind when he says that between God and creature there may be a proportionality but not a proportion, "quae magis dicitur aequivocatio a consilio ab uno aut ad unum, quam analogica significatio."[83] Once more the Cajetanian bias and once more, immediately after, a more independent view. Sylvester cannot ignore the fact that St Thomas holds that God and creature are named analogously because of a relation "unius ad alterum"; he therefore proposes a twofold interpretation of "unius ad alterum," first as distinguished from "multorum ad unum," and secondly as distinguished from analogy of proportionality.[84] In the first way, the phrase is common to proportion and proportionality, that is, either a determinate or indeterminate relation of one thing to another. Thus God and creature involve an analogy "unius ad alterum" because no third thing is prior to them as they receive a common name. Taken in the second way, since there is an infinite distance between them, the common name does not involve the "unius ad alterum" "ita scilicet quod ex uno aliud comprehendi et terminari per intellectum possit."[85] There is, then, no contradiction between the *De veritate* and the text of the *Contra Gentiles* before us.

Sylvester is not finished. In chapter thirty-two of the first book of the *Summa Contra Gentiles*, St Thomas, in speaking of the "analogia Dei ad creaturam," said that it was one "in qua prius ponitur in definitione posterius, sicut substantia in definitione accidentis." But this is elsewhere[86] said to be true of proportion and not of proportionality. Sylvester proposes two solutions of this difficulty, one in the spirit of Cajetan, another more intricate one he feels is better.

First of all, then, it is not necessarily the case that, in a proportionality, what is first is put in the definition of what is secondary. Sylvester warns that he is speaking of names signifying properly and formally both the *prius* and the *posterius* (i.e. denominating both intrinsically) and suggests

    [83] *Ibid.*, n. VII.
    [84] *Ibid.*, n. VII, 2.
    [85] *Ibid.*
    [86] *Q.D. de ver.*, q. 2, a. 11, ad 6.

that all other analogous names are metaphors.[87] The rule[88] that in all things named analogously, the first is placed in the definition of the second, is not universal at all. It can be applied to things related by proportion, like things named being or (by the metaphor?) healthy. As for chapter thirty-two of the first book of the *Contra Gentiles*, St Thomas is making the point that nothing is said of God and creature univocally by appealing to an obvious example of what is said *secundum prius et posterius*, an example of a proportion in which the first happens to be put in the definition of the second. But the divine names involve a proportionality and St Thomas is leaving much unsaid.

A second resolution, one Sylvester feels is closer to the thought of St Thomas, begins by asserting that in every mode of analogy it is true that what is first enters into the definition of the secondary precisely insofar as they are considered as named analogously. There is no difficulty in accepting this when the "ordo secundum rationem nominis" coincides with that "secundum rem." Where these two orders differ, the name imposed to signify that which is posterior in the real order is said of it in two ways, absolutely or analogically. Sylvester distinguishes three steps in naming when the two orders differ. First, what is posterior in reality is considered absolutely and the word is imposed to signify it via that absolute conception of it; then inquiry leads to knowledge of that which is prior in reality and the name is extended to signify it. Finally, seeing the relation of what is posterior in reality to what is prior though named secondarily, we impose the name to signify what is posterior in reality, not absolutely this time, but with reference to what is prior in reality. Take the example of "wisdom." The word is first imposed to signify human wisdom as such, absolutely; when we see that our wisdom proceeds from God's, we extend the term to signify the divine wisdom; finally, it is imposed to signify human wisdom with respect to divine wisdom, its cause and exemplar. According to the first imposition, the primary analogate is not put into the definition of human wisdom, for the latter is named absolutely, univocally, not analogically. "Secundum autem quod analogice sumitur, quod convenit sibi secundum tertium impositionem, perfectio divina ponitur in definitione perfectionis creaturae ut eodem nomine significatur."[89]

This second solution enables Sylvester to save all the texts of St Thomas, even those he has earlier adjudged to be adopting something

---

[87] Sylvester, *loc. cit.*, n. VIII.
[88] Cf. *Ia*, q. 13, a. 6.
[89] Sylvester, *loc. cit.*, n. IX.

less than a universal vantage point. Thus it is true to say, as St Thomas does,[90] that in all things named analogously what is prior enters in the definition of the posterior. So too the statement[91] that whatever is said of God and creature is said insofar as one is ordered to the other is saved. When St Thomas seems to deny this,[92] he only means to stress the infinite distance between God and creature.

Sylvester is drawn in two directions in this commentary. On the one hand, while he will sometimes adopt Cajetan's attitude towards difficult texts, he always retains the commendable desire to honor St Thomas' statements at their face value; on the other hand, he is convinced that Cajetan's opusculum has, in the main, faithfully presented the doctrine of St Thomas on analogous names – to the point of referring his reader to that work for the resolution of any problems he may have left. The result, unfortunately, is hybrid and not a little confusing. Despite the chapter he is commenting, Sylvester continually speaks of two modes of analogy which are not those given by St Thomas. So too, though he faces up to the problem of the "ratio propria," he opts for an understanding of the phrase which has nothing to do with St Thomas' use of it, a preference which can only be explained by the influence of Cajetan. The final conciliation of all the troublesome texts, the highpoint of the commentary, does not erase the memory of what has gone before: it would certainly be wrong to say that Sylvester presents us with a clear alternative to Cajetan's interpretation. Nevertheless, on the points where Sylvester has offered his independent view, a basis is provided for a bifurcation in subsequent interpretations. Yet what we find are not so much different interpretations as different emphases: the basic outlook of Cajetan is retained.

This glance at Cajetan and Sylvester is sufficient to set the stage for our own study; the majority of subsequent interpretations moves within the context of Cajetan's systematization. Where this is less obviously so, even where Cajetan is subjected to severe criticism, Cajetan's elevation of the analogy of names into a metaphysical question is never seriously questioned. We refer the reader to Lyttkens' book for a discussion of some later variations.[93]

To conclude this introductory chapter, we suggest that if, after reading Cajetan, one poses some fundamental questions, he will find

[90] *Ia*, q. 13, aa. 6, 10.
[91] *Ia*, q. 13, a. 5.
[92] *Q.D. de ver.*, q. 2, a. 11, ad 6.
[93] Hampus Lyttkens, *The Analogy between God and the World*, (Uppsala, 1952).

himself rather hard pressed to answer them. For example, what is an analogous name? To what discipline does it belong to answer this question? If there are kinds of analogous name, in terms of what are they distinguished? (Obviously the criteria chosen will follow on our answer to the previous question.) In the following study, we shall try to present the thought of St Thomas on the analogy of names in such a way that the fundamental and basic questions can receive an answer.

CHAPTER II

LOGIC AND ANALOGY

At the beginning of his opusculum, *De nominum analogia*,[1] Cajetan remarks that analogy has great importance for metaphysics, something
which is certainly true, but soon the impression gets fixed that analogical
signification is a metaphysical doctrine. John of St Thomas observes
that there is a logical doctrine of analogy, but feels that in following
Cajetan one is engaged in a metaphysical consideration. Nevertheless,
John stresses something which it is difficult to find in Cajetan and
Sylvester, namely that the doctrine of the analogy of names is a logical
one.

...quia in illo loco 1 p., q. 13 agit de analogia magis dialectice quam metaphysice,
scilicet ut tenet se ex parte nominum, non ex parte rerum (de nominibus Dei ibi
agebat). Sicut autem ad analogiam metaphysice attenditur inaequalitas ex parte
rerum, ita in analogia dialectice considerata attenditur inaequalitas in modo significandi et nominandi.[2]

How curious then that John of St Thomas can begin his discussion of
analogy *as an antepredicament* with these words: "Difficultates de analogia,
quae satis metaphysice sunt, ita copiose et subtiliter ab Caietano disputatae
in opusc. de Analogia nominum, ut nobis locum non reliquerit quid-
quam aliud excogitandi."[3]

What is puzzling about John's attitude here is that he accepts the
view that the analogy of names is metaphysical and that its metaphysical character is made evident in a work whose title indicates that it is
concerned with names. But the analogy of names, John has said, constitutes a dialectical or logical problem. How then can the analogy of
names be metaphysical? And, if it is, why is John introducing a treatment of it into his work on logic?

Analogy as it covers inequality on the part of the signification of a
common name is a logical question according to John of St Thomas, yet
Cajetan's work on the analogy of names presents a metaphysical doctrine. This confusion is not peculiar to John. It is not unusual to find

---

[1] *De nominum analogia, ed. cit.,* nn. 1, 29.

[2] John of St Thomas, *Cursus Philosophicus,* ed. Reiser, (2nd edition, Rome; 1948), Tome I,
p. 490b.

[3] *Ibid.,* p. 481b. Emphasis ours.

an allusion to the logical doctrine on analogical names in studies devoted to analogy, but it is extremely rare that there is something more than an allusion. Most authors prefer to concern themselves with what they feel is the metaphysical doctrine on the analogy of names. In the light of this, we want to stress that, for St Thomas, the analogy of names is a logical doctrine; moreover most texts brought forward in interpretations of analogy as metaphysical are clearly written from a logical point of view. Once it is seen that the analogy of names is a logical doctrine, the present study, whose title might seem to indicate that it offers a partial analysis of analogy, can be seen as an attempt at a formal treatment of the problem.

The analogy of names is a logical question. To this assertion it might be objected that "analogy" is used in many ways, that it is itself an analogous term. This is a very valuable objection because it indicates that, even if there should be a metaphysical problem of analogy, there is a prior problem concerned with words – in this case, with the word "analogy." We are told that analogy is analogous. Now this is like being told that word is a word: we know this means, "word" is a word. So too it is "analogy" that is analogous, and to understand what this means is to understand something about the way this word signifies many things. This is a logical matter. To say this is not to say that "analogy" in every one of its uses signifies a logical relation, but it is to say that one of its uses will tell us how the one term "analogy" can mean many things, one of which is a logical relation. No one who favors a metaphysical interpretation of the analogy of names has ever attempted to apply this to "analogy" itself even while taking obvious delight in reminding us that "analogy" is analogous. It does not seem too much to say that, unless one can explain what he means by saying that "analogy" is analogous, he is begging the whole question of the analogy of names.

St Thomas is hardly ambiguous on the nature of analogical signification. Consider, for example, his remarks on the various modes of unity distinguished by Aristotle.[4] "Primo distinguit modos unius naturaliter, idest secundum conditiones in rebus inventas. Secundo vero logice, idest secundum intentiones logicales..."[5] What are the members of the division according to logical intentions? "Ponit aliam divisionem unius, quae est magis logica; dicens quod quaedam sunt unum numero, quaedam specie, quaedam genere, quaedam analogia."[6] Can this be

---

[4] *Metaphysics*, Delta, 6.
[5] *In V Metaphys.*, lect. 7, n. 848.
[6] *Ibid.*, lect. 8, n. 876.

dismissed as an isolated remark, perhaps dictated by the text being commented rather than by his own views on analogy? Hardly, when we notice that St Thomas usually speaks of analogical signification by comparing it with univocation and equivocity; it is difficult to find a text on the analogy of names where this comparison is not made.[7] The obvious significance of the comparison is that the things compared are in the same order. But to be named equivocally or univocally is surely not something which would be numbered among the accidents of things as they exist *in rerum natura*. To be named happens to things as they are known by us; that is why the modes of signification fall to the consideration of the logician. They are indeed the first consideration of the *Categories* and it was in commenting on that work that Cajetan saw the need for a separate treatise on analogous names. At that time, he experiences no difficulty in recognizing the logical character of the problem.[8] We could safely assume, then, that the analogy of names, like equivocity and univocity, is a logical intention, is in fact an antepredicament. But we do not have to assume that this is the view of St Thomas; he tells us this quite explicitly.

Dicendum quod animal dictum de animali vero et de picto, non dicitur pure aequivoce: sed Philosophus largo modo accipit aequivoca, secundum quod includunt in se analoga. Quia et ens, quod analogice dicitur, aliquando dicitur aequivoce praedicari de diversis praedicamentis.[9]

The point of comparing analogy with equivocation and univocation is that each is a second intention, each falls to the consideration of the logician. Not only is analogical signification an antepredicament, it is as well a kind of equivocation. Thus to remark that we have in the works of St Thomas no formal and per se consideration of the analogy of names is much the same thing as saying that we have no commentary by him on the *Categories* of Aristotle.

St Thomas could not be clearer on the status of the analogy of names: it is a logical doctrine to be discussed in terms of what is formal to logical discussions and, above all, to be divided by properly logical criteria. By attaching nearly every statement on the analogy of names to equivocation, St Thomas makes it difficult for us to treat the analogy of names as something other than a logical intention. And yet the very texts on which this obvious judgment is based have occasioned statements on

---

[7] Cf. *Ia*, q. 13, a. 5; *In IV Metaphys.*, lect. 1, n. 535; *De principiis naturae*, (ed. Spiazzi), cap. 6, n. 366; *In XI Metaphys.*, lect. 3, n. 2197; *Q.D. de pot.*, q. 7, a. 7, etc.

[8] Cajetan, *Commentaria in Praedicamenta Aristotelis, ed. cit.*, pp. 8–14.

[9] *Ia*, q. 13, a. 10, ad 4. Cf. *In I Metaphys.*, lect. 14, n. 224.

the profoundly metaphysical character of the analogy of names. What is the reason for this misunderstanding?

It would be too facile to lay the entire blame for it on Cajetan. There is a host of difficulties in the texts of St Thomas. Generally speaking, this is due to the fact that St Thomas always introduces the doctrine on the analogy of names in function of a particular problem, when he is discussing things which happen to be named analogously. Side by side with quite general statements as to what it means for things to be named analogously are found statements about the determinate things under consideration, things which happen to found the second intention. Because of this, the real considerations can seem to be part and parcel of the mode of signification which is the analogy of names. Thus, because the things named healthy analogically are these particular things with these particular characteristics, and those named being analogically are things with these determinate characteristics, the real differences between these groups of things can seem to be differences in the mode of being named which they have in common. The division of analogy resulting from such confusion can only be regarded as a gross identification of the logical and real orders.

When we add to such contextual difficulties the discrepancy, noted by both Cajetan and Sylvester,[10] between the use of the Greek ἀναλογία and the Latin *analogia*, an almost insuperable obstacle to understanding St Thomas' doctrine is erected – if one forgets that St Thomas must be numbered among the *latini*, not the *graeci*. How often, in commenting on the *Metaphysics* does St Thomas speak of analogy where Aristotle has not used the Greek term, but rather the phrase "things said in many ways."[11] Are we to discount St Thomas' remarks because κατ᾽ἀναλογίαν or ἀναλογία does not occur in Aristotle? How absurd, and yet we have seen that this is precisely the tendency of Cajetan and, less clearly, Sylvester. To strive for a one-to-one correspondence between the use of ἀναλογία and *analogia* is wrong-headed at best, since the correspondence is obviously lacking. This lack of correspondence has nothing to do, need it be said, with the question of a correspondence of doctrine between what Aristotle tends to call πολλαχῶς λέγεται and St Thomas *analogice dicuntur*, a question, moreover, that we are not posing. We hope only to make some small contribution to the effort to rescue St Thomas'

---

[10] *De nominum analogia, ed. cit.*, n. 20; *In I Contra Gentiles*, cap. 34, n. VII: "...sciendum est quod analogiae nomen graecum est vocabulum, et aliter accipitur a Graecis, aliter a nonnullis Latinis." Cf. John of St Thomas, *op. cit.*, p. 512b42.

[11] Notably Aristotle, *Metaphysics*, Gamma, 2, 1003a33 and St Thomas, *In IV Metaphys.*, lect. 1, n. 535.

doctrine on the analogy of names from the vast confusion into which it has fallen in the literature, the more so because we are convinced that, stripped of the accretions of quasi mystical obfuscation, that doctrine will be revealed as an important statement on what might be called the systematic ambiguity of certain words.

The stage having been set, the nature of the study which follows can be at least partially foreseen. If St Thomas makes analogical signification a logical matter, we must determine what for him logic is. Then we must examine his views on signification in general, after which we can profitably turn to an initial statement on the analogy of names. In going on to discuss the division of things named analogically, we shall look at length at the texts which suggested to Cajetan his hybrid, tripartite division. Then, after discussing knowing by analogy and analogical causes, we shall say something about the divine names, a problem which, more than any other, occasioned the remarks of St Thomas which form the basis of the present interpretation.

CHAPTER III

THE NATURE OF LOGIC

The necessity and importance of logic is indicated by the place it occupies in the order of learning. St Thomas tells us that logic must be learned before any other science, and he points out that this has been the usual method of philosophers.

Primo quidem incipientes a logica quae modum scientiarum tradit, secundo procedentes ad mathematicam cuius etiam pueri possunt esse capaces, tertio ad naturalem philosophiam quae propter experientiam tempore indiget, quarto autem ad moralem philosophiam cuius iuvenis esse conveniens auditor non potest, ultimo autem scientiae divinae insistebant quae considerat primas entium causas.[1]

It can be seen that the order of learning is based upon what is more easily known by us as well as on the amount of experience required for the various sciences. Logic, however, does not come first because it is easy to learn; it is most difficult, second only to metaphysics in this regard.[2] The priority of logic is founded on the fact that it is presupposed by every other science. "Et propter hoc debet prius addiscere logicam quam aliis scientiis, quia logica tradit communem modum procedendi in omnibus aliis scientiis."[3] The very nature of the human mind requires logic, for although the object of the intellect is truth, it is not so determined to its object that error is impossible. There are first principles which are known easily and without possibility of error, but they are common and do not of themselves give a determinate and particular knowledge of everything that follows on them. As soon as we move away from these principles, error is possible. With regard to this further knowledge, then, we are not guided by nature so much as by art.[4]

---

[1] *In librum de causis*, (ed. Saffrey), proemium; Cf. *In VI Ethic.*, lect. 7, n. 1211.

[2] "Ad tertium dicendum quod in addiscendo incipimus ab eo quod est magis facile, nisi necessitas aliud requirat. Quandoque enim necessarium est in addiscendo incipere non ab eo quod est facilius, sed ab eo, a cuius cognitione sequentium cognitio dependet. Et hac ratione oportet in addiscendo a logica incipere, non quia ipsa sit facilior ceteris scientiis, habet enim maximam difficultatem, cum sit de secundo intellectis, sed quia aliae scientiae ab ipsa dependet, inquantum ipsa docet modum procedendi in omnibus scientiis." – *In Boethii de trin.*, (ed. Wyser), q. 6, a. 1, qᵃ 2, ad 3.

[3] *In II Metaphys.*, lect. 5, n. 335; *In Boethii de trin.*, q. 5, a. 1, ad 2. The priority of logic is argued for in the *via addiscendi*, not in the *via inveniendi*. Cf. *Q.D. de ver.*, q. 11, a. 1.

[4] Insofar as the intellect, like every potency of the soul, is *quaedam natura*, it has a natural appetite. That is why the grasp of first principles is said to be *per modum naturae*, as opposed

Given the indetermination of the mind apart from its grasp of first principles, some determination is required if it is to proceed easily, in an orderly manner, and without error. This determination is had from the art of logic.

Every art determines human acts in such a way that operation is made easy. In other words, art is a rational direction of human acts whereby they attain their ends by determinate means. However, reason is directive not only of the acts of powers other than itself, but also of its own act: reason can reflect on and reason about reasoning. And, just as reasoning about manual operations is productive of an art which directs such activity in such a way that man can proceed easily and surely in, say, building, so too an art is produced by reason when it reflects on its own activity. This art is logic.[5]

St Thomas maintains that logic is necessary if the act of reason is to achieve its end. Sometimes he speaks of that reflexive act which gives rise to logic as one of discovery, as in the following text.

Uno modo secundum quod iste ordo est adinventus per intellectum et attributus ei quod relative dicitur; et huiusmodi sunt relationes quae attribuentur ab intellectu rebus intellectis, prout sunt intellectae, sicut relatio generis et speciei: has enim relationes ratio adinvenit considerando ordinem eius quod est in intellectu ad res quae sunt extra, vel etiam ordinem intellectuum ad invicem.[6]

Does this mean that logic is a natural product of reasoning and that the art of logic consists in pointing out what is already given? St Albert speaks of a natural logic of human reason, a way any man has of moving from what he knows to knowledge of something new, although this natural logic is exceedingly imperfect and liable to error.[7] On this view, the art of logic would perfect this natural logic by introducing that

---

to *per modum rationis*. However, the grasp of the first principles *per modum naturae* does not imply the will's entering into the specification of the object, as is the case when faith and the moral virtues are said to be *per modum naturae*. In the latter two, the will has an influence on the very object, whereas in the case of first principles, the intellect is moved by the evidence of its proper object. Cf. *III Sent.*, d. 23, q. 3, sol. 2, ad 2.

[5] "Et inde est quod ad actus humanos faciliter et ordinate perficiendos diversae artes deserviunt. Nihil enim aliud ars esse videtur, quam certa ordinatio rationis quomodo per determinata media ad debitum finem actus humani perveniant. Ratio autem non solum potest dirigere inferiorum partium actus, sed etiam actus sui directivus est. Hoc enim est proprium intellectivae partis ut in seipsam reflectatur: nam intellectus intelligit seipsum et similiter ratio de suo actu ratiocinari potest. Si igitur ex hoc quod ratio de actu manus ratiocinatur, adinventa est ars aedificatoria vel fabrilis, per quas homo faciliter et ordinate huiusmodi actus exercere potest; eadem ratione ars quaedam necessaria est, quae sit directiva ipsius actus rationis, per quam scilicet homo in ipso actu rationis ordinate, faciliter et sine errore procedat. Et haec ars est logica, idest rationalis scientia." – *In I Post. Analyt.*, lect. 1, nn. 1–2.

[6] *Q.D. de pot.*, q. 7, a. 11.

[7] St. Albert, *De Praedicabilibus*, tract. 1, cap. 1.

determination which produces facility and freedom from error. This constructive role of logic is suggested by St Thomas.

Alius autem est ordo, quem ratio *considerando facit* in proprio actu, puta cum ordinat conceptus suos adinvicem, et signa conceptuum, quia sunt voces significativae.[8]

The order which is introduced into the act of reason is the proper work of logic. This is not to say that there is something arbitrary about logic, as if a plurality of logics is possible because of the individual differences of men. In reflecting on its own operation, the intellect discovers a foundation for logical relations. We will see later what it is about the human mode of knowing which makes its concepts apt subjects of logical relations. Before discussing that, however, there is a prior problem. Logical relations are said to be beings of reason, *entia rationis*. What is meant by a being of reason?

1. BEINGS OF REASON AND THE SUBJECT OF LOGIC

The being of reason or the relation of reason is often said to be the subject matter of logic. Although this is true, it should be pointed out that there are beings of reason which are not relations and that not just any relation of reason is the concern of the logician. But first of all there is a distinction made between real being and beings of reason. Real being is that which is divided by the ten categories. "The kinds of essential being are precisely those that are indicated by the figures of predication; for the senses of 'being' are just as many as these figures."[9] Real being is that which exists apart from our thought. Beings of reason, on the other hand, would seem by definition to depend upon our minds. To avoid any confusion on this score, it may be well to observe a distinction made by John of St Thomas between kinds of dependence upon reason.

Ens rationis in omni sua latitudine, si nominis significationem attendamus, dicit id, quod dependet aliquo modo a ratione. Potest autem dependere vel ut effectus a causa vel ut obiectum a cognoscente.[10]

Works of art, since they depend upon the mind of the artist, can be

[8] *In I Ethic.*, lect. 1, n. 1. Cf. *Ia* q. 3, a. 4, ad 2.
[9] *Metaphysics*, Delta, 7, 1017a24. Cf. *De ente et essentia*, cap. 1: "Sciendum est quod, sicut in 5 Meta. Philosophus dicit, ens per se dicitur dupliciter: *Uno modo*, quod dividitur per decem genera; *alio modo*, quod significat propositionum veritatem. Horum autem differentia est, quia secundo modo potest dici ens omne illud de quo affirmativa propositio formari potest, etiamsi illud in re nihil ponat; per quem modum privationes et negationes entia dicuntur: dicimus enim quod affirmatio est opposita negationi, et quod caecitas est in oculo. Sed primo modo, non potest dici aliquid quod sit ens, nisi quod in re aliquid ponat."
[10] *Cursus Philosophicus*, T. I, p. 285.

called beings of reason in the first sense. It is the second kind of being of reason that we shall be opposing to real being.[11]

The being of reason so understood can be subdivided into negation and relation. One finds this distinction made in discussions of what are called the transcendental properties of being, namely the one, the true and the good. Although they are the same reality as being, they are said to differ from being *ratione*.

Id autem quod est rationis tantum, non potest esse nisi duplex. Omnis enim positio absoluta aliquid in rerum natura existens significat. Sic ergo supra ens, quod est prima conceptio intellectus, unum addit id quod est rationis tantum, scilicet *negationem*: dicitur enim unum quasi ens indivisum. Sed verum et bonum positive dicuntur; unde non possunt addere nisi relationem quae sit rationis tantum.[12]

In the text of the *De ente et essentia* cited above in note nine, St Thomas points out how negation and privation are said to be. Taking his example, blindness, the privation of sight, is an absence or lack in the real order. In the mind, however, it takes on objective existence and can enter into a proposition.[13] Thus we say, "Blindness is————." Not only privations, but also simple negations are said to be in this way.

Item negationes eorum quae ad substantiam habitudines habent, vel etiam ipsius substantiae esse dicuntur. Unde dicimus quod non ens est non ens. Quod non diceretur nisi negationi aliquo modo esse competeret.[14]

Of course it is only in the mind that non-being enjoys existence.

Although privations and negations are beings of reason, it is not *entia rationis* of this kind which are the subject of logic. That subject is always a relation of reason, and it is by opposing it to non-logical relations of reason that we can isolate it and discover what it is.

It is only in the genus of relation, St Thomas holds, that we can have something of reason alone and not of the real order. In the other genera, such as quantity and quality, what is properly signified is something which inheres in something else. Those things, however, which fall in the genus of relation, which are said *ad aliquid*, properly signify

---

[11] "Quod autem secundo modo ab intellectu dependet, scilicet ut obiectum, dicitur proprie ens rationis, ut pertinet ad praesens, quia nullum esse habet extra rationem, sed solum obiective dicitur esse in ipsa, et sic opponitur enti reali." *Ibid.*

[12] *Q.D. de ver.*, q. 21, a. 1.

[13] Cf. *In V Metaphys.*, lect. 9, n. 896: "Sciendum est autem quod iste secundus modus comparatur ad primum sicut effectus ad causam. Ex hoc enim quod aliquid in rerum natura est, sequitur veritas et falsitas in propositione, quam intellectus significat per hoc verbum Est prout est verbalis copula. Sed, quia aliquid, quod est in se non ens, intellectus considerat ut quoddam ens, sicut negationem et huiusmodi, ideo quandoque dicitur esse de aliquo hoc secundo modo, et non primo. Dicitur enim, quod caecitas est secundo modo, ex eo quod vera est propositio, qua dicitur aliquid esse caecum; non tamen dicitur quod sit primo modo vera. Nam caecitas non habet aliquod esse in rebus, sed magis est privatio alicuius esse."

[14] *In IV Metaphys.*, lect. 1, n. 539.

only a reference to something else. Sometimes this reference is of the very nature of a thing, as when things are by nature mutually ordered to one another so that they have an inclination to each other. These are real relations. Sometimes the reference signified is due to the grasp of reason which refers one thing to another. These relations are of reason alone as, for example, when reason compares man to animal as a species to its genus.[15]

The relations of reason with which the logician is concerned are called *secunda intellecta* or second intentions.[16] The things we know first of all are things outside the mind, and second intentions follow on the way we grasp their natures, namely, by abstracting them from their material conditions. To know these second intentions, the mind must reflect upon itself, know itself as knowing and the way in which it knows.[17] It is the order which is put among things as they are known which is the proper subject of logic.

Ens autem rationis dicitur proprie de illis intentionibus, quas ratio adinvenit in rebus consideratis; sicut intentio generis, speciei, et similium, quae quidem non inveniuntur in rerum natura, sed considerationem rationis consequuntur. Et huiusmodi, scilicet ens rationis, est proprie subiectum logicae.[18]

Although all logical relations are relations of reason, not all relations of reason are logical relations. St Thomas has, in a text which will occupy us for several pages, carefully distinguished logical from non-logical relations of reason. The basis of the distinction will be seen to be that to which the relations are attributed.

Logical relations are attributed to known things precisely insofar as they are known. The intellect forms the relation of species by considering the order of that which is in the mind to that which is in the

---

[15] "Ad cuius evidentiam considerandum est quod solum in his quae dicuntur ad aliud inveniuntur aliqua secundum rationem tantum, et non secundum rem. Quod non est in aliis generibus, quia alia genera, ut quantitas et qualitas, secundum propriam rationem significant aliquid alicui inhaerens. Ea vero quae dicuntur ad aliquid, significant secundum propriam rationem solum respectum ad aliud. Qui quidem respectus aliquando est in ipsa natura rerum; utpote quando aliquae res secundum suam naturam ordinatae sunt, et invicem inclinationem habent. Et huiusmodi relationes oportet esse reales. (...) Aliquando vero respectus significatus per ea quae dicuntur ad aliquid est tantum in ipsa apprehensione rationis conferentis unum alteri; et tunc est relatio rationis tantum; sicut cum comparet ratio hominem animali, ut species ad genus." – *Ia*, q. 28, a. 1.

[16] Cf. *I Sent.*, d. 23, q. 1, a. 3.

[17] *Q.D. de pot.*, q. 7, a. 9: "Prima enim intellecta sunt res extra animam, in quae primo intellectus intelligenda fertur. Secunda autem intellecta dicuntur intentiones consequentes modum intelligendi: hoc enim secundo intellectus intelligit in quantum reflectitur supra se ipsum, intelligens se intelligere et modum quo intelligit. Secundum ergo hanc positionem sequeretur quod relatio (between God and creature) non sit in rebus extra animam, sed in solo intellectu, sicut intentio generis et speciei, et secundarum substantiarum."

[18] *In IV Metaphys.*, lect. 4, n. 574.

real order; it forms the relation of genus by considering the order of one concept to another.[19] To say of a given nature that it is a species or a genus is to attribute a relation to it insofar as it is known. The foundation of the relation is in things as they are known by our minds. This is not the case with non-logical relations of reason.

Non-logical relations of reason are said to follow on our mode of understanding in that the intellect understands one thing as ordered to another. Such relations, although they are not in things as they exist, are nonetheless founded on them as they exist.

Et hoc quidem contingit secundum quod aliqua non habentia secundum se ordinem, ordinate intelliguntur; licet intellectus non intelligat ea habere ordinem, quia sic esset falsus. Ad hoc autem quod aliqua habeant ordinem, oportet quod utrumque sit ens, et utrumque distinctum (quia eiusdem ad seipsum non est ordo) et utrumque ordinabile ad aliud.[20]

Given these three conditions of a real relation, St Thomas goes on to list four non-logical relations of reason which fail to fulfil one or the other of those conditions.

The first such relation does not fulfil the first condition of real relations, namely that both of the things among which the order obtains be real beings.

Quandoque autem intellectus accipit aliqua duo ut entia, quorum alterum tantum vel neutrum est ens: sicut cum accipit duo futura, vel unum praesens et aliud futurum, et intelligit unum cum ordine ad aliud, dicens alterum esse prius altero; unde *istae relationes sunt rationis tantum*, utpote modum intelligendi consequentes.[21]

The second such relation, that of self-identity, does not fulfil the second condition of real relations, namely that the things ordered be two really distinct entities. When something is said to be identical with itself, what is really one is understood as if it were two, and yet it is the existent thing which is said to be identical with itself.[22]

---

[19] *Q.D. de pot.*, q. 7, a. 11.

[20] *Ibid.*

[21] *Ibid.*

[22] "Quandoque vero accipit unum ut duo, et intelligit ea cum quodam ordine: sicut cum dicitur aliquid esse idem sibi; et sic talis relatio est rationis tantum." – *Ibid.* Cf. *In V Metaphys.*, lect. 11, n. 912: "Ex hoc autem ulterius concludit, quod identitas est unitas vel unio; aut ex eo quod illa quae dicuntur idem, sunt plura secundum esse, et tamen dicuntur idem inquantum in aliquo uno conveniunt. Aut quia sunt unum secundum esse, sed intellectus utitur eo ut pluribus ad hoc quod relationem intelligat. Nam non potest intelligi relatio nisi inter duo extrema. Sicut cum dicitur aliquid esse idem sibipsi. Tunc enim intellectus utitur eo quod est unum secundum rem, ut duobus. Alias eiusdem ad seipsum relationem designare non posset. Unde patet, quod si relatio semper requirit duo extrema, et in huiusmodi relationibus non sunt duo extrema secundum rem sed secundum intellectum solum, relatio identitatis non erit relatio realis, sed rationis tantum, secundum quod aliquid dicitur idem simpliciter." Cf. *Ia*, q. 13, a. 12.

The remaining non-logical relations of reason fail to fulfil the third condition of real relations, namely that the two extremes can be ordered to one another. The relation between a relation and the subject of that relation is said to be of reason alone, for if there were really such a relation, we would be involved in an infinite regress. Moreover, it is easy to see that this relation and the possibile infinity to which it leads are due to reason alone.[23] Paternity is a relation, and we can understand it as related to the man who is a father by another relation intermediate between the subject and the relation of paternity.

The fourth kind of non-logical relation of reason is that whereby we understand a mutual relation where there is a real relation in one direction alone.

Quandoque vero accipit aliquid cum ordine ad aliud, in quantum est terminus ordinis alterius ad ipsum, licet ipsum non ordinetur ad aliud: sicut accipiendo scibile ut terminum ordinis scientiae ad ipsum; et sic cum quodam ordine ad scientiam, nomen scibilis relative significat; et est relatio rationis tantum.[24]

Our knowledge, both sense and intellectual, is really related to things, and, because of this, we understand things as related to our knowledge, naming them sensible or knowable. But things are not really related to our knowing powers. Nevertheless, like all such non-logical relations of reason, this is founded on things as they exist; not again because they are really related to our knowledge, but because our knowledge is really related to them. So too something is really identical with itself; it is not such merely in our minds. The relation is of reason alone, but identity is something real.[25] Likewise with the transcendental properties of being; although they differ from being only *ratione*, they are attributed to real being: they are not logical properties, true of being as known but not as it exists. Being is said to be good because it is understood as related to appetite, true because it is understood as related to intellect.

---

[23] St Thomas shows this would follow if we considered identity a real relation. "Si enim identitatis relatio esset res aliqua praeter illud quod dicitur idem, res etiam, quae relatio est, cum sit idem sibi, pari ratione haberet aliam relationem, quae sibi esset idem, et sic in infinitum. Non est autem possibile in rebus infinitum procedere. Nam cum intellectus reflectatur super suum actum, intelligit se intelligere. Et hoc ipsum potest etiam intelligere, et sic in infinitum." – Q.D. de pot., q. 7, a. 11. Cf. Q.D. de ver., q. 1, a. 5, ad 16.

[24] Ibid. Cf. Q.D. de ver., q. 21, a. 1: "Illa autem relatio (...) dicitur esse rationis tantum, secundum quam dicitur referri id quod non dependet ad id ad quod refertur, sed e converso, cum ipsa relatio quaedam dependentia sit, sicut patet in scientia et scibili, sensu et sensibili. Scientia enim dependet a scibili, sed non e converso: unde relatio qua scientia refertur ad scibile est realis; relatio vero qua scibile refertur ad scientiam est rationis tantum."

[25] Q.D. de pot., q. 7, a. 11, ad 3: "...dicendum quod sicut aliquis est idem sibi realiter, et non solum secundum rationem, licet relatio sit secundum rationem tantum, propter hoc quod relationis causa est realis, scilicet unitas substantiae quam intellectus sub relatione intelligit..."

When the appetitive and cognitive powers are ours, these are relations of reason alone, but things are good and true as they exist.

In summary, we can say that the beings of reason which are opposed to real being are negations or privations, on the one hand, relations on the other. Some relations of reason are said to follow on our mode of understanding, but are founded on things as they exist. Logical relations are founded on things as known. We will schematize our findings thus far.

Divisio Entis Rationis

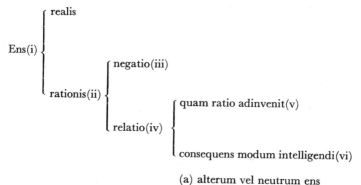

(a) alterum vel neutrum ens
(b) identitas(vii)
(c) relatio relationis
(d) scientia/scibile(viii)

(i) Cf. *De ente et essentia*, cap. 1; *In V Metaphys.*, lect. 9, n. 889.
(ii) Cf. John of St Thomas, *op. cit.*, pp. 285–290. For the division of *ens rationis* into negation and relation, see *Q.D. de ver.*, q. 21, a. 1.
(iii) *In V Metaphys.*, lect. 9, n. 896; *In IV Metaphys.*, lect. 1, n. 539.
(iv) *Ia*, q. 28, a. 1.
(v) *In IV Metaphys.*, lect. 4, n. 574; *Q.D. de pot.*, q. 7, a. 11; *Q.D. de ver.*, q. 1, a. 5, ad 16.
(vi) *Q.D. de pot.*, q. 7, a. 11.
(vii) *In V Metaphys.*, lect. 11, n. 912.
(viii) *Q.D. de ver.*, q. 21, a. 1.

Logical entities or relations are properties of things as known. Just as the reflexive act whereby the intellect knows its own nature presupposes knowledge of something else, so too the reflexive act which logic implies requires knowledge of real entities and these real entities are the remote foundation for logical intentions. Logical beings of reason have as their purpose the ordering of our knowledge of real things. One does not study logic for its own sake, but ultimately as an instrument of science. For this reason, logic is not said to be a speculative science; it is not, however, called a practical science either.[26]

The root of logic is the imperfection of human reason. The indetermination of our intellect requires an art which can guide the very act of reason to its goal of truth. This is accomplished by the formation of second intentions, a realm of entities which are properties of things as known and not as they exist. Our knowledge of logical entities is a mediate knowledge, as we have seen.[27] Furthermore, second intentions have as their purpose the directing of the mind in its knowledge of real things. It can be seen that it is extremely important to respect the difference between the logical and real orders: to confuse them is to court philosophical disaster.

2. THE LOGICAL AND REAL ORDERS

The first problem that the logician must consider, according to St Albert,[28] is that of universality. Universality, as we shall see, is a second intention and in examining an instance where universality was given an ontological status *in rerum natura* we will see the consequences of confusing the real and intentional orders. The Platonic philosophy provides the instance, and by this we mean Plato as Aristotle and St Thomas understood him. For our purposes, it matters little whether or not Plato meant what St Thomas takes him to mean; the criticism of Plato serves to bring out the difference between the logical and real orders.

As has been pointed out above, second intentions are properties of natures as they are known by us: something happens to these natures when they are grasped by our intellect.

Nec oportet, sicut multoties dictum est, quod aliquid eumdem modum essendi habeat in rebus, per quem modum ab intellectu scientis comprehenditur. Nam intellectus immaterialiter cognoscit materialia; et similiter naturas rerum, quae singulariter in rebus existunt, intellectus cognoscit universaliter, idest absque consideratione principiorum et accidentium individualium.[29]

In the real order there are only singular things, and in the realm perceived by the senses, these singulars are material. This man differs from that in such a way that the first man is located here and the other

---

[26] *In Boethii de trin.*, q. 5, a. 1, ad 2: "Res autem de quibus est logica, non quaeruntur ad cognoscendum propter seipsas, sed ut adminiculum quoddam ad alias scientias. Et ideo logica non continetur sub speculativa philosophia quasi principalis pars, sed sicut quoddam reductum ad philosophiam speculativam, prout ministrat speculationi sua instrumenta, scilicet syllogismum et definitiones, et alia huiusmodi, quibus in scientiis speculativis indigemus."

[27] Cf. *ibid.*, q. 6, a. 3.

[28] St Albert, *De Praed.*, tract. 2, cap. 1.

[29] *In III Metaphys.*, lect. 9, n. 446.

there. They are set off from one another, individuated. And yet, in knowing what man is, we form an idea which does not include every particular difference of man and man. Rather our idea expresses what is common and essential to this man, that man and every man. Because our intellect grasps only what is essential to the individuals and leaves aside their individual differences, the nature as known founds a relationship to the many from which it has been abstracted. The property of human nature whereby it is one thing which can be said of many individuals is a property of that nature as it is known. It is the second intention of universality.

Humanitas enim est aliquid in re, non tamen ibi habet rationem universalis, cum non sit extra animam aliqua humanitas multis communis; sed secundum quod accipitur in intellectu, adjungitur ei per operationem intellectus intentio secundum quam dicitur species.[30]

The way in which the nature exists in the mind and the way in which it exists *in rerum natura* differ. This can pose a rather grave problem. If man exists only individually and we grasp human nature as something universal and common to many, it would seem that we understand things otherwise than they are. But truth consists in the conformity of knowledge with reality. So it would seem that intellectual knowledge is radically false and destroys its object in knowing it. We must ask to what "otherwise" refers in the statement, "The intellect understands things otherwise than they are." If the adverb refers to the object known, the objection holds: to understand the object to be otherwise than it is is to have a false understanding. But if "otherwise" refers to our mode of knowing, it does not follow that our understanding things otherwise than they are produces falsity.[31] It is one thing to understand that a material thing is immaterial and quite another to understand a material thing immaterially.

Certain names are imposed to signify the nature with the intention of universality, such as genus, species, etc. These are kinds of logical universal and cannot be predicated of the nature as it exists outside the mind.[32] Sometimes, however, St Thomas refers to the existing nature as

---

[30] *I Sent.*, d. 19, q. 5, a. 1.

[31] *Ia*, q. 85, a. 1, ad 1: "Cum ergo dicitur quod intellectus est falsus qui intelligit rem aliter quam sit, verum est si ly aliter referatur ad rem intellectam. Tunc enim intellectus est falsus quando intelligit rem esse aliter quam sit. (...) Non est autem verum quod proponitur si ly aliter accipiatur ex parte intelligentis. Est enim absque falsitate ut alius sit modus intelligentis in intelligendo, quam modus rei in essendo; quia intellectum est in intelligente immaterialiter per modum intellectus, non autem materialiter per modum rei materialis."Cf. ibid., q. 13, a. 12, ad 3.

[32] "Sic igitur patet, quod naturae communi non potest attribui intentio universalitatis nisi

a universal. There is a universal *in things*, namely the nature which is in particulars, although in them it does not have the note of universality. "Quoddam (universale) est *in re*, scilicet natura ipsa, quae est in particularibus, quamvis in eis non sit secundum rationem universalitatis in actu."[33]

When the different modes of existence which the nature has in reality and in the mind are not distinguished, we have the Platonic confusion. Aristotle's criticism of Plato is that he confused the logical and real orders, that he wanted something real to respond *as such* to the intentions which the mind forms in knowing. This issued in a reification of the logical universal so that not only was there to be a concept of man representing a nature common to many individuals, but there would also be an Idea, Man in himself, which exists apart and by participation in which particular men are. That the World of Ideas arose from the reification of logical entities seems obvious. The Platonist saw that in universals there is something one which is common to many, and it was this one thing which was postulated as enjoying separate existence. Logically, they would be forced to mantain that there must be separate genera as well and the World of Ideas soon becomes more densely populated than the world of singulars it is meant to explain.[34]

We say that universality follows on our mode of understanding: it is in fact a principle or means of knowing for us. What Plato has done, consequently, is to make what is a principle of our knowledge of things, a principle of the being of those things. This can hardly be the case, however, for our concepts are not always representations of what in reality *are* the principles of a thing's being, as when we know causes through their effects and substances through their accidents.[35] Something can be a cause of knowledge even when it is not a cause of being.

---

secundum esse quod habet in intellectu: sic enim solum est unum de multis, prout intelligitur praeter principia, quibus unum in multa dividitur: unde relinquitur, quod universalia, secundum quod sunt universalia, non sunt nisi in anima. Ipsae autem naturae, quibus accidit intentio universalitatis, sunt in rebus. Et propter hoc nomina communia significantia naturas ipsas, praedicantur de individuis; non autem nomina significantia intentiones. Socrates enim est homo, sed non est species, quamvis homo sit species." – *In II de anima*, lect. 12, n. 380; cf. *Q.D. de pot.*, q. 7, a. 6.

[33] *II Sent.*, d. 3, q. 3, a. 2, ad 1.

[34] *In I Metaphys.*, lect. 14, n. 209: "...determinaverunt (Platonici) procedentes de his sensibilibus ad praedictas species, manifestum est si consideretur, qua ratione Platonici ideas induxerunt: hac, scilicet, quia videbant in omnibus univocis unum esse in multis. Unde id unum ponebant esse speciem separatam. Videmus tamen, quod circa omnes substantias rerum aliarum ab ideis invenitur unum in multis per modum univocae praedicationis, inquantum inveniuntur multae unius speciei. (...) Vel ponuntur ideae non solum specierum, sed etiam generum; et sic sunt plures ideae quam species omnes, et praeter haec omnia et singula genera."

[35] *Ia*, q. 85, a. 3, ad 4.

Plato's position does not necessarily entail that our knowledge be causative of things, however. That is, the Platonic position may be seen as a likening of human knowledge, not to the divine, but to the angelic mode of knowing. In the Christian tradition, following the lead of St Augustine, the Platonic Ideas have been interpreted as the divine creative ideas.[36] Angels do not know material things by means of a species abstracted from those things, but by means of an infused species which is prior to things.[37] That universal by which the angel knows is said to be *ad rem* as opposed to our abstracted species which is *a re*. The angelic knowledge, since it is a participation in the divine creative ideas, is said to be operative or practical knowledge. The angels, however, do not have this practical knowledge *modo practico*, since they do not create; rather they are said to possess speculatively a practical knowledge of things.[38] In somewhat the same way, Plato seems to want our knowledge to be *ad rem*. True knowledge of things is had by means of the ideas in which they participate, and not by species abstracted from them. Plato's Ideas are, as it were, concepts existing outside the mind. Aristotle, on the other hand, is quite insistent that the universal nature is for us posterior to things, derived from them.[39]

What Plato has done, in effect, is to make the logical universal, the *universale in praedicando*, a universal cause, an *universale in causando*. "Sed alia est communitas universalis et causae. Nam causa non praedicatur de suis effectibus, quia non sunt idem causa suiipsius. Sed universale est commune quasi aliquid praedicatum de multis; et sic oportet quod aliquo modo sit unum in multis, et non seorsus subsistens ab eis."[40]

There can be principles common to all things in two ways, by predication or by causality. The metaphysician, whose interest is those common causes, must not be waylaid by logical universals.[41] If there is a realm of separate entities, it cannot be attained by Plato's method.

Patet autem diligenter intuenti rationes Platonis, quod ex hoc in sua positione erravit, quia credidit quod modus rei intellectae in suo esse sit sicut modus intelligendi rem ipsam.[42]

---

[36] Cf. *De diversis quaestionibus 83*, q. 46; St Thomas, *Ia*, q. 84, a. 5; *ibid.*, q. 15.

[37] *Ia*, q. 55, a. 2, ad 1.

[38] *II Sent.*, d. 3, q. 3, a. 2, ad 1: "Est autem quoddam universale quod est a re acceptum per abstractionem, et hoc posterius est re; et hoc modo formae angelorum non sunt universales. Est etiam quoddam universale ad rem, quod est prius re ipsa, sicut forma domus in mente aedificatoris; et per hunc modum sunt universales formae rerum in mente angelica existentes, non ita quod sint operativae, sed quia sunt operativis similes, sicut aliquis speculative scientiam operativam habet."

[39] *Ibid.*; cf. *In I de anima*, lect. 1, n. 13; *Ia*, q. 85, a. 3, ad 1.

[40] *In X Metaphys.*, lect. 3, n. 1964. See below, chapter VII.

[41] *In Boethii de trin.*, q. 5, a. 4; cf. *Q.D. de ver.*, q. 7, a. 6, ad 7. The two kinds of community will be discussed in chapters VII and X.

[42] *In I Metaphys.*, lect. 10, n. 158.

CHAPTER IV

THE SIGNIFICATION OF NAMES

To say that some words are analogous is to say something about the way they signify; and, if some words signify analogously while others do not, signification itself is presupposed by a doctrine on analogical words and should be considered first. It seems unwise to assume that it is perfectly clear what St Thomas meant by "sign" and "signification." His teaching on such matters, though initially it seems quite simple, turns out to involve a number of subtleties which must be borne in mind in discussing the analogy of names.

1. LOGIC AND NAMING

Is the matter of the signification of words a legitimate concern of the logician, or does it rather belong to the grammarian? As soon appears, several disciplines concern themselves with the word. The philosophy of nature, when it is involved with animate being, finds it necessary to inquire into vocal sounds, which it deals with as effects of certain kinds of animate being, namely those with respiratory systems.[1] The definition of *vox* given by the philosopher of nature is as follows: "vox sit respirati percussio aeris ad arteriam vocalem, quae quidem percussio fit ab anima, quae est in his partibus, idest principaliter in corde."[2] Not a very interesting definition for our purposes, but it expresses what is physical in the word. It does not, however, permit us to distinguish the cries of animals from the conversation of men.

The word is discussed in grammar and logic as well, St Thomas holds, and before turning to the logic of signification, we want to look at some remarks of his having to do with the distinction between logic and grammar. Actually, these amount to little more than asides; we have no developed treatment on the nature of grammar by St Thomas.

Grammar is said to be "scientia recte loquendi";[3] its concern is the "congrua vocum constructio"[4] and, since any science studies opposites,

[1] *On the Soul*, II, 8.
[2] *In II de anima*, lect. 18, n. 476.
[3] *Q.D. de ver.*, q. 24, a. 6.
[4] *In I Periherm.*, lect. 7, n. 6.

it deals with incongruous constructions as well.[5] Though the grammarian, like the logician, is concerned with words taken alone and in composition with other words, his is, so to say, a more artificial concern than the logician's. Logical relations are founded on concepts and the nature of these concepts dictates the nature of logical relations; grammar on the other hand, deals with the purely conventional, and if it is called a science, "science" must be taken in the broadest sense.[6] Logic is ordered to knowledge of real things, and this makes the written word of slight interest to it, whereas grammar is necessarily concerned with the written language.[7] Indeed, St Thomas will oppose logic and the philosophy of nature to grammar, saying that the former are concerned with the natures of things, while grammar is concerned with the *modus significandi*.[8] Grammar, as pure art, defines in an artistic way; thus the substantive is such because it imitates substance, signifying *per modum substantiae*.[9] Needless to say, a substantive such as whiteness is in reality an accident. The grammarian's use of the terms "substance" and "quality" (we will return to this) does not respond to the categories of the same names which are distinguished by the logician.[10] The conclusion is not that grammar is unimportant. In the order of learning proposed by St Thomas, the trivium of the liberal arts – which included grammar and logic – was presupposed by any further study, and grammar preceded logic.[11] The disciplines concerned with the word, the *artes sermocinales*, had a priority because they dealt with what is most obvious to us or most necessary for learning other things. Not that concern with language disappears after the trivium. Indeed, the wise man, the metaphysician as well as the theologian, will exhibit his own concern with words and signification.[12] Let us turn now to the logical doctrine of signification.

[5] *In IV Metaphys.*, lect. 3, n. 564.

[6] Cf. Sheilah O'Flynn, "The First Meaning of 'Rational Process' According to the *Expositio in Boethium De Trinitate*," *Laval théologique et philosophique*, X, (1954), pp. 167–188.

[7] *In I Periherm.*, lect. 2, n. 3. The difference may be illustrated by noting that, whereas the spoken and written words which signify logical relations are conventional or arbitrary, these relations themselves are not, since they have their foundation in natures as known. The foundation of logical relations introduces the note of necessity thanks to which logic is science in the strict sense, and not merely an art, as grammar is.

[8] Cf. *II Sent.*, d. 35, q. 1, a. 2, ad 5: "...dicendum quod passio potest sumi dupliciter: vel quantum ad naturam rei prout logicus et naturalis passionem considerat, et hoc modo non oportet omnem poenam passionem esse, sed quamdam poenam, scilicet poenam sensus: vel quantum ad modum significandi, prout grammaticus considerat..."

[9] *In V Metaphys.*, lect. 9, n. 894.

[10] *I Sent.*, d. 22, q. 1, a. 1, ad 3.

[11] Cf. *In Boethii de trin.*, q. 5, a. 1, ad 3.

[12] To the objection that the science concerned with *res* will not be concerned with *nomina*, St Thomas replies: "Sed dicendum quod (...) theologia, inquantum est principalis omnium

2. SIGN AND SIGNIFICATION

At the outset of *On Interpretation*,[13] Aristotle discusses vocal sounds as signs, a note which was absent from the definition cited from *On the Soul*. Written words, Aristotle maintains, are signs of spoken words and spoken words are signs of what we know: of *passiones animae*, in the translation used by St Thomas. The noise emanating from the throat can be considered to be a sign, then, but what does it mean to say that vocal sounds signify? "Signum, proprie loquendo, non potest dici nisi aliquid ex quo deveniatur in cognitionem alterius quasi discurrendo."[14] The sign is that which leads to knowledge of something else by a kind of discursive process. Or, in the definition of John of St Thomas, a sign is "id quod potentiae cognoscitivae aliquid aliud a se repraesentat."[15] Signification, then, is to be explained in terms of a kind of *discursus*, coming to know a thing thanks to another which is its sign. The word, which is a conventional sign, because of human institution, does not immediately signify the thing: that this is impossible is taken to be evident from its mode of signification. "Non enim potest esse quod significent immediate ipsas res, ut ex modo significandi apparet: significat enim hoc nomen *homo* naturam humanam in abstractione a singularibus."[16] A groan or other natural sign may immediately signify the thing,[17] but the word relates to what it signifies only via a mental conception; indeed, we shall find it necessary to insist that it is the mental conception which is immediately signified by the word. This should not be interpreted as saying that words do not signify things; the point is the way in which they do so, namely through what we know of things. The word as conventional or arbitrary sign has the will as its source, like any other artifact.[18] No word of human language will as such naturally relate to the thing signified by it.[19]

scientiarum, aliquid in se habet de omnibus scientiis; et ideo non solum res, sed nominum significationes pertractat: quia ad salutem consequendam non solum est necessaria fides de veritate rerum, sed etiam vocalis confessio per nomina." – *I Sent.*, d. 22, *expositio textus*, (ed. Mandonnet), I, p. 543. For the metaphysician's interest in words, see *In V Metaphys.*, lect. 1, n. 749.

[13] 16a1 ff.
[14] *Q.D. de ver.*, q. 9, a. 4, ad 4; cf. *IIIa*, q. 60, a. 4: "Signum autem est per quod aliquis devenit in cognitionem alterius."
[15] *Cursus Philosophicus*, I, p. 9.
[16] *In I Periherm.*, lect. 2, n. 5.
[17] Note that so far as the interpretation of a sign goes, knowledge must always mediate between the natural sign and that of which it is the sign; this it has in common with the conventional sign. It is the *constitution* of the conventional sign which involves the human practical intellect. Of course, insofar as the cause of nature is intelligent, mind is involved in the constitution of the natural sign as well.
[18] *Q.D. de ver.*, q. 4, a. 1.
[19] *In I Periherm.*, lect. 4, nn. 11–12.

This last point indicates a great difference between words and concept *(passiones animae)* as signs. The word is not similar to that of which it is the sign;[20] the concept, on the other hand, is a sign of the thing naturally and by way of similarity. That is why the word is said not to be a sign in the way an image is, for the image involves similarity in species (or in being a sign of the species) with, and origination from, that with which it is similar. The shape of a thing is thought to be more revealing of the nature of a thing than its color (we might distinguish the species of animal by their shapes) and consequently the image is similar in shape rather than in color.[21] But similarity in shape does not suffice for a thing to be an image: two eggs may be similar in shape but one is not the image of the other. Most properly, the image originates from the imaged, as the son is the image of his father.[22] What has this to do with words and concepts? The concept will be called a similitude while written and spoken words are only signs. This seems a long way from attempts to treat language as iconic sign, as that with which we make to ourselves pictures of facts.

Ubi attendendum est quod litteras dixit esse notas, idest signa vocum, et voces passionum animae similiter; passiones autem animae dicit esse similitudines rerum: et hoc ideo quia res non cognoscitur ab anima nisi per aliquam sui similitudinem existentem vel in sensu vel in intellectu. Litterae autem ita sunt signa vocum, et voces passionum, quod non attenditur ibi aliqua ratio similitudinis, sed sola ratio institutionis, sicut et in multis aliis signis: ut tuba est signum belli. In passionibus autem animae oportet attendi rationem similitudinis ad exprimendas res, quia naturaliter eas designant, non ex institutione.[23]

Earlier we quoted a definition of sign which is the *ratio propria* of the name. "Signum, proprie loquendo, non potest dici nisi aliquid ex quo deveniatur in cognitionem alterius quasi discurrendo."[24] Properly speaking, then, there are signs only where there is discursive knowledge, i.e. only in human knowledge. As we shall see later,[25] discursive knowledge involves coming to know one thing from knowledge of another; further-

---

[20] We will not be detained here by the difficulty presented by such words as "susurrus," "whisper," etc., except to note that they do not function in the same way as imitations of bird calls. But "Ulalume"?

[21] The terms *species* and *forma* originally signified shape.

[22] *Ia*, q. 35, a. 1; cf. ibid., q. 93, a. 9.

[23] Cf. *In I Periherm.*, lect. 2, n. 9; Cf. *In de sensu et sensato*, (ed.Spiazzi), lect. 2, n. 31: "...et dicit quod auditus multum confert ad prudentiam. Et accipitur hic prudentia pro quadam intellectiva cognitione, non solum prout est recta ratio agibilium, ut dicitur in sexto Ethicorum. Sed hoc est per accidens, quia sermo, qui est audibilis, est causa addiscendi non per se, *id est secundum ipsas sonorum differentias*, sed per accidens, inquantum scilicet nomina, quibus sermo est, id est locutio componitur, sunt symbola, idest signa intentionum intellectarum, et per consequens rerum." (Emphasis ours.)

[24] *Q.D. de ver.*, q. 9, a. 4, ad 4.

[25] Chapter VIII.

more, discursive knowledge implies a dependence on the senses, something important for the notion of sign. "Et propter hoc etiam in nobis signa sunt sensibilia, quia nostra cognitio, quae discursiva est, a sensibilibus oritur."[26] Properly speaking, a sign is sensible. If something is to lead to knowledge of something else, it must be more knowable to us; but sensible things are most easily known, so far as we are concerned, and will therefore serve as signs of other things. True enough, the notion of sign is broadened and made common so that the concept too is called a sign, but it must be stressed that this involves an extension of the meaning of "sign,"[27] that sensible things are most properly signs.[28] Thus, since all our knowledge takes its rise from the senses, it is from the sensible effects or qualities of things that we proceed to knowledge of quiddity, of what things are.[29] These sensible effects are signs of the nature since, being known, they lead to knowledge of what a thing is. It is interesting to note that, since signs in the most proper sense of the term are sensible, words are properly signs. St Thomas stresses this in his *De magistro*, where he argues that teaching, like medicine, is an art which cooperates with nature in order that nature may more surely and easily attain its end. The proper instruments of this art are those signs we call words.[30] Just as sensible things generally lead us to knowledge of what is not sensible, so do words heard or seen; moreover, words are more efficacious signs of the intelligible.

Unde ipsa verba doctoris audita, vel visa in scripta, hoc modo se habent ad causandum scientiam in intellectu sicut res quae sunt extra animam, quia ex utrisque intellectus intentiones intelligibiles accipit; quamvis verba doctoris propinquius se habeant ad causandum scientiam quam sensibilia extra animam existentia inquantum sunt signa intelligibilium intentionum.[31]

Thus words as sensible signs of intelligible concepts involve and indeed

---

[26] *Q.D. de ver.*, q. 9, a. 4, ad 4.

[27] *Ibid.* "Sed communiter possumus signum dicere quodcumque notum in quo aliquid cognoscatur; et secundum hoc forma intelligibilis potest dici signum rei quae per ipsum cognoscitur."

[28] Cf. *IIIa*, q. 60, a. 4, ad 1: "Effectus autem sensibilis per se habet quod ducat in cognitionem alterius, quasi primo et per se homini innotescens: quia omnis nostra cognitio a sensu initium habet. Effectus autem intelligibiles non habent quod possint ducere in cognitionem alterius nisi inquantum sunt per aliud manifestati, idest per aliqua sensibilia. Et inde est quod primo et principaliter dicuntur signa quae sensibus offeruntur..."

[29] What is proper to the sign is not to be an effect, but to be more easily known than what it signifies. "...de ratione signi proprie accepta non est quod sit vel prius vel posterius in natura, sed solummodo quod sit nobis praecognitum..." – *Q.D. de ver.*, q. 9, a. 4, ad 5.

[30] *Q.D. de ver.*, q. 11, a. 1: "...unde et secundum hoc unus alium docere dicitur, quod istum discursum rationis, quem in se facit ratione naturali, alteri exponit per signa et sic ratio naturalis discipuli, per huiusmodi sibi proposita, sicut per quaedam instrumenta, pervenit in cognitionem ignotorum."

[31] *Ibid.*, ad 11.

perfect the process whereby the intelligible is grasped from the sensible. If this is true in the sublimest areas – *fides ex auditu* – it is not surprising to have it recalled that "nos enim per auditum scientiam ab aliis accipimus."[32]

We name as we know; words are imposed as signs of what we know and if what we know first are sensible things, the word, being sensible, will always be a reminder of the origin of our knowledge. Even when a word is imposed to signify what is intelligible, its very nature recalls the trajectory of our knowledge, from the sensible to the intelligible. To see how this is so, we must consider the question of the imposition of names.

3. THE IMPOSITION OF NAMES

In speaking of the imposition of words or names,[33] St Thomas distinguishes between that from which *(id a quo)* and that which the name is imposed to signify *(id ad quod nomen imponitur ad significandum)*. The name is imposed from that which is most knowable to us, since we name as we know. The sensible effects of things are first and most easily known by us and the *id a quo* will often be that which is grasped by the senses. What is signified, however, need not be these sensible effects.

> Dicendum quod in significatione nominum aliud est quandoque a quo imponitur nomen ad significandum, et aliud ad quod significandum nomen imponitur: sicut hoc nomen *lapis* imponitur ab eo quod laedit pedem; non tamen imponitur ad hoc significandum, quod significet *laedens pedem*, sed ad significandum quamdam speciem corporum; alioquin omne laedens pedem esset lapis.[34]

By saying that sometimes there is a difference between the *id a quo* and the *id ad quod*, St Thomas suggests that it can happen that there is no difference. We can see that these can be the same wherever what is signified is so manifest that there is no need to impose the word from something more manifest. The examples St Thomas gives of words whose *id a quo* and *id ad quod* are identical are things which are absolutely rock-bottom. "Si qua vero sunt quae secundum se sunt nota nobis, ut calor, frigus, albedo et huiusmodi, non ab aliis denominantur. Unde in talibus idem est quod nomen significat et id a quo imponitur nomen ad significandum."[35] Hot, cold, smooth, rough, etc. cannot be denominated from something more manifest; indeed, other things will be denominat-

---

[32] *Q.D. de ver.*, q. 9, a. 4, ad 12.
[33] On the use of "word" and "name," see below, note 52.
[34] *Ia*, q. 13, a. 2, ad 2.
[35] *Ia*, q. 13, a. 8.

ed from them. When it is a question of naming what is the object of intellect as such, our names are often imposed from that which is grasped by the senses and by which we come to knowledge of substance. Thus we grasp sensible properties and operations of substance and the priority of this kind of knowledge will be manifest in the word we use to signify the substance. St Thomas makes frequent use of the example of *lapis* to make this point.[36] It hardly matters that the etymology he assigns to the word is nowadays considered dubious.

As our knowledge must always have its principle in what is grasped by the senses, so too our words have the sensible as their *id a quo*: "secundum autem quod res sunt nobis notae, secundum hoc a nobis nominantur."[37] But just as our knowledge is not restricted to what can be known by the senses, so too the names which are imposed from the sensible manifestations of things can be made to signify the substance which underlies sensible accidents.

When names imposed in this fashion are taken as signifying the *id a quo* rather than the *ad quod*, they are said to signify less properly. Thus, the word "life" is imposed from an effect, self-movement, a vital operation, but the term is imposed to signify the substance which has the ability to move itself, not the operation. Sometimes, however, "life" is taken to signify vital operations as such, and is then said to signify less properly. "Quandoque tamen vita sumitur minus proprie pro operationibus vitae, a quibus nomen vitae assumitur, sicut dicit Philosophus in *IX Ethic.* quod 'vivere principaliter est sentire et intelligere.' "[38]

The distinction, then, is clear. For the most part, we must distinguish in names between that in sense experience from which the name is taken and that which it is imposed to signify. Sometimes, as is the case with the proper objects of the senses, the *id a quo* and *id ad quod* are the same. The distinction would seem to be the same as that St Thomas makes between the etymology and the signification of a word. Thus, in the example of *lapis*, the *id a quo* is the putative etymology of the word, i.e. *laedens pedem*. So too the etymology of "participate" is said to be *partem capere;* that of "principle" priority.[39] *Lapis*, the favorite example,

---

[36] "Dicendum quod non est semper idem in a quo imponitur nomen ad significandum, et id ad quod significandum nomen imponitur. Sicut enim substantiam rei ex proprietatibus vel operationibus eius cognoscimus ita substantiam rei denominamus quandoque ab aliqua eius operatione vel proprietate: sicut substantiam lapidis denominamus ab aliqua actione eius, quia laedit pedem; non tamen hoc nomen impositum est ad significandum hanc actionem, sed substantiam lapidis." – *Ia*, q. 13, a. 8.

[37] *In V Metaphys.*, lect. 1, n. 751.

[38] *Ia*, q. 18, a. 2.

[39] *Ia*, q. 33, a. 1, ad 3: "Dicendum quod licet hoc nomen principium, quantum ad id a quo imponitur ad significandum, videatur a prioritate sumptum: non tamen significat priori-

makes it clear that a word does not properly signify its etymology,[40] and it does it particularly well because it is, if its etymology were correct, a composite term. In *On Interpretation*, it is said of the noun that none of its parts signify separately, a claim it may seem difficult to honor when one thinks of such nouns as "breakfast." This term is composite, is drawn from "break" and "fast," each of which signifies by itself. Why doesn't this observation destroy Aristotle's definition of noun? St Thomas argues that the composite term signifies a simple conception and that, although its parts taken separately signify something, they do not signify part of what the composite noun signifies. For example, "break" does not signify part of the morning meal. The composite signified by the sentence or *oratio* is such that a part of the *oratio* signifies part of the composite conception. Thus the etymology of the word does not function as do the parts of, say, a sentence. St Thomas' example in arguing this is, again, *lapis*.[41]

The distinction between the *id a quo* and *id ad quod* seems to be such that the *id a quo* is the etymology of the word and not what is properly signified by it. Nevertheless, St Thomas will sometimes say that the *id a quo* is what the name properly signifies.[42] There is no question in this text of such proper sensibles as *frigus, calor et alia huiusmodi*. Apparently, unless there is here a flat contradiction, a distinction must be made between various meanings of the phrase *id a quo* if we are to reconcile the texts involved.

Fortunately, St Thomas himself points out the necessary distinction.[43] That from which the name is imposed can be understood either from the point of view of the one imposing the name, which is the way we have hitherto considered it and the way in which it is opposed to the *id ad quod*, or on the part of the thing, *ex parte rei*. In the latter sense, the *id a quo* is the specific difference and what the name properly signifies. "Dicitur autem nomen imponi ab eo quod est quasi differentia constitutiva generis."[44]

tatem, sed originem. Non enim idem est quod significat nomen, et a quo nomen imponitur, ut supra dictum est." For *partem capere*, cf. *In Boethii de hebdomadibus*, lect. 2.

[40] Cf. *Q.D. de pot.*, q. 9, a. 3, ad 1; *IIaIIae*, q. 92, a. 1, ad 2; *I Sent.*, d. 24, q. 2, a. 2, ad 2.

[41] *In I Periherm.*, lect.4,n. 9: "Cuius ratio est quod nomen imponitur ad significandum unum simplicem intellectum; aliud autem est id a quo imponitur nomen ad significandum, ab eo quod nomen significat: quod tamen imponitur ad significandum conceptum cuiusdam rei. Et inde est quod pars nominis compositi, quod imponitur ad significandum conceptum simplicem, non significat partem conceptionis compositae, a qua imponitur nomen ad significandum. Sed oratio significat ipsam conceptionem compositam: unde pars orationis significat partem conceptionis compositae."

[42] Cf. e.g. *III Sent.*, d. 6, q. 1, a. 3.

[43] *Q.D. de ver.*, q. 4, a. 1, ad 8.

[44] *I Sent.*, d. 4, q. 1, a. 1. Cf. *Q.D. de ver.*, q. 4, a. 1, ad 8: "...nomen dicitur ab aliquo imponi

The same distinction appears if we examine what St Thomas has to say of denomination. On the one hand, he can say, "…denominatio proprie est secundum habitudinem accidentis ad subiectum";[45] on the other, in a plethora of texts, he says, "Denominatio fit a forma, quae det speciem rei."[46] If this last remark were taken without any possible qualification, few things would be named by us. But the form from which something is denominated can be understood in a wider sense: "…dicendum est quod illud a quo aliquid denominatur non oportet quod sit semper forma secundum rei naturam, sed sufficit quod significetur per modum formae, grammatice loquendo. Denominatur enim homo ab actione et ab indumento, ab aliis huiusmodi, quae realiter non sunt formae."[47] And, as the first text quoted in this paragraph indicates, denomination is had properly where something is named from its accidents, although it is also applied to the designation of something from its matter.[48] That is why, in the commentary on the *Physics*, denominative predication is distinguished from both essential predication and from that which is predicated *ut inhaerens*.[49] Nevertheless, denomination can be intrinsic as well as extrinsic: the point is that, properly speaking, "denomination" refers to the latter. We will be looking more deeply into the question of intrinsic and extrinsic denomination in Chapter VI, since the distinction plays a prominent role in Cajetan's division of the analogy of names.

4. MODUS SIGNIFICANDI; RES SIGNIFICATA

The notion of the *id a quo nomen imponitur* leads to several other considerations suggested in the following remark. "Dicendum quod in quolibet nomine est duo considerari: scilicet id a quo imponitur nomen, quod dicitur qualitas nominis, et id cui imponitur, quod dicitur substantia

dupliciter: aut ex parte imponentis nomen, aut ex parte rei cui imponitur. Ex parte autem rei nomen dicitur ab illo imponi per quod completur ratio rei quam nomen significat; et haec est differentia specifica illius rei. Et hoc est quod principaliter significatur per nomen. Sed quia differentiae essentiales sunt nobis ignotae, quandoque utimur accidentibus vel effectibus loco earum, ut VII Metaphys. dicitur; et secundum hoc nominamus rem; et sic illud quod loco differentiae essentialis sumitur, est a quo imponitur nomen *ex parte imponentis*, sicut lapis imponitur ab effectu, qui est laedere pedem. Et hoc non oportet esse principaliter significatum per nomen, sed illud loco cuius hoc ponitur."

[45] *I Sent.*, d. 17, q. 1, a. 5, ad 2.

[46] *In I Periherm.*, lect. 8, n. 9; *In II de anima*, lect. 9, n. 347; Ia, q. 33, a. 2, ad 2; *ibid.*, q. 115, a. 2; *II Sent.*, d. 9, q. 1, a. 4.

[47] *Q.D. de pot.*, q. 7, a. 10, ad 8. The significance of this *grammatice loquendo* will become clear in a moment when we examine the notion of the *qualitas nominis*.

[48] Thus, to say of the table that it is wooden, is to denominate it from its matter. Cf. *In IX Metaphys.*, lect. 6, nn. 1839–1843; *In VII Metaphys.*, lect. 2, nn. 1287–9.

[49] Cf. *In III Physic.*, lect. 5, n. 15.

nominis. Et nomen proprie loquendo dicitur significare formam sive qualitatem a qua imponitur nomen; dicitur vero supponere pro eo cui imponitur."[50] The first thing which must be determined in discussing the phrase "nomen significat substantiam cum qualitate,"[51] is the meaning of *nomen*. Sometimes *nomen* signifies with an extension comparable to that of the English "word." When it does, we have for the most part been using "name"; at other times *nomen* has the more restricted meaning of the English "noun."[52] In the phrase quoted above, *nomen* has the second more restricted meaning of a word which is other than the verb, for example. The statement, then, is a grammatical one,[53] something which affects the meaning of "substance" and "quality." These are not to be understood as they are distinguished in the *Categories*. There, substance is that which neither exists in another nor is said of another. The grammarian, aware that accidents can function as subjects in a sentence, as that of which something else is predicated, finds that a sufficient reason for calling them substances or substantives. For him, substance is that which can be the subject of a sentence. A quality, then, would be that which modifies a subject, i.e. can be predicated of it.[54]

The quality of a noun is that from which the word is imposed, that which is the principle of knowing the thing named. In other words, the quality is the *id a quo ex parte rei* and is what is properly signified by the term.[55] In the noun "man, "the quality of the term is human nature, the substance is the supposit subsisting in that nature. "Dicendum quod significare substantiam cum qualitate, est significare suppositum cum natura vel forma determinata in qua subsistit."[56] So too "white" signifies that which has whiteness; the latter is the quality of the term, that which has whiteness is the substance of the noun. It is the form or quality, the principle of knowing the thing, that the noun principally signifies.[57]

The *id a quo ex parte rei*, the specific difference, that in virtue of which the thing is intelligible, is what the name principally signifies. The form

---

[50] *III Sent.*, d. 6, q. 1, a. 3.
[51] *Ia*, q. 13, a. 1, ad 3.
[52] *In I Periherm.*, lect. 5, n. 15: "Nomen dupliciter potest sumi: prout communiter significat quamlibet dictionem impositam ad significandum aliquam rem. Et quia etiam ipsum agere vel pati est quaedam res, inde est quod et ipsa verba, inquantum nominant, idest significant agere vel pati, sub nominibus comprehenduntur communiter acceptis. Nomen prout a verbo distinguitur, significat rem sub determinato modo, prout scilicet potest intelligi ut per se existens."
[53] *I Sent.*, d. 9, q. 1, a. 2.
[54] *I Sent.*, d. 22, q. 1, a. 1, ad 3.
[55] *III Sent.*, d. 6, q. 1, a. 3.
[56] *Ia*, q. 13, a. 1, ad 3.
[57] *I Sent.*, d. 22, q. 1, a. 1, ad 3.

principally signified is either the simple form of the abstract term, or
the form by which the composite is known in concrete terms. But the
significance of that remark requires an understanding of the notion of
modes of signifying in order to be grasped. Before discussing modes of
signification, it may be well to say something of "mode" itself. A text
which brings out its meaning is that concerned with ranging the speculative sciences according to the dignity of their objects and according
to modes.

In the specification of a potency or habit, the object is assigned the
principal role, so that science will be called the best which has the most
worthy object. Thus metaphysics, since it is concerned with things
higher than man and most perfect in themselves, is the science most
worthy of pursuit. However, the mode of attaining the object, the certitude of the science, produces a different order of precedence; the most
perfect science we have is not concerned with things in themselves most
noble. Indeed, the science which is first in dignity, in object, would be
last from the point of view of certitude and evidence, of mode.[58] The mode
follows on the science; generally speaking, any modification presupposes its subject and does not constitute it. "Quia modificare proprie
dicatur aliquid, quando redditur aliquale, non quando fit secundum
suam substantiam."[59] Thus we come to speak of a distinction between
what is signified by a word and the mode of signifying it.

Names signify things as they are known and not immediately as they
exist. The fact that all our knowledge takes its rise from the senses, so
that the quiddity of material things is the proper object of our intellect,
has an effect on the way or mode we know whatever we know, even when
what we know is not the quiddity of a material thing. Because in the
material thing to which our mind is naturally proportioned, there is a
difference between the form and the one having the form, we have one
mode of signifying the composite of matter and form and another of
signifying the form as such. This is precisely the distinction between
concrete and abstract modes of signification.[60] Names which signify
forms do not signify them as subsisting since what is signified as subsisting
is the composite which has the form.

Et quia in huiusmodi creaturis, ea quae sunt perfecta et subsistentia, sunt composita;
forma autem in eis non est aliquid completum subsistens, sed magis quo aliquid est:
inde est quod omnia nomina a nobis imposita ad significandum aliquid completum
subsistens, significant in concretione, prout competit compositis; quae autem impo-

[58] Cf. *In I de anima*, lect 1, nn. 4–5; *I Sent., prolog.*, q. 1, a. 3, sol. 2.
[59] Cajetan, *In II Periherm.*, lect. 8, n. 3.
[60] *I Contra Gentiles*, cap. 30.

nuntur ad significandas formas simplices, significant aliquid non ut subsistens, sed ut quo aliquid est: sicut albedo significat ut quo aliquid est album.[61]

"Humanity" signifies human nature abstractly, not as something which subsists but as that by which a man is a man; "man" signifies the same nature concretely, as that which has humanity, a subsistent thing which might be encountered in the world around us. Concrete terms imply a composition of the form and a subject and for the moment it does not matter whether our examples are "humanity" and "man" or "whiteness" and "white." Human nature is signified by "humanity" *per modum partis*, since it is that whereby man is man. A man, however, is many things besides what is signified by "humanity," e.g. fat, white, etc. The abstract term is said to signify the nature with precision, that is, it prescinds in its mode of signification from everything but the essential principles of the nature signified.[62] From the point of view of the concrete whole, man, humanity is but a part. Yet humanity is what is formal to the composite: that is why it is called the *forma totius* as opposed to the *forma partis*.[63] "Man," the concrete term, is said to signify *per modum totius*, since it means the one who has humanity, that which subsists in the nature, without prescinding from what is not of the essence. That is why "man" can be predicated of Socrates and "humanity" cannot, directly *(in recto)*, although "man" does not include in its signification the accidents of such individuals as Socrates. "Unde licet in significatione hominis non includantur accidentia eius, non tamen homo significat aliquid separatum ab accidentibus; et ideo homo significat ut totum, humanitas significat ut pars."[64] Thus, it is the same nature which is signified by the abstract and concrete term, but the mode of signifying differs. As we shall see later,[65] no matter how perfect the *res* signified by a name attributed to God, with respect to its mode of signifying, *omne nomen cum defectu est.*

---

[61] *Ia.* q. 13, a. 1, ad 2.

[62] *Quodl. IX*, q. 2, a. 1, ad 1: "...dicendum quod ex unione animae et corporis constituitur et homo et humanitas: quae quidem duo hoc modo differunt: quod *humanitas* significatur *per modum partis*, eo quod humanitas dicitur qua homo est homo, et sic praecise significat essentialia principia speciei, per quae hoc individuum in tali specie collocatur; unde se habet per modum partis, cum praeter huiusmodi principia multa alia in rebus naturae inveniuntur. Sed *homo* significatur *per modum totius*: homo enim dicitur habens humanitatem, vel subsistens in humanitate, sine praecisione quorumcumque aliorum supervenientium essentialibus principiis speciei; quia per hoc quod dico: Habens humanitatem, non praeciditur, qui habet colorem, et quantitatem et alia huiusmodi." Cf. *De ente et essentia*, cap. 3.

[63] *In VII Metaphys.*, lect. 9, nn. 1467–9.

[64] *In VII Metaphys.*, lect. 5, n. 1379.

[65] Chapter IX.

5. RATIO QUAM SIGNIFICAT NOMEN [66]

As our analysis of the text from the commentary on *On Interpretation* made clear, St Thomas' doctrine on signification is simply Aristotle's: the word signifies the thing *(res)* not directly, but via a conception of the mind. This conception, which is directly and immediately signified by the word, is given the technical logical designation, *ratio*. "Ratio enim quam significat nomen, est conceptio intellectus de re significata per nomen."[67] In order to isolate the *conceptio* or *ratio*, we note, with St Thomas, that a man can be considered as related to four things when he understands: to the thing understood, to the intelligible species by which the intellect is actualized, to the act of understanding and, finally, to the conception.

Quae quidem conceptio a tribus praedictis differt. *A re* quidem intellecta, quia res intellecta est interdum extra intellectum, conceptio autem intellectus non est nisi in intellectu; et iterum conceptio intellectus ordinatur ad rem intellectam sicut ad finem: propter hoc enim intellectus conceptionem rei in se format ut rem intellectam cognoscat. Differt autem *a specie* intelligibili, nam species intelligibilis qua fit intellectus in actu, considerat ut principium actionis intellectus, cum omne agens agat secundum quod est in actu; actu autem fit per aliquam formam, quam oportet esse actionis principium. Differt autem *ab actione* intellectus, quia praedicta conceptio consideratur ut terminus actionis, et quasi quoddam per ipsam constitutam.[68]

The conception produced by the act of understanding is what the word signifies; indeed, the conception itself is called a word. "Haec autem conceptio intellectus in nobis proprie *verbum* dicitur: hoc enim est quod verbo exteriori significatur: vox enim exterior neque significat ipsum intellectum, neque speciem intelligibilem, neque actum intellectus, sed intellectus conceptionem, qua mediante refertur ad rem."[69] The inner word is said to be both the efficient and final cause of the spoken word. It is the final cause for the reason just given: the purpose of the spoken word is to express and signify the concept or inner word. It is the efficient cause of the spoken word "quia verbum prolatum exterius, praeexistit in mente artificis, ita in mente proferentis verbum exterius, praeexistit quoddam exemplar exterioris verbi."[70] The conception is called the *verbum cordis* whereas as exemplar of the spoken word it is called the *verbum interius*.[71] What now is the significance of calling the conception a *ratio?*

[66] *In IV Metaphys.*, lect. 16, n. 733.
[67] *Ia*, q. 13, a. 4.
[68] *Q.D. de pot.*, q. 8, a. 1; ibid., q. 9, a. 5.
[69] *Q.D. de pot.*, q. 8, a. 1.
[70] *Q.D. de ver.*, q. 4, a. 1.
[71] *Ibid.* We might mention that St Thomas is here presenting *verbum* as an analogous name; ibid., ad 8 gives the etymology of the term: "...a verberatione vel a boatu."

St Thomas gives us an extensive and exhaustive statement of what is meant by *ratio* in this regard, as well as the manner of its reference to the real order. "Ratio nihil aliud est quam id quod apprehendit intellectus de significatione alicuius nominis."[72] Sometimes, but not always, the *ratio* signified by the name is a definition; we know and name many things which cannot be defined, properly speaking, notably, substance, quantity and the other supreme genera. (Properly speaking, of course, the definition consists of the proximate genus and specific difference.) Now if that which the word signifies is sometimes a definition, *ratio* like definition must be a second intention. The conception, considered as a definition, is a *secundum intellectum*,[73] a second intention. So too *ratio* in the phrase: *ratio quam nomen significat est definitio. Ratio*, of course, can mean other things,[74] but we are presently interested in it insofar as it is a *nomen intentionis*.[75] To be a *ratio* is something which happens to a thing insofar as it is conceived by our intellect: it is a relation following on our mode of knowing just as species, genus, difference and definition are.[76] "Nec tamen hoc nomen ratio significat ipsam conceptionem, quia hoc significatur per nomen rei, sed significat intentionem huius conceptionis, sicut et hoc nomen definitio, et alia nomina secundae impositionis."[77] "Man" would be an example of a *nomen rei*. What does it signify? Rational animal. This is the nature grasped in the

---

[72] I Sent., d. 2, q. 1, a. 3.

[73] Q.D. de pot., q. 7, a. 9: "Prima enim intellecta sunt res extra animam, in quae primo intellectus intelligenda fertur. Secunda autem intellecta dicuntur intentiones consequentes modum intelligendi: hoc enim secundo intellectus intelligit inquantum reflectitur supra se ipsum, intelligens se intelligere et modum quo intelligit."

[74] Cf. *In de divinis nominibus*, lect. 5, n. 735. "Ratio" can mean, (a) quaedam cognoscitiva virtus, (b) causa, ut, e.g., "qua ratione hoc fecisti?," (c) computatio, (d) aliquid simplex abstractum a multis, sicut dicitur ratio hominis id quod per considerationem abstrahitur a singularibus, ad hominis naturam pertinens. It is with this last sense that we are presently concerned.

[75] *I Sent.*, d. 33, q. 1, a. 1, ad 3; cf. *ibid.*, d. 25, q. 1, a. 1, ad 2, for "definitio."

[76] Q.D. de pot., q. 7, a. 6.

[77] *I Sent.*, d. 2, q. 1, a. 3. On the difference between *nomen rei* and *nomen intentionis*, see *Ia*, q. 30, a. 4. Andre Hayen, S.J., in *L'Intentionnel selon saint Thomas*, Paris, Bruges, Bruxelles, deuxième édition, 1954, seems not to take sufficiently into account the distinction between *ratio* as a *nomen intentionis* and *ratio* as the known nature to which being a *ratio* happens. On p. 180, for example, he quotes St Thomas, "Ratio autem se tenet magis ex parte rei." St Thomas is comparing *ratio, scientia* and *idea*, and his complete sentence is as follows: "Ratio autem se tenet magis ex parte rei, ut consignificari et significari possit; dicimus enim rationes plures." (*I Sent.*, d. 36, q. 2, a. 2, ad 4) Or consider this remark. "La théorie psychologique de la première et de la seconde intention met en relief la propriété de notre connaissance intellectuelle, qui est de s'opposer à son objet en lui attribuant une *intentio prima*, si cet objet est une chose extérieure ou une *intentio secunda*, si cet objet est un autre concept de l'esprit, la *ratio* de la chose déjà investie d'une *intentio prima*." (pp. 192–3) The reader, finding the distinction between first and second intentions becoming progressively hazier, is somewhat abashed to find his objection anticipated (p. 194), but handled in a yet more hazy manner. But of course there can be no question here of giving Father Hayen's book the attention it undoubtedly deserves.

concept and verified in the real order. The term *ratio* applied to "rational animal" signifies a relation which attaches to the nature as it exists in the mind, the relation of the nature conceived to the word imposed to signify it.

This is a difficult but important doctrine. St Thomas points out that it underlies every discussion of the Divine names. The sublety involved is apparent when we watch St Thomas handle the question which asks if the *ratio* exists in reality. In a sense, we can say it does, but the reservations are most significant.

> Non enim hoc dicitur, quasi ipsa intentio quam significat nomen rationis, sit in re; aut etiam ipsa conceptio cui convenit talis intentio, sit in re extra animam, cum sit in anima sicut in subjecto: sed dicitur esse in re, inquantum in re extra animam est aliquid quod respondet conceptioni animae, sicut significatum signo.[78]

Notice that the nature conceived can be called the *ratio* of a given name, but what *ratio* names is the relation, or the known nature as subject of the logical relation. The relation itself does not exist "out-there" anymore than the concept does; but the nature conceived and as such the subject of such intentions as species, genus, *ratio*, etc. may exist "out-there." There are degrees of dependence on or reference to reality in names. The concept is a sign of a real nature and the name signifying it is called a *nomen rei* (e.g. "man.") The concept does not exist in reality, in the sense of outside the mind, since it is precisely an accident of intellect,[79] but something in reality answers directly to it as the signified to the sign. Second intentions, on the other hand, have as their proximate foundation the nature existing in the mind, the nature as known; there is nothing in reality which answers immediately and directly to logical relations. If we add to names of first and names of second intentions the names of fictive entities, we can distinguish with St Thomas three ways in which names refer to reality.[80]

The foregoing enables us to see what is meant by saying that the signification of names is a logical question. Insofar as we speak of the nature signified by the word as a *ratio*, we are adequately put on notice that we are engaged in a logical discussion; that is, we are considering natures, not as they exist *in rerum natura*, but from the point of view of the relations they take on as known by us. "Logicus enim considerat modum preaedicandi, et non existentiam rei."[81] The nature as signified by the name, as well as the different way words signify – univocally,

[78] *I Sent.*, d. 2, q. 1, a. 3.
[79] *Q.D. de pot.*, q. 8, a. 1.
[80] *I Sent.*, d. 2, q. 1, a. 3.
[81] *In VII Metaphys.*, lect. 17, n. 1658.

equivocally, analogically – are logical considerations and they are carried on in logical terminology.

6. SIGNIFICATION AND SUPPOSITION

We have distinguished the *id a quo* which is the etymology of the word from the *id a quo* which is its quality, that is, the form principally signified by it. We must now distinguish the *id a quo* in this second sense from the supposition of the term, for supposition, like etymology, differs from signification. The need for this further distinction is clear from a text already quoted from the *Sentences*.[82] "Dicendum quod in quolibet nomine est duo considerare: scilicet id a quo imponitur nomen, quod dicitur qualitas nominis, et id cui imponitur, quod dicitur substantia nominis. Et nomen, proprie loquendo, dicitur significare formam sive qualitatem a qua imponitur nomen; dicitur vero supponere pro eo cui imponitur." The significance of this distinction for our purposes is that a diversity of supposition will not give rise to equivocation. "...aequivocatio inducitur ex diversa forma significata per nomen, non autem ex diversitate suppositionis: non enim hoc nomen homo aequivoce sumitur ex eo quod quandoque supponit pro Platone, quandoque pro Sorte."[83] Moreover, as we shall argue later, metaphor is a question of supposition rather than of signification. On this basis, the distinction of signification and supposition will be relevant in evaluating the position that metaphor is a kind of analogous name.

In the following text, St Thomas compares signification with supposition and what is called *copulatio*.

...propria ratio nominis est quam significat nomen, secundum Philosophum. Id autem *cui* attribuitur nomen, si sit recte sumptum sub re significata per nomen, sicut determinatum sub indeterminato, dicitur supponi per nomen; si autem non sit recte sumptum sub re nominis, dicitur copulari per nomen; sicut hoc nomen *animal* significat substantiam animatam sensibilem, et *album* significat colorem disgregativum visus: *homo* vero recte sumitur sub ratione animalis, sicut determinatum sub indeterminato. Est enim homo substantia animata sensibilis tali anima, scilicet rationali; sub albo vero, quod est extra essentiam eius, non directe sumitur. Unde homo supponitur nomine animalis, copulatur vero nomine albi.[84]

[82] *III Sent.*, d. 6, q. 1, a. 3.

[83] *IV Contra Gentiles*, cap. 49. Cf. *Compendium theologiae*, cap. 211; *Q.D. de unione verbi incarnati*, a. 2, ad 4: "Dicendum quod univocatio et aequivocatio attenditur secundum quod ratio nominis est eadem vel non eadem. Ratio autem nominis est quam significat definitio; et ideo aequivocatio et univocatio secundum significationem attenditur et non secundum supposita."

[84] *Q.D. de pot.*, q. 9, a. 4; cf. *III Sent.*, d. 7, q. 1, a. 1, ad 5. In *Ia*, q. 39, a. 5, ad 5, St Thomas attributes the distinction between supposition and copulation to sophists, which is why we are excusing ourselves from any discussion of *copulatio*.

Supposition presupposes the signification of the term and concerns its use to stand for what falls under its signification as the determinate under the indeterminate. Thus the species can be supposed for by the generic name, as in the text just cited, and the individuals can be supposed for by the specific name.[85] The supposition of a term, its supposits, are the things it stands for given its signification. A term has supposition, it would seem, only as used in a proposition. Thus, in "Some animals are rational," the subject of the proposition signifies "animate sensitive substance" and supposes for men. Such a use of the term does not constitute its signification, since its signification must be presupposed if we are to understand the use. It is fairly clear that it is the abstractive mode of our understanding which gives rise to what is called the supposition of a term. Given the universal signification, the term can be used to stand for things in which what it signifies is found. As used in a proposition, a term will normally suppose or stand for the things in which its *res significata* is saved. Nevertheless, a term may suppose in other ways as well.

Sometimes a word stands for itself, as in the sentence, "To run is a verb."

Sed dicendum est quod in tali locutione, hoc verbum *curro* non sumitur formaliter, secundum quod eius significatio refertur ad rem, sed secundum quod materialiter significat ipsam vocem quae accipitur ut res quaedam. Et ideo tam verba quam omnes orationis partes, quando ponuntur materialiter, sumuntur in vi nominum.[86]

This is what, in systematic discussions of supposition, is called the material supposition of a term.[87] Sometimes a term is taken to stand for the nature it signifies insofar as that nature is considered as common or universal.

Unitas autem sive communitas humanae naturae non est secundum rem, sed solum secundum considerationem; unde iste terminus homo non supponit pro natura communi, nisi propter exigentiam alicuius additi, ut cum dicitur, homo est species.[88]

This use of a term is called simple supposition in systematic treatises on supposition. It is clear that material and simple supposition are possible and important uses of a term, but it is equally clear that a term will normally be taken to suppose in the way we spoke of suppo-

[85] See references in note 83 above; see as well, *Ia*, q. 13, a. 10, ad 1.
[86] *In I Periherm.*, lect. 5, n. 6.
[87] John of St Thomas, *Cursus Philosophicus*, T. I, p. 29 ff; Ph. Boehner, O.F.M., *Medieval Logic*, Chicago, 1952, pp. 27–51; E. A. Moody, *Truth and Consequence in Mediaeval Logic*, Amsterdam, 1953, pp. 18–23; J. P. Mullally, *The Summulae Logicales of Peter of Spain*, Notre Dame, 1945.
[88] *Ia*, q. 39, a 4. Cf. *IIIa*, q. 16, a. 7.

sition at the outset, a type of supposition called personal supposition in systematic treatises. Nonetheless, the signification of a term does not decide the use it may have in a proposition. It is a fairly common tenet[89] that a term has supposition only in a proposition; if this is accepted, and doubtless it should be, supposition will be a logical intention falling to the logic of the second operation of the mind; signification, and this will include equivocation and consequently analogy, pertains to the logic of the first operation. For, again, the meaning of a term is presupposed by the use of a term in a proposition and not constituted by that use. There can be diversity of supposition in the realm of personal supposition (e.g. "man" standing now for Socrates, now for Plato) without equivocation ensuing, for in each of these uses "man" has the same signification. Equivocation, of course, involves diversity of signification.

It may be that what St Thomas has to say about supposition is the same as what can be found in treatises devoted to this matter; we are not prepared to say that this is so, or that it is not so. If we assume that John of St Thomas has accurately systematized his mentor on this matter, however, a rather curious result follows. John groups material, simple and personal supposition under the heading of proper supposition. Metaphor, he adds, is an instance of improper supposition.[90] Furthermore, he will say that supposition is a second intention arising from the second operation of the mind.[91] Equivocation, on the other hand, follows on the first operation. How then can he maintain that metaphor is a type of analogous name? We will agree that metaphor is rather a question of supposition than of signification, but we will go on to take this as indication enough that metaphor must be distinguished from analogy. And we will show how this is done.

---

[89] John of St Thomas, loc. cit., p. 30. See Moody, op. cit., p. 21. Possible corroboration in St Thomas is had in III Sent., d. 7, q. 1, a. 1, ad 5.

[90] Loc. cit., p. 31.

[91] There is a special problem connected with the term suppositum, a problem we only allude to here. This term is sometimes a nomen rei as opposed to a nomen intentionis. Cf. I Sent., d. 23, q. 1, a. 3; Q.D. de unione verbi incarnati, a. 2; a. 3 c. et ad 5; Ia. q. 29, a. 1, ad 3.

CHAPTER V

THE ANALOGY OF NAMES

We are now in a position to examine the doctrine of the analogy of names. Since, as we have already pointed out, the analogy of names is for St Thomas a kind of equivocation, it will be well to examine in some detail the logical doctrine of equivocation and univocation. These matters are discussed at the outset of the *Categories* and they are numbered among the considerations which have come to be called the antepredicaments.

1. THINGS NAMED EQUIVOCALLY

"Things are said to be named equivocally when, though they have a common name, the definition corresponding with the name differs for each."[1] This is the first sentence in the Aristotelian corpus and, like every statement which follows, its meaning must be carefully unpacked. The translation given is not entirely happy. The Latin rendering is as follows: "Aequivoca dicuntur quorum solum nomen commune est, secundum nomen vero substantiae ratio diversa."[2] Both translations indicate that the definition begins with the things named and not from the name itself. A recent book insists on this in a rather curious way, and its author would have us believe that for Aristotle equivocation is something of things and not of terms.[3] It is Aristotle, however, who points out that our names refer to things insofar as they are known,[4] and when we are talking about equivocals, we are talking about something which happens to things thanks to our mode of knowing, not something which

---

[1] *Categories*, lal–2: Ὁμώνυμα λέγεται ὧν ὄνομα μόνον κοινόν, ὁ δὲ κατὰ τοὔνομα λόγος τῆς οὐσίας ἕτερος.

[2] It will be helpful to have the complete Latin text. "Aequivoca dicuntur quorum solum nomen commune est, secundum nomen vero substantiae ratio diversa, ut animal homo et quod pingitur. Horum enim solum nomen commune est, secundum nomen vero substantiae ratio diversa. Si quis enim assignet quid sit utrumque eorum, quo sint animalia propriam assignabit utriusque rationem."

[3] Joseph Owens, C. SS. R., *The Doctrine of Being in the Aristotelian Metaphysics*, Toronto, (1951), pp. 49–53. But see his, *A History of Ancient Western Philosophy*, New York, (1959), pp. 297–8.

[4] *On Interpretation*, 16a3–4: Ἔστι μὲν οὖν τὰ ἐν τῇ φωνῇ τῶν ἐν τῇ ψυχῇ παθημάτων σύμβολα.

belongs to them as they exist *in rerum natura*. Nevertheless, it is true that Aristotle is speaking of things, not of names, when he says, "aequivoca dicuntur." This does not mean that things are equivocal apart from being known and named; they are *said* to be equivocal: *dicuntur, et non sunt*.[5] If man with his distinctive mode of knowing did not exist, there would be no equivocals, that is, things named equivocally. But this is quite obvious from our previous considerations.

Things named equivocally are said to have only a name in common: as soon as one goes beyond the name, there is diversity, for the common name does not signify the same definition with each use. The English here relies on our rather loose use of "definition," something which is avoided in the Latin *ratio*.[6] A definition in the strict sense of a proximate genus and specific difference is not necessarily intended by *ratio* in the definition of equivocals. Indeed, if it were, the apparent purpose of speaking first of equivocals and then of univocals would be defeated. Aristotle is preparing to speak of the ten supreme genera of which "being" is said, not univocally, but equivocally. And, since the supreme genera cannot have a definition in the strict sense, they could not be said to be named equivocally if *ratio* had the restricted sense.

Aristotle's definition begins from things; these things are said to be equivocal: they are not equivocal in themselves, but they are named equivocally. Nevertheless, Aristotle is not talking about equivocation, but about equivocals, about things named equivocally. The *Categories* divides things, but not things as they exist, for then it would not be a logical work. Rather, the division is in terms of the different mode of existence (and hence of signification) which things have in our mind. Things are said to be equivocal or univocal, then, because of what happens to them due to our mode of knowing.[7] This is the reason for

[5] Boethius, *In Categorias Aristotelis*, Migne, *Patrologia Latina*, vol. 64, col. 164B: "Aequivoca, inquit, dicuntur res scilicet, quae per se ipsas aequivoce non sunt, nisi uno nomine praedicentur: quare quoniam ut aequivoca sint, ex communi vocabulo trahunt, recte ait, aequivoca dicuntur. Non enim sunt aequivoca, sed dicuntur."

[6] Notice the similarity between the various meanings of *ratio* given by St Thomas in his commentary on the *De divinis nominibus*, lect. 5, n. 735, and those given by Boethius. "Ratio quoque multimode dicitur. Est enim ratio animae, et est ratio computandi, est ratio naturae, ipsa nimirum similitudo nascentium, est ratio quae in diffinitionibus vel descriptionibus redditur. Et quoniam¦ generalissima genera genere carent, individua vero nulla substantiali differentia descrepant, diffinitio vero ex genere et differentia trahitur, neque generalissimorum generum, neque individuorum ulla potest diffinitio reperiri. Subalternorum vero generum, quoniam et differentias habent et genera, diffinitiones esse possunt. At vero quorum diffinitiones reddi nequeunt, illa tantum descriptionibus terminatur. Descriptio autem est, quae quamlibet rem proprie quadam proprietate designat. Sive ergo diffinitio sit, sive descriptio, utraque rationem substantiae designat." – *loc. cit.*, col. 166A.

[7] "Et dicuntur univoca per oppositum modum ad aequivoca, res scilicet univocatae in nomine uno, ut res ipsa ad dici et ad sermonem referatur, quia aliter non esset logicum quod

the distinction, mentioned by Cajetan[8] and John of St Thomas,[9] between *aequivoca aequivocans* (the name) and *aequivoca aequivocata*. The latter are the things named, and they are equivocal, not as things, but as named. This is a logical discussion.

There is a difficulty which can arise in trying to understand Aristotle's statement that things named equivocally have the same name. What constitutes a name as a name is the fact that it signifies something. But how can it be said that a sound which signifies different *rationes* is the same name? It would seem that something designating the merely physical aspect of the word should have been used, so that the Latin, for instance, would read, "quorum solum vox est commune."

St Albert goes into this problem at some length, distinguishing between a first and a second form of the name. The physical sound, the *vox*, is what is material, but the first form to determine it is an accent, a pronunciation, and, as written, letters and syllables. This first form of the *vox* introduces something besides the merely physical, and the result of this formation is a word or name. In this sense, St Albert says, things named equivocally can be said to have the same name.[10] The idea is that, unless the *vox* has received the first form, it is not apt to take on the further form of signification, and, since it can retain this first form even when its significations vary, we can say that the same name is retained. It is of course essential to the understanding of the definition of equivocals that the second form of the *vox*, its signification, be understood as well. In things named equivocally, not only has the *vox* received the first determination of accent, letters and syllables, but it is also taken as signifying. The point is that it signifies different things. Support for this explanation of St Albert can be found in St Thomas.[11]

With regard to the phrase in the definition, "secundum nomen substantiae ratio diversa," St Albert seems to be the only one who has referred this to the classical dictum: "omne nomen substantiam signifi-

dicitur: quia res in se considerata, non secundum quod stat sub dictione, non ad logicum, sed ad Philosophum pertinet. Et ideo additur, *dicuntur*, et non dicitur univoca *sunt*. – St Albert, *In praedicamenta Aristotelis*, tract. 1, cap. 3. Cf. Cajetan, *Commentaria in praedicamenta Aristotelis*, p. 9: "Signanter quoque dixit ,dicuntur' et non dixit ,sunt', quia rebus non convenit aequivocari ut sunt in rerum natura, sed ut sunt in vocibus nostris. Aequivocari enim praesupponit vocari, quod rebus ex nobis accidit."

[8] Cajetan, *loc. cit.*, p. 8.

[9] John of St Thomas, *Cursus Philosophicus*, T. I, p. 478: "Sed quia non dicuntur aequivocata nisi ratione intentionis alicujus, quae dicitur aequivocatio, et haec, ut statim dicemus, non convenit rebus significatis nisi ut subsunt nomini, non vero conceptui ultimato, ideo traditur definitio per nomen, in ordine ad quod sumitur intentio aequivocationis."

[10] St Albert, *loc. cit.*, cap. 2.

[11] John of St Thomas directs our attention (*loc. cit.*, p. 479) to *Quodl. IV*, q. 9, a. 2: "Manifestum est autem quod unitas vocis significativae vel diversitas non dependet ex unitate vel diversitate rei significatae; *alioquin non esset aliquod nomen aequivocum*: secundum hoc enim si sint diversae res, essent diversa nomina, et non idem nomen."

cat cum qualitate."[12] The *ratio substantiae* is that which the name is imposed to signify; the quality of the name, we recall, is that *a quo nomen imponitur*. The substance of the name is that to which it is attributed, or that for which it supposes; it underlies the quality which is the *ratio* signified by the name. In things named equivocally, therefore, there is the same name, but it signifies different *rationes*.

Aristotle insists, in his definition, that it is according to the name which equivocals have in common that they are said to be named equivocally. Given another name, it could happen that things now named equivocally, could be named univocally. It is according to the proper signification of the common name that univocals are said to be such. It is because the common name signifies different notions that other things are said to be named equivocally.[13]

What things named equivocally have in common, then, is the name itself; there is simply a community of the name. When one looks to what the name signifies, it is found that now it signifies this *ratio*, now another different from the first. Let this suffice for a preliminary glance at things named equivocally.

2. THINGS NAMED UNIVOCALLY

"On the other hand, things are said to be named univocally which have both the name and the definition answering to the name in common."[14] Once again Aristotle begins from the things named, and once again there is a community of the name. But here, in opposition to equivocals, the community extends beyond the name to the definition or *ratio* signified by it. When a man and an ox are named animals, they have the name "animal" in common, but that which is signified by the name is also shared by each, and, from this point of view, shared equally.

---

[12] St Albert, *loc. cit.*, cap. 2. "...et id quidem cui imponitur nomen est significata substantia ipsius; proprietas autem ejusdem rei sive substantiae quae afficit imponentem dum nomen imponit, est qualitas significata per nomen."

[13] Cf. Boethius, *loc. cit.*, col. 165C: "Idem etiam in his nominibus quae de duabus rebus communiter praedicantur, si secundum nomen substantiae ratio non reddatur, potest aliquoties fieri, ut ex univocis aequivoca sint, et ex aequivocis univoca; namque homo atque equus cum secundum nomen animalis univoca sint, possunt esse aequivoca, si secundum nomen minime diffinita sint. Homo namque et equus communi nomine animalia nuncupantur, si quis ergo hominis reddat diffinitionem dicens, animal rationale mortale, et equi, animal irrationale hinnibile, diversas reddidit diffinitiones, et erunt res univocae in aequivocas permutatae. Hoc autem idcirco evenit, quod diffinitiones non secundum animalis nomen reditae sunt, quod eorum commune vocabulum est, sed secundum hominis et equi."

[14] "Univoca dicuntur quorum nomen commune est, et secundum nomen eadem ratio substantiae." – *Categories*, 1a6–7: συνώνυμα δὲ λέγεται ὧν τό τε ὄνομα κοινὸν καὶ ὁ κατὰ τοὔνομα λόγος τῆς οὐσίας ὁ αὐτός.

Both man and ox are "animate sensitive substance." The term "animal" is imposed to signify what man and ox have in common with a generic community.

The difference between things named equivocally and those named univocally is now clear. The latter have a common name and the *ratio* signified by the name is common to them all. In equivocals, on the other hand, although they have a common name, that name signifies different *rationes* as applied to them. A point of extreme importance which warrants repetition is that things are said to be *(dicuntur)* equivocals or univocals. In themselves, *in rerum natura*, they are neither, for in order to be univocals or equivocals they must be known and named by us. We are talking about the things signified insofar as they are signified. The problem of equivocals is a logical problem; the problem of univocals is a logical one.

At this point it is of interest to note the fourfold way in which things can be named. This is found in Boethius,[15] who observes that things are *univoca, diversivoca, multivoca* or *aequivoca*. That is, they either have one name which signifies the same *ratio ;* or they have different names which signify different *rationes ;* or one thing receives many names which signify the same *ratio* (thus *multivoca* are those things *we* would say are named by synonyms; συνώνυμα is Aristotle's word for univocals.) Finally, many things have one name which signifies diverse *rationes*. It is with the latter, the equivocals, that analogy is numbered.

3. THINGS NAMED ANALOGICALLY

We have already seen that for St Thomas analogy is a kind of equivocation, but when we were discussing the equivocals we said nothing about analogy. We must now return to the definition of things named equivocally and see how it leaves room for things named analogically. In doing so, we will draw on the commentaries of Boethius, St Albert and Cajetan before turning to St Thomas. St Thomas did not comment on the *Categories*, but by referring the analogy of names to the definition of things named equivocally he explicitly calls into play the doctrine of Aristotle on this point. It is for that reason that we have found it advisable to spend time on that doctrine; only by understanding equivocation and its status as a logical doctrine can we come to an adequate understanding of St Thomas' teaching on the analogy of names.

Things are said to be named equivocally which have a common name,

[15] Boethius, *loc. cit.*, cols. 164–5.

although they differ with regard to what the name signifies in each case. Obviously things can receive a common name which, as it is said of each of them, does not signify entirely different notions. The clearest example of equivocation is had when the notions are entirely diverse, of course. For example, "pen" used to signify a writing instrument and an enclosure for pigs is an equivocal name. When, however, a cow and a picture of it are named "animal," the notions signified by the name are not wholly diverse. The example of "pen" is one of pure equivocation, that of "animal" is not. In such cases as that of "pen," it would seem that the same name just happens to be imposed to signify different things; it is completely adventitious. We would not feel, however, that "animal" is imposed fortuitously to signify the cow and its picture. True, "animal" won't mean exactly the same thing in each case, but its meanings are not unrelated. Such considerations as these are behind Boethius' division (garnered from Aristotle elsewhere) of equivocals into those which are such by chance and those which are such by design.[16]

It is interesting that commentators seem unanimous in pointing out that the example given by Aristotle in defining things named equivocally is not one of pure equivocation. It is only fitting that it not be, of course, when we consider the purpose of the discussion for the doctrine of the supreme genera. The definition, then, covers things named purely equivocally as well as those which are not, depending on whether the diversity of the notions signified is complete or partial.[17]

Where there is only partial diversity in things named equivocally, there must also be partial sameness. The sameness is had, St Albert notes, in this that the name principally signifies one of the equivocals and the others insofar as they refer in some way to what is principally signified. He illustrates this with the familiar Aristotelian examples of "being," "medicine" and "medical." "Et hic quidem modus vocatur

---

[16] *Ibid.*, col. 166: "Aequivocorum alia sunt casu, alia consilio, ut Alexander Priami filius et Alexander Magnus. Casus enim id egit, ut idem utrique nomen poneretur. Consilio vero, ea quaecumque hominum voluntate sunt posita."

[17] St Albert spells this out in his prolix fashion. "Quando ergo idem est nomen quantum ad ea quae sint nominis in littera et accentu: et id quod significatur in nomine, non est idem vel aeque participatum ab illis quibus nomen imponitur, nec etiam proprietas a qua impositum est omnino eadem est, quamvis forte referatur ad unum: tunc nomen est aequivocum, quia ratio substantiae cui nomen imponitur (quae est ratio substantialis a qua nomen imponitur) sic duobus modis est secundum aliquid vel simpliciter diversa: substantia enim aliqua (ut diximus) est secundum aliquid per modum quo rationi substat, cui nomen ipsum imponitur: et illius ratio diversa est quando non penitus est eadem: et adhuc a quo nomen imponitur quod est nomen qualitas, est substantialis ratio quae datur de nomine secundum illud quod nomen est. Quando ergo illa etiam non penitus est eadem, iterum ratio substantiae, hoc est, substantialis ratio nominis diversa: ita quod nihil rei cui imponitur nomen, aequaliter participant significata per nomen." – *loc. cit.*, cap. 2.

multiplex dictum secundum analogiam, sive proportionem ad unum quod principaliter in nomine significatur."[18]

We might point out here that Cajetan, in his commentary on the *Categories*, is quite explicit about the fact that analogy is a kind of equivocation. Having pointed out that *diversa* in the definition of things named equivocally should be understood as comprising both complete and partial diversity on the part of the *rationes* signified by the common name, he goes on to say that the example given by Aristotle is one of "aequivocatio a consilio seu analogia."[19] It is precisely here that he promises a separate treatise on this type of equivocation.[20] That separate treatise was to be the *De nominum analogia* and in it analogy, which is a kind of equivocation, unaccountably becomes something metaphysical. In turning now to the texts of St Thomas, we will begin the study which will enable us to see if Cajetan was explaining equivocation or employing it.

At this point, we must reiterate that St Thomas did not devote any separate treatise to the subject of the analogy of names. His thought on the matter must be drawn from the many places where he is discussing the application of analogy, or an instance of it. Because of this, we should keep in mind what has gone immediately before. There is little danger that equivocation or univocation will be considered metaphysical rather than logical. Analogy, however, is constantly treated as if it were something metaphysical. We are not here concerned with other interpretations of St Thomas, but it should be clear throughout what follows that the analogy of names is something of logic. This is obvious enough in St Thomas.

It was in commenting on the example Aristotle gives in the *Categories* of things named equivocally that St Thomas referred analogy to equivocation.[21] Just as Aristotle sometimes says that "being" is predicated equivocally of substance and the other categories, so too he says that "animal"

---

[18] *Ibid.* Boethius too speaks of equivocals by design which represent an *aequivocatio secundum proportionem*. Cf. *loc. cit.*, col. 166: "...secundum proportionem, ut principium, namque principium est in numero unitas, in lineis punctum. Alia vero sunt quae ab uno descendunt... Alia quae ad unum referuntur..." It is interesting to see Boethius moving easily from what could be called the proportionality of "principle" to proportions *ad unum* and *ab uno*. It is noteworthy that Boethius distinguishes equivocation *secundum proportionem* from that *secundum similitudinem*. It is the last kind of equivocation which he feels is involved in the example given by Aristotle in the *Categories*.

[19] Cajetan, *loc. cit.*, p. 10.

[20] *Ibid.*, p. 11. "Quot autem modis contingat variari analogiam et quomodo, nunc quum summarie loquimur, silentio pertransibimus, specialem de hoc tractatum, si Deo placuerit, cito confecturi."

[21] *Ia*, q. 13, a. 10, ad 4. Why does the theologian concern himself with the analogy of names? Cf. *I Sent.*, d. 22, q. 1, a. 4, *divisio textus*. In seeming contradiction to this, St Thomas elsewhere says, "sapientis non est curare de nominibus." (Cf. *II Sent.*, d. 3, q. 1, a. 1) The theologian is concerned with the *meanings* of words, in the sense of the *ratio* attached to this burst of sound,

is said equivocally of an animal and a painting of one. In both cases, St Thomas remarks, it is a question of analogy. As other commentators had before him, St Thomas distinguishes between things named equivocally by chance and those which are not chance equivocals.[22] Chance equivocals are things which receive the same name, but the name signifies something entirely different in each case. The most obvious example of chance equivocals, according to St Thomas, are two men who receive the same name quite accidentally.[23] Things which are named equivocally by design are said to be named according to analogy so as to distinguish them from pure or chance equivocals.

As we have already noted, St Thomas seldom mentions analogy without contrasting it with pure equivocation and univocation. Pure equivocation, again, is had when several things receive the same name which signifies totally different notions or *rationes* in each case. St Thomas' example is usually "dog" said of an animal and a star.[24]

Quandoque vero secundum rationes quae partim sunt diversae et partim non diversae: diversae quidem secundum quod diversas habitudines important, unae autem secundum quod ad unum aliquid et idem istae diversae habitudines referuntur; et illud dicitur analogice praedicari, idest proportionaliter, prout unumquodque secundum suam habitudinem ad illud unum refertur.[25]

In contrast to pure equivocation, analogical signification entails a certain unity among the many *rationes* signified by the common name. Things named purely equivocally have a common name, but that is all they have in common, for as soon as we go beyond the name to the notions signified there is total diversity. This is not the case with things named analogically, for such a name involves an order among the *rationes* signified. There is diversity because the name signifies different proportions or relations or references; there is unity because these proportions or relations or references are to one and the same thing. The diverse *rationes* or definitions are attributed[26] to one and the same thing. The analogous

that pile of ink. Thus, in disputes as to whether the potency in angels should be called matter or not, it is the meaning "matter" is thought to have which, in the final analysis, matters – not the *vox* itself. Nevertheless, we should bear in mind that the meanings which have previously been attached to a given *vox* can make it a more adaptable instrument for what the theologian wants to say. But this should not lead the theologian into purely verbalistic disputes.

[22] *In I Ethic.*, lect. 7, n. 95; cf. *I Sent.*, d. 31, q. 2, a. 1, ad 2.
[23] *In I Ethic.*, lect. 7, n. 95.
[24] *In IV Metaphys.*, lect. 1, n. 535; *In XI Metaphys.*, lect. 3, n. 2197; *I Sent.*, d. 31, q. 2, a. 1, ad 2.
[25] *In IV Metaphys.*, lect. 1, n. 535.
[26] *De principiis naturae*, cap. 6, n. 366: "Analogice dicitur praedicari quod praedicatur de pluribus quorum rationes et definitiones sunt diversae, sed attribuuntur uni alicui eidem: sicut sanum dicitur de corpore animalis et de urina et de potione, sed non ex toto idem significat in omnibus tribus. Dicitur enim de urina ut signo sanitatis, de corpore ut de subjecto, de potione ut de causa; sed tamen omnes istae rationes attribuuntur uni fini, scilicet sanitati."

name is one of multiple signification but that multiplicity is reduced to a certain unity because the name signifies many relations to one and the same thing. The example to which St Thomas returns again and again to show the mutiplicity of the analogous name is "healthy." The term "healthy" can signify many things, such as medicine, urine, food, etc. This is not the chance multiplicity of things named equivocally in the sense of pure equivocation. All of these things are said to be healthy because they refer or are proportioned or attributed to the same health. The different relations involved are that of restoring, of signifying and of sustaining health.[27]

It is well to notice that *analoga dicuntur* just as *aequivoca dicuntur* and *univoca dicuntur*. The contrast between *dicuntur* and *sunt* must be retained in things named analogically just as it is in things named equivocally or univocally. As such, there is nothing analogical in being a sign of something else, or in causing or sustaining it, anymore than there is anything as such equivocal about being a star and being an animal which barks. The last two are said to be equivocal *(aequivoca dicuntur)* if the same word "dog" is taken to signify them both. So too a thing and its cause and its sign will be analogates if the same name is imposed to signify them all. Of course, unless things are related in some way we would not purposely impose a common name on them. Nevertheless, the question of analogy does not arise in discussing things as they exist, but as they are known and named. That is why St Thomas compares the analogy of names with equivocation and univocation. They are all three second intentions.

When things are named analogically, the multiple signification of the common name can be reduced to a certain unity. But, if this is the case, it would seem that we are reducing analogy to univocity. When things are named univocally, the common name signifies the same *ratio* in each case. Does not the unity of the many *rationes* signified by the analogous name imply univocity? The answer to this lies in the different ways in which what is univocally common and what is analogously common are divided.

Dicendum quod duplex est divisio: una qua dividitur genus univocum in suas species, quae ex aequo participant genus, sicut animal in bovem et equum; alia est divisio communis analogi in ea de quibus dicitur secundum prius et posterius; sicut ens

[27] *In XI Metaphys.*, lect. 3, n. 2197: "In his vero quae praedicto modo dicuntur, idem nomen de diversis praedicatur secundum rationem partim eamdem, partim diversam. Diversam quidem quantum ad diversos modos relationis. Eamdem vero quantum ad id ad quod fit relatio. Esse enim significativum, et esse effectivum, diversum est. Sed sanitas una est. Et propter hoc huiusmodi dicuntur analoga, quia proportionantur ad unum."

dividitur per substantiam et accidens, et per potentiam et actum; et in talibus ratio communis perfecte salvatur in uno; in aliis autem secundum quid et posterius...[28]

Things named univocally participate equally in the common notion signified by their common name. The notion signified by "animal" is "animate sensitive substance" and it is participated in equally by man and horse. In things named analogically, on the other hand, the common notion signified by the name is not shared equally by all the things which receive the name; only one of the analogates is signified perfectly by the name. The others are signifies imperfectly and in a certain respect, that is, insofar as they refer in some way to what is perfectly signified. For example, the word "being" signifies "id quod habet esse." Of the various things which are named being, only substance saves the common notion perfectly. The other genera save it imperfectly, insofar as their *rationes* refer in some way to that of substance. Thus there is an order in the multiple signification of the analogous name. One *ratio* is signified perfectly and most properly; other *rationes* are signified less perfectly and less properly and with reference to the *ratio propria* of the name. Although there can be inequality among things named univocally, this inequality is not signified *secundum nomen commune*. The analogous name signifies precisely an inequality of significations, but according to a certain order. This is a difference on which we will dwell at length in our exegesis of a controversial text.[29] We can note now that this difference between things named univocally and things named analogically is brought out in a striking way by St Thomas in his commentary on the *Metaphysics*,[30] where he observes that the one to which the secondary analogates refer is "unum numero et non solum ratione." In things named analogically, one of the things is primarily signified, and others are signified insofar as they refer in some way to this thing. The unity of the univocal name, on the other hand, is solely due to reason. Man and horse are specifically different, but animal nature is something generically common to both. Animal nature is not something that could be numerically distinct from man and horse; its unity is due to reason alone. In things named analogically, the one which is principally signified is not an aspect of the secondary analogates, separated from them only by the operation of reason.

Analogy, like equivocation and univocation, is a way of naming

---

[28] *Q.D. de malo*, q. 7, a. 1, ad 1.

[29] See below, chapter VI.

[30] *In IV Metaphys.*, lect. 1, n. 536. "Item sciendum quod illud unum ad quod diversae habitudines referuntur in analogicis, est unum numero, et non solum ratione, sicut est unum illud quod per nomen univocum designatur."

things. St Thomas insists that equivocal, analogical and univocal names are each divided differently. The equivocal name is divided according to the things signified; the univocal name is divided according to specific differences; the analogical name is divided according to different modes.[31] Analogy is midway between equivocation and univocation.

Et iste modus communitatis medius est inter puram aequivocationem et simplicem univocationem. Neque enim in his quae analogice dicuntur, est una ratio, sicut est in univocis; nec totaliter diversa, sicut in aequivocis; sed nomen quod sic multipliciter dicitur, significat diversas proportiones ad aliquid unum; sicut sanum, de urina dictum significat signum sanitatis animalis, de medicina vero dictum significat causam eiusdem sanitatis.[32]

It is noteworthy that when St Thomas says something about analogy as such, his statements are always made in strict logical terminology. The emphasis is always on *dicuntur* as opposed to *sunt*, on *ratio* as opposed to the mode of existence which things enjoy apart from being known and named. The example of "healthy" which St Thomas so often employs is meant to exemplify the logical doctrine. Many things receive the common name "healthy," but they do not participate equally in the *ratio* signified by the name. The concrete term *sanum* is imposed to signify from *sanitas* which we will take to mean "that whereby there is a proper proportion of the humors." The *ratio propria* of the term is saved perfectly by one of the analogates, namely, animal; the animal is *id quod habet sanitatem*. The other analogates will be signified by *sanum* insofar as they refer in some way to that which perfectly saves the *ratio propria;* it is due to this reference to what the name properly signifies that they receive the common name.

Ad cuius evidentiam, sciendum est quod, quando aliquid praedicatur univoce de multis, illud in quolibet eorum secundum propriam rationem invenitur, sicut animal in qualibet specie animalis. Sed quando aliquid dicitur analogice de multis, illud invenitur secundum propriam rationem in uno eorum tantum, a quo alia denominantur.[33]

Only one of the things of which "healthy" is said saves the *ratio propria* of the term; only one of the things called "true" analogically saves the *ratio propria* of that term. This diversity of the *rationes* signified by the analogous name (e.g. *quod habet sanitatem, quod causat sanitatem*) is on

---

[31] *I Sent.*, d.22, q. 1, a. 3, ad 2: "…dicendum quod aliter dividitur aequivocum, analogum et univocum. Aequivocum enim dividitur secundum res significatas, univocum vero dividitur secundum diversas differentias; sed analogum dividitur secundum diversos modos. Unde cum ens praedicetur analogice de decem generibus, dividitur in ea secundum diversos modos. Unde unicuique generi debetur proprius modus praedicandi."

[32] *Ia*, q. 13, a. 5.

[33] *Ia*, q. 16, a. 6.

the plane of the *ratio* and not as such on the level of things as they exist. Quite apart from the various examples which can be given of things named analogically, what is proper to this logical intention is the unity of reference to the *ratio propria* which is participated unequally, *per prius et posterius* by the analogates. This is a wholly formal statement concerning the analogy of names.

> Dicendum quod in omnibus quae de pluribus analogice dicuntur, necesse est quod omnia dicuntur per respectum ad unum; et ideo illud unum oportet quod ponitur in definitione omnium. Et quia "ratio quam significat nomen est definitio," ut dicitur in IV Metaph., necesse est quod illud nomen per prius dicatur de ea quod ponitur in definitione aliorum, et per posterius de aliis, secundum ordinem quo appropinquant ad illud primum vel magis vel minus; sicut sanum quod dicitur de animali, cadit in definitione sani quod dicitur de medicina, quae dicitur sana inquantum causat sanitatem in animali; et in definitione sani quod dicitur de urina, quae dicitur sana inquantum est signum sanitatis animalis.[34]

This is an absolutely universal rule of things named analogically and not, as seems sometimes suggested, a universal rule of the particular example of "healthy." Things which are named analogically are so named because of a community among them. This community is not simply one of the name, as is the case with pure equivocation, nor is exactly the same *ratio* signified by the name as it is predicated of each of them, as is the case with the univocal name. The analogous name names one thing primarily, and others insofar as they relate in some way to what it principally names. The *rationes* of the secondary analogates will express their reference to the thing which perfectly saves the *ratio propria* of the word. This is just what is meant by the analogy of names: "hoc est, secundum ordinem vel respectum ad aliquid unum."[35]

The fact that the analogous name names one thing primarily is manifested by the fact that, if the name is used simply, it will be taken to mean that thing.[36] We have seen that this thing is principally named because it perfectly saves the *ratio propria* of the name whereas the secondary analogates do so only imperfectly, that is, with reference to what saves it perfectly. There is no question of such an inequality among things

---

[34] *Ia*, q. 13, a. 6.

[35] *I Contra Gentiles*, cap. 34.

[36] *Q.D. de ver.*, q. 7, a. 5, ad 3: "...dicendum quod aliquid simpliciter dictum intelligitur quandoque de eo quod per posterius dicitur, ratione alicuius additi; sicut ens in alio intelligitur accidens; et similiter vita ratione eius quod adiungitur, scilicet liber, intelligitur de vita creata, quae per posterius vita dicitur." – Cf. *In XI Metaphys.*, lect. 3, n. 2197: "Nam ens simpliciter dicitur id quod in se habet esse, scilicet substantia. Alia vero dicuntur entia, quia sunt huius quod per se est, vel passio vel habitus, vel aliquid huiusmodi. Non enim qualitas dicitur ens quia ipsa habet esse, sed per eam substantia dicitur esse disposita. Et similiter est de aliis accidentibus. Et propter hoc dicit quod sunt entis. Et sic patet quod multiplicitas entis habet aliquid commune, ad quod fit reductio." Cf. *In I Periherm.*, lect. 5, n. 19.

named univocally. That is why we must never confuse the *ratio communis* of an analogous name (e.g. *id quod habet esse*) with the *ratio communis* of the univocal name.[37] Analogates do not participate equally in the *ratio communis* of the analogous name. The *ratio* of the univocal name, on the other hand, is saved perfectly and equally by all univocals. It is the inequality among the things named as named by it which makes the analogous name analogous; it names one thing principally.[38]

The analogous name is a name of multiple signification, but the multiplicity has a unity of order, *secundum prius et posterius*. Moreover, this multiplicity is one of signification, not of supposition. "Nominum multiplicitas non attenditur secundum nominis praedicationem, sed secundum significationem."[39] The univocal name has a multiplicity of supposits, but it always signifies the same form. Supposition is attached rather to predication than to signification, to the second operation rather than to the first, as we indicated in the previous chapter.

These remarks are sufficient for a preliminary understanding of the analogy of names. We turn now to the division of the analogy of names and the difficulties attendant on that and subsequent discussions will enable us to flesh out what is thus far but a skeletal statement on analogy.

---

[37] This is shown in the example of the analogous name "principle." "Respondeo dicendum quod idem iudicium est de principio et de origine super quam fundatur ratio principii. Potest autem origo considerari dupliciter: aut secundum *communem rationem* originis, quae est aliquod ab aliquo esse, et sic una ratio est communis ad originem personarum et originem creaturarum, non quidem communitate univocationis, sed analogiae: et similiter etiam nomen principii. Potest etiam considerari secundum determinatum modum originis; et sic sunt diversae speciales rationes originis et principii; sed hoc non facit aequivocationem: quia sic etiam secundum Philosophum I de anima, text 8, animalis ratio secundum unumquodque est alia." – *I Sent.*, d. 29, q. 1, a. 2, sol. 2. Cf. as well, *I Sent.*, d. 25, q. 1, a. 2, ad 5: "...dicendum quod ratio personae importat distinctionem in communi; unde abstrahitur a quolibet modo distinctionis; et ideo potest esse una ratio analogice in his quae diversimode distinguuntur." See below, chapter VIII, section 4.

[38] *Q.D. de malo*, q. 7, a. 1, ad 1.

[39] *Ia*, q. 13, a. 10, ad 1.

CHAPTER VI

THE DIVISION OF ANALOGY

How many kinds of analogous name are there? If we should put this question to Cajetan, the answer received could be that there are four kinds, or it could be that there is but one. Recent interpreters have often proposed different types than Cajetan; some even tend to treat every instance of analogous name as a special type. The texts of St Thomas, at first reading, give us a straightforward answer to our question. In the majority of texts, we find a twofold division of analogous names. However, on one occasion,[1] St Thomas gave a threefold division and, as it happened, it is that division which forms the structure of Cajetan's *De nominum analogia*. Indeed, when the threefold division is considered together with *Quaestio Disputata de veritate*, question two, article eleven, the interpretation of Cajetan seems to command assent; we find ourselves disposed to accept his way of treating the twofold division which is to relegate it to the status of a subdivision of what is not really analogy at all, namely, "analogy of attribution." In this chapter, we shall first examine the texts in which the twofold division is given; the other two texts will then be taken up as difficulties to be resolved in the light of the twofold division. The result of this analysis should make it clear that Cajetan has based his opuscle on texts which adopt a very special point of view and do nothing towards calling into question the fact that, for St Thomas, there are but two kinds of analogous name.

1. MULTORUM AD UNUM, UNIUS AD ALTERUM

Things are named analogically when they have a common name which signifies neither the same *ratio* nor wholly diverse *rationes* as said of each of them. Analogous signification is said to be as it were midway between univocal and equivocal signification, participating something of each.[2]

Et iste modus communitatis medius est inter puram aequivocationem et simplicem univocationem. Neque enim in his quae analogice dicuntur, est una ratio, sicut est in univocis; nec totaliter diversa, sicut in aequivocis; sed nomen quod sic multipliciter dicitur, significat diversas proportiones ad aliquid unum; sicut sanum de urina dictum

[1] *I Sent.*, d. 19, q. 5, a. 2, ad 1.
[2] *II Sent.*, d. 42, q. 1, a. 3.

significat signum sanitatis animalis, de medicina vero dictum, significat causam eiusdem sanitatis.[3]

That which saves the *ratio propria* of "healthy" is the thing which has
the quality from which the word is imposed to signify, and normally we
will take the word to mean that thing.[4] The things which do not so save
the *ratio propria* will be referred to what does insofar as they receive
the common name. The *rationes* signified by the common term as applied
to these secondary things will not be utterly other than its *ratio* as applied
to what it principally signifies, precisely because of the reference, stated
in the secondary *rationes*, to what is chiefly signified by the term.[5] There
is therefore an order among the various notions signified by an analogous
name; and, if there are types of analogous name, they will be distinguished with reference to what is formal and proper to analogical signification. It is this kind of formal difference St Thomas has in mind when
he says that several things are named analogically in either of two ways.

It can happen that what a name properly signifies is not one of the
things which are said to be named analogically. For example, if urine
and food are said to be healthy, they receive the common name because
of their reference to a third thing, to that which "healthy" signifies *per
prius* and most properly. So too, quality and relation are named being
because of their proportions to what that term signifies *per prius* and
most properly, namely, substance. This type of analogy is called that of
several to one *(multorum ad unum)*. Sometimes, on the other hand, two
things receive a common name because one has a proportion to the
other. For example, when food and animal are said to be healthy, this
is because food has a proportion to the health of the animal. Animal,
of course, is not called healthy with reference to some other thing. So
too when substance and quantity are named being; quantity has a
proportion to substance. This type of analogy is called that of one thing
to another *(unius ad alterum)*.[6]

This twofold division of things named analogically does not go beyond
the logical doctrine of signification. What is important here is not the

---

[3] *Ia*, q. 13, a. 5.
[4] Lyttkens several times raises the objection that if the analogous name signifies things
insofar as they refer to some first thing, that first thing is not signified by the analogous name.
Cf. Lyttkens, *op. cit.*, pp. 55–8. As we shall see below in Chapter VIII, a name first has a
ratio propria and then acquires the *ratio communis* which renders it analogous. Obviously what
saves the *ratio propria* of the name is not named with reference to what saves the *ratio propria*.
A name is analogous when it signifies things which do not save its proper notion, and these
things are signified by it precisely insofar as they are referred to what does save that proper
notion.
[5] *Ia*, q. 13, a. 6.
[6] This division is found in *Ia*. q. 13, a. 5; *Q.D. de pot.*, q. 7, a. 7; *I Contra Gentiles*, cap. 34.

examples, but what they exemplify. We name things as we know them and sometimes things have a common name which is neither univocal nor purely equivocal. If we ask what the name means, we sometimes find that the different notions include a reference to a third thing, sometimes that one notion refers to the other. It is difficult to envisage any other type of analogical community. Doubtless this is why, in the texts with which we are now concerned, St Thomas seems so emphatic in saying that things can be named analogically in either of two ways. He clearly intends the division to be exhaustive. Nevertheless, there is a series of difficulties to be faced before the exhaustiveness of this division can be accepted, difficulties which arise from other texts of St Thomas.

St Thomas often speaks of the proportions of things named analogically as *ad unum, ab uno* or *in uno*.[7] Is this a division of the analogy of names? Cajetan seems to feel it is a division of his "analogy of attribution."[8] But if this were a division of the analogy of names, it would have to introduce some differences into what is proper to that mode of signifying. And this it does not do. A cursory examination of a text where this division of what can be the *per prius* of the analogous name is used suffices to show this.

The listing of the various causes which can serve as the primary analogate of an analogous name is in function of showing that the unity of analogous names is not a oneness of *ratio*, as is the case with univocal names. "Item sciendum quod illud unum ad quod diversae habitudines referuntur in analogicis, est unum numero, et non solum unum ratione, sicut est unum illud quod per nomen univocum designatur."[9] Things named being which do not perfectly save the *ratio propria* of that term are referred to what does, "quod est unum sicut una quaedam natura." So too with urine, food and medicine when they are called healthy: they are referred to one end. "Nam ratio sani secundum quod dicitur de diaeta, consistit in conservando sanitatem."[10] Sometimes several things are referred to one efficient cause: the doctor is said to be medical, and when instruments and potions are called medical, it is by reference to the doctor as efficient cause. (Notice that the efficient cause to which the things secondarily signified refer is not here *their* efficient cause.[11]) Sometimes many things are referred to one subject, as in the case of "being."

[7] Cf. *In IV Metaphys.*, lect. 1, nn. 537–9.
[8] Cf. *De nominum analogia*, nn. 9, 18.
[9] *In IV Metaphys.*, lect. 1, n. 536; cf. *In VII Metaphys.*, lect. 4, n. 1337.
[10] *I Sent.*, d. 19, q. 5, a. 2, ad 1.
[11] *Q.D. de ver.*, q. 1, a. 2.

That this division of the various causes which can be the *per prius* of an analogous name does not divide the logical notion itself is clear from the fact that as analogous names they are all explained in the same way. Whether it is a material, efficient or final cause to which other things are proportioned, their notions will include it insofar as they share a common name with it. Thus, no difference in the logic of analogy is generated. Moreover, the twofold division already discussed can be exemplified no matter what kind of cause is the *per prius*. For example, "medical" said of scalpel and aspirin gives us an instance of *multorum ad unum*, whereas said of Doctore Kildare and the scalpel it gives us an instance of *unius ad alterum*.

2. PROPORTION AND PROPORTIONALITY

The texts presenting the twofold division of things named analogically are emphatic and clear. Yet the knowledgeable reader will be annoyed by the prominence we give this division; must we not distinguish between proportion, which can be divided in the manner discussed, and proportionality, which seemingly cannot? As soon as one moves from the *Summa theologiae* to the texts which play a privileged role in Cajetan's opuscle, the clarity of the twofold division begins to blur and one becomes sensible of the attractiveness of Cajetan's schema. That succumbing to this attractiveness can be fatal is revealed by a close exegesis of the main texts. We want now to examine them, first *Quaestio Disputata de veritate*, question two, article eleven, and then the exposition of *Sentences*, Book One, distinction nineteen, question five, article two, the reply to the first objection. Let it be understood that the cogency of our interpretation is intended to be cumulative and cannot be fully assessed until the end of Chapter X.

In the *Summa theologiae*, St Thomas introduces the twofold division we have discussed in order to make a precision about names common to God and creatures. These names are said to involve an analogy *unius ad alterum*.

Et hoc modo aliqua dicuntur de Deo et creaturis analogice, et non aequivoce pure, neque pure univoce. Non enim possumus nominare Deum nisi ex creaturis, ut supra dictum est. Et sic hoc quod dicitur de Deo et creaturis, dicitur secundum quod est aliquis ordo creaturae ad Deum, ut ad principium et causam in qua praeexistunt excellenter omnes rerum perfectiones.[12]

There is no third thing to which God and creature could be referred

[12] *Ia*, q. 13, a. 5.

in receiving a common name, for whatever is not a creature is God, whatever is not God is a creature.[13] Let us turn now to *Quaestio Disputata de veritate,* question two, article eleven.

St Thomas is asking whether "science" is predicated univocally of God and creature. In the body of the article, he rejects the possibility on grounds that the result would be pantheism. Whatever is in God is identical with his existence, something which would be true of his knowledge or science, and creatures could only attain "ad eamdem rationem habendi aliquid quod habet Deus" if they were identical with God's existence. Terms common to God and creature need not be equivocal, however; if there were no similarity *(convenientia)* between God and creature, we could neither know nor name God. The only possibility remaining is that such names as "science" are common "secundum analogiam, quod nihil est aliud dictu quam secundum proportionem." But he adds immediately, "Convenientia enim secundum proportionem potest esse duplex: et secundum hoc duplex attenditur analogiae communitas." Mathematical examples exhibit this division.

Est enim quaedam convenientia inter ipsa quorum est ad invicem proportio, eo quod habet determinatam distantiam vel aliam habitudinem ad invicem, sicut binarius cum unitate, eo quod est eius duplum: convenientia etiam quandoque attenditur duorum ad invicem inter quae non sit proportio, sed magis similitudo duarum ad invicem proportionum, sicut senarius convenit cum quaternio ex hoc quod sicut senarius est duplum ternarii, ita quaternarius binarii.

The first type of similarity *(convenientia)* is one of proportion, the second of proportionality. Some things have a name in common because one is proportioned to the other: it is in this way that "being" is said of substance and accident and "healthy" of urine and animal. But things can also have a common name, not because one is proportioned to the other, but because they are proportioned in similar ways to different things. That is, one proportion is similar to the other. Thus is "sight" said of the eye and the mind.[14]

In the *Summa theologiae,* St Thomas spoke of names common to God and creature in terms of a proportion of one to the other. Is he denying

---

[13] *Q.D. de pot.,* q. 7, a. 7.

[14] *Q.D. de ver.,* q. 2, a. 11: "Prima ergo convenientia est proportionis, secunda autem proportionalitatis; unde et secundum modum primae convenientiae invenimus aliquid analogice dicitur de duobus quorum unum ad alterum habitudinem habet; sicut ens dicitur de substantia et accidente ex habitudine quam substantia et accidens habent; et sanum dicitur de urina et animali, ex eo quod urina habet aliquam similitudinem ad sanitatem animalis. Quandoque vero dicitur aliquid analogice secundo modo convenientiae; sicut nomen visus dicitur de visu corporali et intellectu, eo quod sicut visus est in oculo, ita intellectus est in mente."

this in the text before us? This conclusion has sometimes been drawn and it leads in turn to a strange issue. We might be told in the present case, for example, that the analogous word "science" means that "as our science is to our intellect, so is God's to his." To this may be added, "– only proportionally," a curious addendum to the statement of a similarity of proportions. Now this does not seem to be a particularly enlightening statement, anymore than "as sight is to the eye, so is understanding to the mind" seems to say what the common word "sight" means. What is lost sight of when such statements are taken to give the meanings of analogous names is that one proportion is the means of knowing and naming the other. God's knowledge is known and named from ours just as, when we speak of understanding as seeing, we are moving from something obvious to something less so, a movement which should be revealed in the notions signified by the common name. In other words, where there is a similarity of proportions, one is very often the *per prius* with respect to the signification of a common name. But we shall return to this.

Why is there no conflict between the proportion of the *Summa* and the proportionality of the *De veritate?* We must notice, first of all, that proportion is an analogous name. According to its first signification, it means a determinate relation of one quantity to another, e.g. double, triple, equal. Secondly, it signifies any relation among things, and in this extended sense we can speak of a proportion of creature to God.[15] Since neither the relation of accident to substance nor that of creature to God are quantitative ones, neither is a proportion in the first sense of the term. Moreover, the extended meaning of "proportion" is *any* relation of one thing to another *(quaelibet habitudo unius ad alterum)* ; given this, the phrase "secundum proportionem" in the *Summa theologiae* covers both determinate and indeterminate proportions. There is surely no contradiction in saying that in names common to God and creature, there is a community "secundum proportionem" and that this community is "non secundum proportionem, sed secundum proportionalitatem." Proportion in the common sense cannot be divided against its subjective part. It is very much like saying, on one occasion, "Man is an animal" and, on another, "Man is not an animal." The first statement is true when "animal" is the name of the genus; the second is true when "ani-

---

[15] *Ia*, q. 12, a. 1, ad 4: "Dicendum quod proportio dicitur dupliciter. Uno modo, certa habitudo unius quantitatis ad alteram: secundum quod duplum, triplum et aequale sunt species proportionis. Alio modo, quaelibet habitudo unius ad alterum proportio dicitur. Et sic potest esse proportio creaturae ad Deum, inquantum se habet ad ipsum ut effectus ad causam, aut potentia ad actum."

mal" is the name of the species opposed to man.[16] But of course this is
clear from the *De veritate* itself. We are told that "science" is said of God
and creature according to analogy "quod nihil est aliud dictu quam
secundum proportionem." Only then is proportion subdivided into proportion and proportionality. What St Thomas is getting at is that
between some things named analogously there is a finite distance or
other determinate relation while between others there is not. It is interesting that he manifests both determinate and indeterminate relations
by quantitative, numerical relations. In a numerical proportionality,
however, 4 can be like as astronomical a number as you wish, not
because there is a determinate distance between them, but because the
astronomical number, like 4, is double another number. Thus 4:2 ::
2,000,000,000: 1,000,000,000.[17] Of course there is a determinate distance between four and two billion, but the point is that no determinate
relation between *them* is envisaged when both are called double. Are
they called double univocally?[18] St Thomas seems to suggest that
"double" is an analogous term. On this basis, when 2 and 6 are called
double in 2:1 :: 6:3, we have an analogy *unius ad alterum* and in 6:3 ::
4:2, the example of the text, we have an analogy *multorum ad unum*,
since 6 and 4 receive the name "double" by reference to 2.

A similarity of proportions whereby one thing is referred to another
is not as such the explanation of an analogically common name. "As
seeing is to the eye so is understanding to the mind" expresses a similarity
of proportions which permits us to say we *see* the answer to a problem
in geometry. But is this use of the term metaphorical or analogical? A
repetition of the proportionality is hardly an answer to this question,
nor does adding "– only proportionally" help, since our question is
posed on the assumption of the proportionality. What we must decide
is the meaning or *ratio* of "seeing" as applied to understanding. We
may find a common notion shared *per prius et posterius* by the activity of
eye and intellect, or we may decide that the similarity of proportions
gives rise to only metaphor. Or both, depending on our point of view;[19]

---

[16] The recognition of the common notion of "proportion" does not mean that the term is
univocally common to determinate and indeterminate relations. See below, Chapter VIII.

[17] *Q.D. de ver.*, q. 2, a. 11, ad 4.

[18] As I suggested in "The Logic of Analogy," *The New Scholasticism*, XXXI, (1957), pp.
149–171. Cf. *In V Metaphys.*, lect. 17, n. 1015: "Primi autem termini in quibus invenitur
aliqua proportio, dant speciem ipsi proportioni. Unde in quibuscumque aliis terminis consequenter inveniatur, in venitur in eis secundum rationem primorum terminorum. Sicut
proportio dupla primo invenitur inter duo et unum. Unde ex hoc proportio recipit rationem
et nomen. Et propter hoc, si etiam unus numerus respectu alterius numeri sit duplus, tamen
hoc est secundum quod minor numerus accipit rationem unius, et maior rationem duorum."

[19] See below, Chapter VIII, section 4.

even, let it be conceded, neither, for we may want to allow the view of one who feels there is no difference. In any case, it is not the similarity of proportions alone which decides the signification of the common name.

The text of the *De veritate* does not deny that there is a proportion *unius ad alterum* in names common to God and creature. Rather it stresses that some things named analogically are separated infinitely, something clearly the case with God and creature. Yet, even here, one is known and named from the other: could we explain what we meant by the divine science without appeal to human science? It is just this that St Thomas seems to deny in the text before us. The sixth objection maintains that "in omnibus analogicis" it is the case that one enters into the definition of the other or some third thing into the definition of both (our twofold division). "Sed creatura et Deus non hoc modo se habent, neque quod unum ponatur in definitione alterius, neque quod unum ponatur in definitione utriusque, *eo quod sic Deus definitionem haberet.*" The concluding phrase is not unimportant. The objection ends by denying that "science" is analogically common to God and creature. Here is St Thomas' reply.

Dicendum quod ratio illa procedit de communitate analogiae quae accipitur secundum determinatam habitudinem unius ad alterum: tunc enim oportet quod unum in definitione alterius ponatur, sicut substantia in definitione accidentis; vel aliquid unum in definitione duorum, ex eo quod utraque dicuntur per habitudinem ad unum, sicut substantia in definitione quantitatis et qualitatis.[20]

This text has been taken to be proof positive that the twofold division is the result of a limited view and not a division based on what is formal to the analogy of names. There are several things to keep in mind at this point. First of all, the twofold division is presented in the *Summa theologiae* precisely in discussing the divine names. This has led some interpreters to the "mixed case" theory, something Lyttkens has effectively called into question.[21] The only conclusion to be drawn is either (1) the division has relevance for the divine names, or (2) St Thomas is hopelessly confused (whether simultaneously or, at one time not confused, later confused). That the second alternative does not impose itself is clear from a diligent reading of the troublesome text. Names common to God and creature are not purely equivocal; if they were it wouldn't matter what name we applied to God. But it does matter and therefore we must be able to know and name God from

[20] *Q.D. de ver.*, q. 2, a. 11, ad 6.
[21] Cf. Lyttkens, *op. cit.*, pp. 298–300.

creatures because of a "habitudo unius ad alterum." What St Thomas is stressing in the *De veritate* is that this proportion or relation is indeterminate; it is not determinate as if by moving from our knowledge we could know *what* God's knowledge is. Note that this is the tenor of the objection and the response. God cannot be defined, cannot be expressed determinately in a *ratio*. Properly speaking, substance and the other supreme genera cannot be defined either,[22] but the *rationes* signified by their names express determinately what they are. No *ratio* of "science" can express determinately the nature of God's knowledge, which is one with his existence. But the *ratio* the name expresses when it is applied to God is dependent on that which it signifies as applied to our knowledge: God is known and named on an analogy with creatures. Our first chapter has indicated the difficulties which attend this matter; we shall give an explanation of the divine names in Chapter IX when we will have in hand more of the elements required for an adequate statement of the doctrine.

Now we must face a further difficulty in the text before us, a difficulty which will lead us into our discussion of *I Sent.*, d. 19, q. 5, a. 2, ad 1. We have in mind an apparently flagrant contradiction between the *Summa theologiae* and the *De veritate*. In the former, St Thomas writes:

dicendum quod animal dictum de animali vero et picto, non dicitur pure aequivoce; sed Philosophus largo modo accipit aequivoca, secundum quod includunt in se analoga. Quia et ens, quod analogice dicitur, quandoque dicitur aequivoce praedicari de diversis praedicamentis.[23]

In the *De veritate* we read:

dicendum quod hoc nomen animal imponitur non ad significandam figuram exteriorem, in qua pictura imitatur animal verum, sed ad significandum naturam, in qua pictura non imitatur; et ideo nomen animalis de vero et picto aequivoce dicitur; sed nomen scientiae convenit creaturae et Creatori secundum id in quo creatura Creatorem imitatur; et ideo non omnino aequivoce praedicatur de utroque.[24]

At the sure risk of over explicitness, let us underline the contradiction. First we are told that "animal" is analogically and not purely equivocally common to the animal and its picture; then we are told that "science" is analogically common to God and man and, unlike "animal" in the case mentioned, *non omnino aequivoce praedicatur*. Which leaves us with the statement that "animal" said of a beast and its picture is *omnino*, that is, *pure aequivoce* so said. What are we to make of this?

Let it be said, first of all, that the difference between the texts just

[22] Cf. e.g. *I Sent.*, d. 2, g. 1, a. 3.
[23] *Ia*, q. 13, a. 10, ad 4.
[24] *Q.D. de ver.*, q. 2, a. 11, ad 8.

cited brings out in an unmistakable fashion the difference between the treatment of analogy in the *Summa*, question thirteen, and this article from the *De veritate*. In the former, St Thomas gives us the characteristics of the logical intention of analogical signification, an intention discussed formally on the level of the diverse *rationes* signified by a word. From this vantage point, it is clear that when "animal" is said of the picture because it is a representation of the real animal, its *ratio* will include the *ratio propria* of the name. Thus the term is analogous and based on the relation *unius ad alterum*. Now, if we ask what in fact the similarity is between Peter and his portrait, the similarity which founds the analogy of the term "animal" as common to them, we must admit that it is an imperfect similarity.[25] The picture resembles Peter via his shape, which is a sign of his nature (since their various shapes enable us to distinguish species of animal.)[26] The picture resembles the man in that which is only a sign of the form which is the *id a quo* of the word.[27] It is this similarity at third remove which is stressed in the answer to the eighth objection of article eleven, question two, *De veritate*. "Science," on the other hand, is common to God and creature because of a similarity in that from which the name is imposed to signify.[28] In the case of the animal, then, St Thomas is stressing the dissimilarity between the image and the imaged, something which can also be done with respect to human and divine science.[29] Moreover, St Thomas can be said to be more concerned here with the *esse horum rationum*[30] than with the *rationes* themselves when he says that "animal" is said purely equivocally of the animal and its picture. On the level of *rationes*, there is no doubt that "animal" is an analogous name in the use in question. It is only when attention is shifted from *rationes* to their foundation in reality that the community can seem so tenuous as to evaporate completely. The significance of this shift of attention is something we shall be discussing at great length later in this chapter. This being the case, we can leave the present analysis, recognizing its incompleteness. Some things, however, seem already clear. There is no need to see an opposition between proportion and proportionality. Names analogically common to God

---

[25] *Q.D. de ver.*, q. 2, a. 11, ad 1: "...homo non dicitur suae imagini similis, sed e converso: si autem imperfecte imitetur, tunc potest dici simile et dissimile id quod imitatur ei ad cuius imitationem fit: simile secundum quod repraesentat; sed non simile, inquantum a perfecta repraesentatione deficit."

[26] *Ia*, q. 35, a. 1.

[27] Cf. *Q.D. de pot.*, q. 7, a. 7, ad 3 *in contr*.

[28] That is, the *id a quo ex parte rei*. Cf. *Q.D. de ver.*, q. 4, a. 1, ad 8.

[29] *Q.D. de ver.*, q. 2, a. 11, ad. 1.

[30] Cf. *I Sent.*, d. 19, q. 5, a. 2, ad 1, See below, Chapter IX.

and creature involve a proportion *unius ad alterum*. What St Thomas is
after in the *De veritate* is the recognition that such a proportion does not
put us in possession of determinate knowledge of God. Furthermore,
when the analogical community of the name is based on one thing's
imitation of another, this similarity can be more or less perfect depending
on whether the imitation is in terms of *id a quo nomen imponitur* in the rich
sense, or a sign of the form from which the name is imposed. This is
not constituitive of a gradation of analogous names nor, as we shall
point out later, can it be said that in names common to God and creature,
both God and creature save the *ratio propria* of the name. Cajetan
maintained this and then tried to show, unsuccessfully we think, that
this does not make such names univocal. Nonetheless, as we shall see,
there are extenuating circumstances for his attempt. As for proportionality, we shall attempt to put its role in the divine names into a new
perspective in Chapter VIII, section 4.

3. EXTRINSIC DENOMINATION AND ANALOGOUS NAMES

The first condition of what Cajetan calls analogy of attribution is that
it is according to extrincic denomination only.[31] That is, the *per prius*
of the name realizes the perfection formally and the others have it only
by extrinsic denomination. We have seen in our first chapter that Cajetan wants this rule to be understood "formally," a counsel which turned
out to be somewhat baffling, since "healthy" and "medical" only happen
(accidit)[32] to involve extrinsic denomination, a curious way to speak of
what is supposed to be a condition of "analogy of attribution" formally
as such. We want now to point out that intrinsic and extrinsic denomination are accidental, not to a putative type, but to the analogy of
names formally as such.

First of all, a brief recalling of what is meant by these two kinds of
denomination. Being is divided into the ten categories not univocally,
"sed secundum diversum modum essendi."[33] But modes of being are
proportional to modes of predication and it is according to the latter
that the genera of being are disinguished. St Thomas distinguishes three
major types of predication in this connection, the first being had when
the predicate expresses the essence of that of which it is said; the second
is had when the predicate pertains to the essence. "Tertius autem modus

[31] Cajetan, *op. cit.*, n. 10.
[32] *Ibid.*, n. 11.
[33] *In III Physic.*, lect. 5, n. 15. Our discussion follows this text, but see as well, *In V Metaphys.*,
lect. 9, n. 892; *I Sent.*, d. 32, q. 1, a. 1.

praedicandi est, quando aliquid extrinsecum de aliquo praedicatur per modum alicuius denominationis: sic enim et accidentia extrinseca de substantiis praedicantur; non tamen dicimus quod homo sit albedo, sed quod homo sit albus."[34] Extrinsic denomination, in things other than man, is of two kinds. "Communiter autem invenitur aliquid denominari ab aliquo extrinseco, vel secundum rationem causae, vel secundum rationem mensurae; denominatur enim aliquid causatum et mensuratum ab aliquo exteriori." St Thomas argues that the effect is denominated only from efficient cause and that the exterior measures are place and time.

It should be noticed that extrinsic denomination is here spoken of only as it applies to substance. Properly speaking, denomination is based on the relation of accident to substance.[35] That is, denomination is extrinsic denomination. In a wide sense, however, we can speak of intrinsic denomination, something involved in the *id a quo ex parte rei*. St Thomas has distinguished two ways in which something can be denominated by reason of a relation to another. First, when the relation itself is the cause of the denomination. It is in this way that urine is said to be healthy, i.e. it is the sign of the health of the animal and a sign is in the genus of relation.[36] Thus, urine is not denominated healthy from any form inherent in it.[37] Secondly, when it is not from the reference to the other, but from the other as cause that a thing is denominated.[38] Here there must be a similitude of effect to cause, so there will be an inherent form whereby the effect is denominated from its cause. In this second case, Cajetan denies that there is extrinsic denomination and claims that, in fact, we have an analogy not of "attribution" but of "proper proportionality."[39]

---

[34] *In III Physic.*, lect. 5, n. 15.

[35] *I Sent.*, d. 17, q. 1, a. 5, ad 2: "...denominatio proprie est secundum habitudinem accidentis ad subjectum..."

[36] Cf. *IV Sent.*, d. 4, q. 1, a. 1; *IIIa*, q. 63, a. 2, ad 3.

[37] It seems to be the case that, of the secondary analogates of "healthy," urine would fall under the first member of the division quoted in the following note, medicine in the second. Cf. *Q.D. de ver.*, q. 1, a. 4.

[38] *Q.D. de ver.*, q. 21, a. 4, ad 2: "...dicendum quod dupliciter denominatur aliquid per respectum ad alterum: uno modo, quando ipse respectus est ratio denominationis, sicut urina dicitur sana per respectum ad sanitatem animalis. Ratio enim sani, secundum quod de urina praedicatur, est esse signum sanitatis animalis. Et in talibus, quod denominatur per respectum ad alterum, non denominatur ab aliqua forma sibi inhaerente, sed ab aliquo extrinseco ad quod refertur. Alio modo denominatur aliquid per respectum ad alterum, quando respectus non est ratio denominationis, sed causa, sicut si aer dicatur lucens a sole; non quod ipsum referri aerem ad solem sit lucere aeris, sed quia directa oppositio aeris ad solem est causa quod luceat. Et hoc modo creatura dicitur bonum per respectum ad bonum; unde ratio non sequitur."

[39] Perhaps it would be more accurate to say he would claim we have both.

The striking thing about Cajetan's treatment of the analogy of names is that he interprets in terms of extrinsic denomination the statement that, in things named analogically, the *ratio propria* of the name is saved in one alone. Let us look again at the text involved. Is there but one truth in terms of which every being is said to be true? Well, yes and no, St Thomas replies. In things named univocally the *ratio propria* of the name is found in each of them.

> Sed quando aliquid dicitur analogice de multis, illud invenitur secundum propriam rationem in uno eorum tantum, a quo alia denominatur. Sicut sanum dicitur de animali et urina et medicina, non quod sanitas sit nisi in animali tantum, sed a sanitate animalis denominatur medicina sana, inquantum est illius effectiva, et urina, inquantum est illius significativa. Et quamvis sanitas non sit in medicina neque in urina, tamen in utroque est aliquid per quod hoc quidem facit, illud autem significat sanitatem.[40]

In his commentary, Cajetan rejects this rule as something applicable to analogous names; rather, he says, it applies to things which have a common name because they are *ad unum* or *in uno* or *ab uno*. He denies that "true" is analogous as said of things and judgments of our mind, but is analogous as said of various minds. "Veritas autem, respectu intellectu divini et aliorum, proportionale nomen est."[41] The reason for this is that the *ratio propria* of truth is found in the mind but not in things. The difficulty with Cajetan's view, of course, is that "true" cannot mean the same thing as said of our judgments and God's knowledge – in other words, it signifies different *rationes* and one of these will be the *ratio propria*, the other will not.[42] "Illud invenitur secundum propriam rationem in uno eorum tantum" and the other will be denominated from it. Where there is no denomination of one thing from another according to diverse *rationes*, there is no analogy of names: notice that, on this basis and so understanding extrinsic denomination, every analogous name involves extrinsic denomination. Things are said to be named analogically when they have a common name which signifies one of them principally, *secundum rationem propriam*, and the other secondarily and with reference to the first – that is, the second is denominated from the first. This is as true of "true" as it is of "healthy." If truth is a reflexive recognition of the conformity of thought and reality, simple apprehension and extramental things will not save the *ratio propria* of the term.[43] When the name is extended to God, the term will not signify the same *ratio* as when said of creature, anymore than it signifies the

[40] *Ia*, q. 16, a. 6.

[41] Cajetan, *In Iam*, q. 16, a. 6, n. VI.

[42] As we shall see in Chapter IX, section 4, in names common to God and creature, there is special need to distinguish the *per prius secundum rationem nominis* from the *per prius secundum rem*.

[43] *Q.D. de ver.* q. 1, a. 3.

same *rationes* as said of our judgments and of extramental things. In both cases there is something in each of the analogates which founds the extension of the name to include them; but only one of them will found the *ratio propria*. In names common to God and creature, the underlying reference of effect to cause always explains the community of the name. And, since *omne agens agit sibi simile*, the similarity of effect to cause must be based on something intrinsic to the effect.[44] This is not to say, of course, that the analogy of names demands that the *per prius* be the efficient cause of what is denominated from it. In the examples of "healthy" and "true" (said of judgments and things), the causes are denominated from their effects.[45] The point is this: it does not matter that our judgments can be denominated "true" without reference to God because of their intrinsic possession of this perfection; when the name is common to our judgments and God, there will be a *per prius* from which the other is denominated true.

What we are suggesting is that the intrinsic possession of the perfection is irrelevant to the intent of the phrase that something said analogically of many is found in only one of them with respect to its proper notion. Cajetan, speaking of "analogy of attribution," holds that only the primary analogate realizes the prefection formally while the others have it by extrinsic denomination. But what are we to make of an analogous name which applies to its *per prius* by extrinsic denomination? Place is an extrinsic measure of body; consequently to say of a body that it is located is to denominate it extrinsically.[46] But to be in place is analogically common to bodies and angels: "angelo convenit esse in loco: aequivoce tamen dicitur angelus esse in loco, et corpus."[47] The *ratio propria* of "located" will be saved only by bodies; in an extended sense, intelligible only by reference to the proper signification of the name, the angel is in place. Surely this example does nothing towards diminishing or changing the formal rules of the analogy of names; neither do the examples of "being," "good," "true" and "science" said of God and creature.

In his commentary on Aristotle's *Ethics*,[48] St Thomas says some things

---

[44] *Q.D. de ver.*, q. 21, a. 4: "...omne agens invenitur sibi simile agere; unde si prima bonitas sit effectiva omnium bonorum, oportet quod similitudinem suam imprimat in rebus effectis; et sic unumquodque dicetur bonum sicut forma inhaerente per similitudinem summi boni sibi inditam, et ulterius per bonitatem primam, sicut per exemplar et effectivum omnis bonitatis creatae."

[45] *Q.D. de ver.*, q. 1, a. 2.

[46] *In III Physic.*, lect. 5, n. 15.

[47] *Ia*, q. 52, a. 1.

[48] *Nicomachean Ethics*, 1, 6.

which have always been of interest to students of his doctrine of analogy, particularly because the text in question is one of the few which figure explicitly in Cajetan's *De nominum analogia*. Aristotle is making the point, against Plato, that if the good is separated as Man is supposed to be, "good" would signify univocally whatever it is said of.[49] But that cannot be, nor can "good" be a purely equivocal term. So it would seem to be a name signifying many as from one cause or ordered to one cause or, better, things which are one according to analogy.[50] Let us look at St Thomas' commentary.

He begins by pointing out that a name is said of many things according to diverse *rationes* in two ways, either according to wholly diverse *rationes* (and then we have pure equivocation and things so named are *aequivoca a casu*), or the *rationes* are not wholly diverse but agree in some one thing.[51] He goes on to subdivide this last possibility. (1) Sometimes several things are referred to one principle, e.g. "military" as said of weapons and armor refers them to him who has the art of making war. (2) Sometimes several things are referred to one end, e.g. "healthy." (3) Sometimes according to proportion, and this either (a) by diverse proportions to the same subject, e.g. quantity and quality to substance in the case of "being," or (b) by one proportion to different subjects, e.g. sight to eye, understanding to mind.

This division is reminiscent of those we found in the commentary on the *Metaphysics* and in the *De principiis naturae*.[52] The primary analogate may be either an efficient, final or material cause. As we have seen, this is not a division of the analogy of names as such, since it intro-

---

[49] 1096b25.

[50] 1096b25–30: οὐκ ἔστιν ἄρα τὸ ἀγαθὸν κοινόν τί κατὰ μίαν ἰδέαν. ἀλλὰ πῶς λέγεται; οὐ γὰρ ἔοικε τοῖς γε ἀπὸ τύχης ὁμωνύμοις, ἀλλ᾽ ἆρά γε τῷ ἀφ᾽ ἑνὸς εἶναι; ἢ πρὸς ἓν ἅπαντα συντελεῖν; ἢ μᾶλλον κατ᾽ ἀναλογίαν; ὡς γὰρ ἐν σώματι ὄψις, ἐν ψυχῇ νοῦς, καὶ ἄλλο δή ἐν ἄλλῳ. Cf. *Q.D. de ver.*, q. 21, a. 4.

[51] *In I Ethic.*, lect. 7, n. 95: "Et haec quidem quaestio locum habet, quia aliquid dici de multis secundum diversas rationes dupliciter. (A) Uno modo secundum rationes omnino diversas non habentes respectum ad unum. Et ista dicuntur *aequivoca a casu*, quia scilicet casu accidit, quod unum nomen unus homo imposuit uni rei, et alius alii rei, ut praecipue patet in diversis hominibus uno nomine nominatis. (B) Alio modo unum nomen dicitur de multis secundum rationes diversas non totaliter, sed in aliquo uno convenientes. (1) Quandoque quidem in hoc quod referuntur ad unum principium, sicut res aliqua dicitur militaris, vel quia est instrumentum militis, sicut gladius, vel quia est tegumentum eius sicut lorica, vel quia est vehiculum eius, sicut equus. (2) Quandoque vero in hoc quod referuntur ad unum finem sicut medicina dicitur sana, eo quod est factiva sanitatis, dieta vero eo quod est conservativa sanitatis, urina vero eo quod est sanitatis significativa. (3) Quandoque (a) secundum proportiones diversas ad idem subiectum, sicut qualitas dicitur esse ens, quia est dispositio per se entis, idest substantiae, quantitas vero eo quod est mensura eiusdem, et sic de aliis, (b) vel secundum unam proportionem ad diversa subiecta. Eamdem enim habent proportionem visus quoad corpus, et intellectus ad animam. Unde sicut visus est potentia organi corporalis, ita etiam intellectus est potentia animae absque participatione corporis."

[52] *In IV Metaphys.*, lect. 1, nn. 537–9; *De principiis naturae*, cap. 6.

duces no difference into the common doctrine. In any case, the *ratio propria* of the common name is saved in one alone and others are denominated from it. There is, however, an added note in the text before us, namely that of similar proportions to different subjects. Since the other subdivisions do not alter the common doctrine of the analogy of names, that is, are not types of analogous name, it is unlikely that this added note will do anything different. Now what is added is precisely the *similtudo proportionum* and it is exemplified here, as it was in the *De veritate*, by seeing and understanding, but now insofar as both can be called good. When they are so named, the one is not referred to the other as to its efficient or final cause. So it is, in the text of Aristotle, that, having rejected the Platonic separated good from which all things might be denominated good as from their efficient or final cause, Aristotle prefers to stay in the order of things more accessible to him (and more relevant to ethics); concern with things existing separately in the manner of the idea of good belongs to another branch of philosophy.[53] The similarity of proportions, as we have seen and will see again, does not involve another doctrine of the analogy of names: if "good" means one thing with reference to sense, and another with reference to mind, and these meanings are not wholly diverse, they will be related *per prius et posterius*. It is very important to notice that St Thomas makes the phrase *secundum analogiam* common to every nonchance equivocation, something Aristotle does not do with the phrase κατ᾽ ἀναλογίαν.[54] The text of the commentary hardly provides a basis for the claim that "good" is common to God and creature according to a similarity of proportions. On the contrary, it is only when that community of the name has been set aside that the question of similarity of proportions, of similar proportions to different subjects, comes into the picture. And this, note, both in the text of Aristotle and in the commentary of St Thomas.

---

[53] 1096b30–1: ἀλλ᾽ ἴσως ταῦτα μὲν ἀφετέον τὸ νῦν, ἐξακριβοῦν γὰρ ὑπὲρ αὐτῶν ἄλλης ἂν εἴη φιλοσοφίας οἰκειότερον.

[54] *In I Ethic.*, lect. 7, n. 96: "Sic ergo dicit, quod bonum dicitur de multis, non secundum rationes penitus differentes, sicut accidit in his quae sunt a casu aequivoca, sed magis *secundum analogiam*, idest proportionem eamdem, inquantum omnia bona dependent ab uno primo bonitatis principio, vel inquantum ordinantur ad unum finem. Non enim voluit Aristoteles quod illud bonum separatum sit idea et ratio omnium bonorum, sed principium et finis. Vel etiam dicuntur omnia bona magis secundum analogiam, idest proportionem eamdem, sicut visus est bonum corporis, et intellectus est bonum animae. Ideo hunc tertium modum praefert quia accipitur secundum bonitatem inhaerentem rebus. Primi autem duo modi secundum bonitatem separatam, a qua non ita proprie aliquid denominatur." See once more *Q.D. de ver.*, q. 21, a. 4, quoted above in note 44.

4. ALIQUID DICITUR SECUNDUM ANALOGIAM TRIPLICITER

While moving from "analogy of inequality" through "analogy of attribution" to "analogy of proportionality," Cajetan pauses at each step to discuss the terminology of St Thomas with respect to these three, which are and are not, according to Cajetan, types of analogous name. In each case, it is the same text of St Thomas to which appeal is made, a text in which we are told that something is said according to analogy in three ways.[55] Now, as it happens, the text in question is the answer to an objection and consequently must be read in terms of that objection, the more so because the division given is to be found nowhere else in St Thomas. The objection occurs in an article which asks a question St Thomas often poses, viz. whether all things are true by uncreated truth.[56] The first objection is an attempt at an affirmative answer.

Videtur quod omnia sint vera veritate quae est veritas increata. Sicut enim dictum est (*I Sent.*, d. 19, q. 5, a. 1), verum dicitur analogice de illis in quibus est veritas, sicut sanitas de omnibus sanis. Sed una est sanitas numero a qua denominatur animal sanum, sicut subjectum ejus, et medicina sana, sicut causa ejus, et urina sana, sicut signum ejus. Ergo videtur quod una sit veritas qua omnia dicuntur vera.

Before turning to St Thomas' highly nuanced discussion of this argument, there are a few things to be said by way of preliminary. What is the meaning of "una est sanitas numero" in the objection? If it should be understood in the sense examined earlier where the one to which analogates refer is *unum numero* and not only *unum ratione*, as is the case with univocals, it will be difficult to understand the example of "being" in the third member of this division. It will be recalled that the distinction of *unum numero* and *unum ratione* figures in a context which would explain the many meanings of "being." What the objector has in mind is this. In the example of "healthy" only the primary analogate possesses the form in virtue of which it is denominated healthy. "Healthy" is an analogous name, but so too is "true." Since they have this in common, it would seem that they should also have in common the fact that only one of the things can be denominated "true" in virtue of an intrinsic form. Now this, we shall argue, is to argue from what they do have in common, the logical intention of analogy, to something which, though true of things named healthy, is not true of them insofar as they are named analogically. That is, it is accidental to the analogy of names.

[55] *I Sent.*, d. 19, q. 5, a. 2, ad 1.
[56] Cf. *II Contra Gentiles*, cap. 35; *III Contra Gentiles*, cap 82, 84; *Ia*, q. 16, a. 6; *Q.D. de ver.*, q. 1, a. 5.

If it were not, the argument would be valid. If it is accidental, and the reply of St Thomas will be seen to be arguing just this, to confuse the logical intention and the extralogical properties of the things which happen to be named analogically, is to exhibit a faulty understanding of the logical intention. Moreover, the claim of the objector will be seen not to be merely a restatement of the law that, in all things named analogically, the *ratio propria* of the name is saved only in one.

And yet St Thomas begins his answer with the observation that "aliquid dicitur secundum analogiam tripliciter." What we must come to grips with is the significance of the couplet in terms of which this division is made, *secundum intentionem*, on the one hand, *secundum esse*, on the other. Furthermore, much will depend on our identification of the *logicus* of the second member of the division, for it is he who is at work in the objection.

(a) Secundum intentionem, non secundum esse

Ad primum igitur dicendum quod aliquid dicitur secundum analogiam tripliciter: vel secundum intentionem tantum, et non secundum esse; et hoc est quando una intentio refertur ad plura per prius et posterius, quae non habet esse nisi in uno; sicut intentio sanitatis refertur ad animal, urinam et dietam diversimode, secundum prius et posterius; non tamen secundum diversum esse, quia esse sanitatis non est nisi in animali.

The familiar example in the setting of this division has some unfamiliar things said about it, though they may seem to be the same things said in a text we were looking at a moment ago.[57] There is no need to repeat why "healthy" is an analogous name. Given the fact that it is, we know that it will name something primarily, that which saves its *ratio propria*. Let us say that that *ratio propria* is "the quality whereby there is a proper equilibrium of the humors." Of animal, urine and diet, only animal is chiefly denominated from this quality; the others do not possess this quality and are called "healthy" only with reference to the animal.[58] Of course there must be something in the diet and in urine which founds the *rationes* signified by "healthy" as said of them. This is generally true of analogates – it is generally true of names. However, when we inquire into what founds the various *rationes* of this analogous name as opposed to that, (and by "founds" we mean the remote foundation), we are concerned with differences, not in the logical order, but among the *res* as such. Some things are named analogically which have such

---

[57] *Ia*, q. 16, a. 6.
[58] Should "healthy" be taken to mean "that which is so disposed as to live well," the grain in the field could be called healthy, not insofar as it is food, but from its own condition or quality.

and such ontological characteristics, others which do not have those characteristics. Some things can save the *ratio propria* of a name and yet be said to receive the name with reference to something else.[59] This is true of "true" and of all names common to God and creature. Our judgments save the *ratio propria* of the term "true" and, as created judgments, can be called true with reference to God. This does not mean that both our judgments and God found the *ratio propria* of a term common to them, for then it would be a univocal term. So too creatures, that is substances, can found the *ratio propria* of "good" insofar as they have existence, but they can also be called good with reference to God who is Goodness and the exemplar, efficient and final cause of created goods. Yet we cannot say that both God and creature found the *ratio propria* of the term, for this would make it univocal. The phrase "illud invenitur secundum propriam rationem in uno eorum tantum" has nothing to do with possessing the perfection intrinsically. To say that, among things called healthy, only animal can be so denominated from a perfection intrinsic to it, is to say more than is said when we are told that animal, urine and food are called healthy analogically. Whether this ontological situation holds or not, all the rules given for the analogy of names are valid and unchanged. We cannot argue from the fact that things are named analogically to one ontological situation or the other, for what they have in common is to be named analogically – not *to be* this way or that, but *to be named* in this way.

(b) Secundum esse, non secundum intentionem

Vel secundum esse et non secundum intentionem; et hoc contingit quando plura parificantur in intentione alicujus communis, sed illud commune non habet esse unius rationis in omnibus, sicut omnia corpora parificantur in intentione corporeitatis. Unde logicus qui considerat intentiones tantum, dicit, hoc nomen, corpus, de omnibus corporibus univoce praedicari: sed esse huius naturae non est ejusdem rationis in corporibus corruptibilibus et incorruptibilibus, ut patet in X Metaph.

Several things can be made equal in this that they are all signified by a name signifying a common notion or intention even though that common note has a different kind of being in each of them. For example, all bodies are made equal, are one, insofar as each is signified by "body" the *ratio* of which is the notion or intention of corporeity. What all bodies have in common is what is signified by "body." The *logicus*, noting this, says that the term is predicated of all bodies univocally; or, conversely, that they are all named body univocally. What else could he say if the same intention or notion is signified each time something is

[59] This paradoxical statement will be explained in Chapter IX.

called a body? What is this example doing in a discussion of the way things are said to be *secundum analogiam?*

Let us look closely at the verb, *parificantur*. There is equality on the level of the intention or *ratio* when things are named univocally. Now this is not true of things named analogically: they are not equalized in a common notion, but share in it *per prius et posterius*, unequally. Thus, in things named analogically, there is inequality on the level of the common intention or notion. In the second division of the text before us, we are faced with an example of things named univocally. That is, they are made equal on the level of the common intention: if there is analogy or inequality, if in some way they are related *per prius et posterius*, this will not be according to the common intention. Their inequality is said to obtain in the *esse hujus rationis*, and not on the level of the intention, that is, the common intention, itself.

What does it mean to say that things named univocally are analogous because "illud commune non habet esse unius rationis in omnibus"? Does this mean that bodies are named both univocally and analogically? Not that such a claim would in itself be surprising. Things can be named univocally with respect to one name and analogically with respect to another. For example, man and herb are named univocally with respect to "substance" and analogically with respect to "healthy." But we are not at present asking if several things can be called "body" univocally and be named analogically with respect to some other name. Rather we must ask if the text before us says that bodies are named "body" univocally and analogically, depending on our point of view.

The *logicus* says that the name "body" is univocal; it satisfies the definition of things named univocally. Will the observation that the notion signified by "body" enjoys a different mode of existence in celestial and terrestial bodies, following Aristotle's hypothesis,[60] lead to the view that the same word "body" is analogous? St Thomas, we see, refers us to the tenth book of the *Metaphysics* for light on the subject.

In the text referred to it is again a question of celestial and terrestial bodies being named body univocally. We will be returning to the context of the discussion, but right now we want to cite a passage which clarifies the distinction made in the second division of our text in the *Sentences*. Contrariety is sometimes the cause of specific diversity, sometimes of generic diversity.

---

[60] Cf. *On the Heavens*, I, 3, 270b10. In commenting on this passage, St Thomas stresses that the incorruptibility of heavenly bodies is only a hypothesis. Cf. *In I de coelo*, lect. 7, n. 6.

...corruptibile et incorruptibile sunt genere diversa. Manifestum est enim quod contraria quae sunt in uno genere, non sunt de substantia illius generis. Non enim rationale et irrationale sunt de substantia animalis, sed animal est potentia utrumque. Quodcumque autem genus accipiatur, oportet quod corruptibile et incorruptibile sunt de intellectu eius. Unde impossibile est quod communicent in aliquo genere. Et hoc rationabiliter accidit. Nam corruptibilium et incorruptibilium non potest esse materia una. Genus autem, *physice loquendo*, a materia sumitur. Unde supra dictum est, quod ea quae non communicant in materia, sunt genere diversa. *Logice autem loquendo*, nihil prohibet quod conveniant in genere, in quantum conveniant in una communi ratione, vel substantiae, vel qualitatis, vel alicuius huiusmodi.[61]

The genus can be considered from a physical as well as from a logical point of view. Obviously an understanding of this option will clarify the whole division in the text of the *Sentences*.

(1) Genus logice loquendo

Since we have already discussed the manner in which genus is a second intention, a logical relation, it will seem redundant to speak of the genus *logice*. Let us recall what the logical relation of genus is. We saw that second intentions are accidents which accrue to natures as they exist in our mind. We say, for example, "Animal is a genus." What is the meaning of this predicate? A genus is that which is said of many things which differ in species and which expresses what they are.[62] Obviously, in order to be thus predicable, the nature must be in our mind.[63] To be generically common is something which belongs to animal as it is known by us; to be a genus does not belong to "animate sensitive substance" as such, nor to this animal or that. In the *De ente et essentia*, where he is interested in showing the relationship between essence and such intentions as genus, species and difference, St Thomas distinguishes carefully between the nature as such, the *natura absolute considerata*, and the accidents which accrue to it as it exists in singulars or in our intellect. Thus, it is not of the essence of animal to be a genus; nevertheless, it is the nature, not the logical intention, which is predicated of many.[64]

Since we name things as we know them, it is the nature as known that

---

[61] *In X Metaphys.*, lect. 12, n. 2142. Why does St Thomas say of the *genus physicum* alone that it *a materia sumitur?* The physical genus is based in a special way on matter, since in "illud materiale unde sumitur genus," there is both form and matter and the physical genus comprises both. Cf. *In Boethii de trin.*, q. 4, a. 2.

[62] *Topics*, I, 4; Porphyry, *Isagoge*, chap. 4.

[63] One might recall the diverse kinds of supposition mentioned in Chapter IV, section 6.

[64] *De ente et essentia*, cap. 4: "Praedicatio enim est quoddam quod completur per actionem intellectus componentis et dividentis, habens tamen fundamentum in re, ipsam unitatem eorum quorum unum de altero dicitur. Unde ratio praedicabilitatis potest claudi in ratione huius intentionis quae est genus, quae similiter per actionem intellectus completur; nihilominus id cui intellectus intentionem praedicabilitatis attribuit, componens id cum altero, non est ipsa intentio generis, sed potius id cui intellectus intentionem generis attribuit, sicut quod significatur hoc nomine animal."

is named. What is immediately signified by the word "animal" is, as we have seen, the *ratio* of the name. And, again, things are said to be named univocally when the name they have in common signifies the same *ratio* as applied to each of them. Thus "animal" as applied to man or brute signifies "animate sensitive substance." This notion expresses something of the essence or quiddity of those things to which the name is applied. It is of the essence of genus to signify univocally.[65]

Those things which are in the same genus are said to be made equal thanks to an intention or concept of something common. Man and brute are made equal thanks to the common notion, "animate sensitive substance." All bodies are made equal in the common intention of corporeity. We might wonder why the genus is singled out for attention here, for the same thing would seem to be true of species. Are not all men made equal in the common intention signified by the term "man?" There is, however, an important difference between genus and species in this regard, if by species we mean the *species specialissima*, the common notion which is not further divisible by formal differences.[66] Obviously "animal" is a species with respect to "living body," but it has in common with its genus that the things signified by it are made equal thanks only to the intention of something common. The *species specialissima* has a greater unity than the genus because it is based on something which is absolutely one in nature.

Et huius ratio est, quia species sumitur a forma ultima quae simpliciter una est in rerum natura, genus autem non sumitur a forma aliqua quae sit una in rerum natura sed secundum rationem tantum: non est enim aliqua forma ex qua homo sit animal praeter illam ex qua homo sit homo. Omnes igitur homines, qui sunt unius species, conveniunt in forma quae constituit speciem, quia quilibet habet animam rationalem; sed non est in homine, equo aut asine aliqua anima communis quae constituat animal, praeter illam animam quae constituit hominem, vel equum vel asinum: quod si esset, tunc genus esset unum et comparabile, sicut et species; sed in sola consideratione accipitur forma generis per abstractionem intellectus a differentiis. Sic igitur species est unum quid a forma una in rerum natura existente, genus autem non est unum: quia secundum diversas formas in rerum natura existentes diversae species generis praedicationem suscipiunt. Et sic genus est unum logice et non physice.[67]

The unity of the genus follows in a special way on our mode of knowing since it does not signify the same form or essence in each of the things which fall under it. The form of man and the form of horse differ formally in reality; they are unified in the generic notion only because

---

[65] *Q.D. de pot.*, q. 7, a. 3, ad 6.
[66] See below, note 100.
[67] *In VII Physic.*, lect. 8, n. 8.

we do not attend to what is formally peculiar to each, but seize upon that which they have in common. Thus, the common notion is not based on some one form *in rerum natura* and its unity is due in a special way to our mind. "Animal" and "man" do not signify different forms,[68] but the same form from the vantage point of different degrees of understanding. The possibility of the generic notion lies in the fact that, viewed in a confused manner, things with different forms can be made equal.[69] Moreover, this confusion and the hierarchy of genera to which it gives rise is seen to follow necessarily on the kind of intellect we have.[70] St Thomas gives us a lengthy statement on the hierarchy of genera and we want to examine it closely, particularly since it leads us into a consideration of the genus *physice loquendo*.

This statement is to be found in a commentary on Boethius[71] where the question is raised as to whether accidental differences are the cause of the numerical distinction of substances. In addressing himself to that question, St Thomas discusses generic, specific and numerical diversity. The composite which falls in the genus of substance involves three things: form, matter and the composite itself, and it is in these that we must seek the causes of the various kinds of diversity. "Sciendum igitur quod diversitas secundum genus reducitur in diversitatem materiae: diversitas vero secundum speciem in diversitatem formae, sed diversitas secundum numerum partim in diversitatem materiae, et partim in diversitatem accidentis."[72] It is the widening of the question to include the cause of generic diversity which makes this article relevant to our inquiry. The assignment of matter as the cause of generic diversity raises a serious problem. The genus is a principle of knowing, a sign of which is that it is the first part of the definition of anything. Matter, however, is said to be unknowable in itself. Nevertheless, St Thomas states, matter can be known, and in either of two ways.

First of all, matter can be known by analogy; in another way, it can be known through the form which makes it to be in act.[73] It is the

---

[68] *Q.D. de spirit. creat.*, a. 1, ad 3: "...dicendum quod cum animal sit id quod vere est homo, distinctio naturae animalis ab homine non est secundum diversitatem realem formarum, quasi alia forma sit per quam sit animal, et superaddatur altera per quam sit homo; sed secundum rationes intelligibiles. Secundum enim quod intelligitur corpus perfectum in esse sensibili ab anima, sic comparatur ad perfectionem ultimam quae est ab anima rationali inquantum huiusmodi, ut materiale ad formale. Cum enim genus et species significent quasdam intentiones intelligibiles, non requiritur ad distinctionem speciei et generis distinctio realis formarum, sed intelligibilis tantum."

[69] Cf. *II Sent.*, 17, q. 1, a. 1.

[70] *Ia*, q. 85, a. 3.

[71] *In Boethii de trin.*, q. 4, a. 2 (ed. Calcaterra: lect. 1, q. 2, a. 2).

[72] *Ibid.*

[73] On knowing matter by analogy, see below, Chapter VIII, section 3.

second way of knowing matter which gives rise to a hierarchy in the genus of substance.

Alio modo penes materiam sumitur generis diversitas, secundum quod materia est perfecta per formam. Et cum materia sit potentia pura, et Deus sit actus purus, nihil aliud est materiam perfici in actu, qui est forma, nisi quatenus participat aliquam similitudinem actus primi, licet imperfecte; ut scilicet id quod est iam compositum ex materia et forma, sit medium inter potentiam puram et actum purum.[74]

There is, however, an unequal participation in actuality on the part of matter, for some material things possess perfection in this that they subsist, some in that they live, others in that they know, yet others in that they have reason. The similitude with First Act in all of these is their form. "Sed forma talis in quibusdam facit esse tantum, in quibusdam esse et vivere; et sic de aliis in uno et eodem. Similitudo perfecta habet omne id quod habet similitudo minus perfecta, et adhuc amplius."[75] It is thanks to one substantial form that man is, lives, senses and understands. A stone is matter in act to the degree that it subsists. Matter taken with this common perfection, subsistence, gives rise to a notion which is material with respect to further perfection, in the case of man, to imperfection in the case of the stone. That is, "that which has exist-ence in itself" when taken as common to stones and living things is material with respect to the perfection "living" and the imperfection "non-living": "et ex hoc materiali sumitur genus: differentia vero ex perfectione et imperfectione praedicata."[76]

Sicut ex hoc communi materiali quod est habere vitam, sumitur hoc genus quod est animatum corpus; ex perfectione vero superaddita, haec differentia, sensibile: ex imperfectione vero haec differentia, insensibile: et sic diversitas talium materialium inducit diversitatem generis, sicut animalis a planta. Et propter hoc dicitur materia esse principium diversitatis secundum genus.[77]

Thus the tree of Porphyry has its roots in the imperfection of our mode of knowing which is such that we first form confused notions whereby things of diverse perfections are made equal "in intentione alicujus communis." This concept or intention to which the logical intention of generic community attaches is one thanks in a special way to the operation of our mind; unlike the specific notion it is not based on some one type of form *in rerum natura*.[78]

---

[74] *In Boethii de trin.*, q. 4, a. 2.
[75] *Ibid.*
[76] *Ibid.*
[77] *Ibid.*
[78] An important precision on the way things made equal in a generic notion are said to be one is found in *Metaphysics*, Delta, 6. Figure is divided by such species as circle, triangle, etc. Triangle, in turn, is generic with respect to isosceles and scalene. Isosceles and scalene

It must not be thought that, because the generic notion does not express the full perfection of the things it signifies, it signifies only a part of these things. If this were the case, the genus could not be predicated of them,[79] surely a strange pass for something of whose very nature it is to be predicable. The species does not differ from the genus by signifying the whole as opposed to a part. We can say both, "Socrates is man" and "Socrates is animal." Both predicates signify the whole, but they differ in that the genus is indeterminate, confused, *non signatum*, and the species is determinate, distinct, *signata*.[80] The genus "body" signifies the whole of that of which it is said.

Or does it? St Thomas has said that the genus cannot signify a part because no integral part is predicated of its whole. He has in mind the fact that we are unlikely to say, "The house is lumber" or "Man is bone." However, though we do say, "Man is a body," we can also say, "Man is composed of body and soul," and we would mean composed as of integral parts. Doesn't this make the genus an integral part? Furthermore, the genus enters into the definition of a thing, but shouldn't the parts of the definition relate to the parts of the thing defined as the whole definition relates to the whole *definitum?* This last question is raised in the *Metaphysics*,[81] and it receives a decisively negative answer. When he comments on the *Metaphysics*, St Thomas remarks that it is patently false that the parts of the definition are the parts of the thing defined. His reason is again that the integral parts of a thing cannot be predicated of it as a whole; but genus and difference, the parts of the definition, are predicated of the whole thing: Man is animal, Man is rational.[82]

Sed dicendum est quod partes definitionis significant partes rei, inquantum a partibus rei sumuntur partes definitionis; non ita quod partes definitionis sint partes rei. Non

are not one and the same triangle (proximate genus), but rather one and the same figure (remote genus), "Cuius ratio est quia hi duo trianguli non differunt per differentias quibus dividitur figura. Differunt autem per differentias quibus dividitur triangulus. Idem autem dicitur a quo aliquid non differt differentia." – *In V Metaphys.*, lect. 7, n. 863.

[79] "Si enim animal non esset totum quod est homo, sed pars eius, non praedicaretur de eo; cum nulla pars integralis praedicetur de suo toto." – *De ente et essentia*, cap. 3; cf. *In X Metaphys.*, lect. 10, nn. 2113–9.

[80] Cf. *De ente et essentia*, cap. 3.

[81] A somewhat similar question is asked in the third book of that work. Do genera amount to principles of the being of things? St Thomas, anticipating the later solution, argues that genera are principles of knowledge and could only be principles of being if they existed separated from the things of which they are the genera. "Quia enim separatim accipitur a ratione genus sine speciebus, est principium in cognoscendo. Et eodem modo esset principium in essendo, si haberet esse separatum." – *In III Metaphys.*, lect. 8, n. 442; cf. *Ia*, q. 85, a. 3, ad 4. We are now asking if the genus is an intrinsic principle, an intergal part, of the thing defined.

[82] *In VII Metaphys.*, lect. 9, n. 1462.

enim animal est pars hominis, neque rationale, sed animal sumitur ab una parte et rationale ab alia. Animal enim est quod habet naturam sensitivam, rationale vero quod habet rationem. Natura autem sensitiva est ut materialis respectu rationis. Et inde est quod genus sumitur a materia, differentia a forma, species autem a forma et materia simul. Nam homo est quod habet rationem in natura sensitiva.[83]

The genus is part of the definition, an integral part of the species, but not of the thing defined.[84] That it is not a component or integral part is clear from the fact that it signifies the whole *definitum*. "Animal" means "animate sensitive substance" or "what has a sensitive nature" and this signifies Socrates as a whole, not just part of him. We must, then, distinguish between the integral parts of the definition and the integral parts of the thing defined.[85] The thing defined is composed of matter and form, but the genus is not matter, the difference is not form.

Unde dicimus hominem esse animal rationale, et non ex animali et rationali, sicut dicimus eum esse ex anima et corpore. Ex corpore enim et anima dicitur esse homo, sicut ex duabus rebus quaedam tertia res constituta, quae neutra illarum est. Homo enim nec est anima neque corpus. Sed, si homo aliquo modo ex animali et rationali dicatur esse, non erit sicut res tertia ex duabus rebus, sed sicut intellectus tertius ex duobus intellectibus.[86]

What then of the difficulty we posed a moment ago? Body is a genus and yet the animal is composed of body and soul. But body as a component part of man cannot be a genus. Precisely, and it is because it is not that we must ask after the meaning of "body" in these two uses. What has happened is that the same word is taken to signify the generic notion and matter, an integral part of the thing defined. St Thomas likens this situation to the taking of the word signifying matter to signify as well matter together with a privation. Thus, we might say, "The statue came to be from bronze." Despite their grammatical similarity, we would not want to interpret that statement as we would this one:

---

[83] *Ibid.*, n. 1463.

[84] Since the species is also said to be part of the genus, we may seem to be faced with a contradiction. But there are wholes and wholes, parts and parts. The genus is a predicable whole of which the species is a subjective part. That is, the genus can be predicated of the species, and it is predicated of the whole of the species. The species, on the other hand, is a whole of which the genus is a component or integral part. If the species were taken to be integral parts of the genus, the genus would be a contradictory notion – as if animal were composed of rational and irrational, Cf. *In V Metaphys.*, lect. 21, nn. 1094–7; *Ia*, q. 85, a. 3, ad 2; *In X Metaphys.*, lect. 12, n. 2142.

[85] For example, in commenting on the fourth way in which something can be said to come from something else, according to Aristotle, St Thomas notes a twofold way we can understand that the species comes from parts of the species. "Secundum rationem, sicut bipes est pars hominis, quia est pars definitionis eius, quamvis secundum rem non sit pars, quia aliter non praedicaretur de toto. Toti enim homini competit habere duos pedes. Secundum rem vero sicut 'syllaba est ex elemento,' idest ex littera sicut ex parte speciei." – *In V Metaphys.*, lect. 21, n. 1088.

[86] *De ente et essentia*, cap. 3; cf. *I Sent.*, d. 25, q. 1, a. 1, ad 2.

"The musical comes from the non-musical" or "The shaped comes from the unshaped." In the statement about the statue, bronze does not disappear when the statue is finished, but is a component of the product. Musical, on the other hand, displaces non-musical as shaped does unshaped. If we use "bronze" as we do in the first sentence, it is because we have no word for the opposite of statue.[87] So too when we have no special word for a form, we sometimes use the name of matter, understanding it to mean the matter together with a common perfection.[88] St Thomas gives two examples of this state of affairs. One is vocal sound *(vox)*.[89] This may mean the sound which is the subject and thus other than its determination into various syllables, and then *vox* names matter. On the other hand, *vox* may mean the sound together with the determination into syllables and divisible into the various species of syllables, and thus it is the name of a genus. The other example is that of "body."

Si enim in intellectu corporis intelligatur substantia completa ultima forma, habens in se tres dimensiones, sic corpus est genus, et species eius erunt substantiae perfectae per has ultimas formas determinatas, sicut per formam auri, vel argenti, aut olivae, aut hominis. Si vero in intellectu corporis non accipiatur nisi hoc, quod est habens tres dimensiones cum aptitudine ad formam ultimam, sic corpus est materia.[90]

But let us return to the other way of looking at genus.

(2) Genus physice loquendo

Logically speaking, genus is a relation which attaches to a common notion susceptible of further determination in somewhat the same way as matter is subject to form. Thus the genus is said to be material. We remember that this material notion amounts to a grasp of matter together with a common determination. In other words, the generic notion comprises a form, the determination, and matter: it is this composition

---

[87] See *In I Physic.* lect. 12, n. 9, and below, Chapter VIII, section 3.
[88] "Sciendum est autem quod licet idem secundum nomen possit esse genus et materia, non tamen idem eodem modo acceptum. Materia enim est pars integralis rei, et ideo de re praedicari non potest. Non enim potest dici quod homo sit caro et os. Genus autem praedicatur de specie. Unde oportet quod significet aliquo modo totum. Sicut enim propter hoc quod est innominata privatio, aliquando simplici nomine materiae significatur materia cum privatione, ut supra dictum est, quod aes accipitur pro aere infigurato cum dicimis quod ex aere fit statua; ita etiam quando forma est innominata, simplici nomine materiae intelligitur compositum ex materia et forma, non quidem determinata, sed communi; et sic accipitur ut genus. Sicut enim compositum ex materia et forma determinata est species, ita compositum ex materia et forma communi est genus." – *In VII Metaphys.*, lect. 12, n. 1546. Think of St Albert's discussion of "quorum vox est commune" in the definition of equivocals.
[89] *Ibid.*, n. 1548.
[90] *Ibid.*, n. 1547; cf. *De ente et essentia*, cap. 3; *I Sent.*, d. 25, q. 1, a. 1, ad 2.

which is the basis for the distinction between the *genus logicum* and the *genus physicum*. "Sciendum tamen quod cum illud materiale unde sumitur genus, habeat in se formam et materiam, logicus considerat genus solum ex parte eius quod formale est, unde eius definitiones dicuntur formales; sed naturalis considerat genus ex parte utriusque."[91] Logically considered, the genus is abstract, formal; physically speaking, the genus is concrete, taking into account both form and matter. This gives rise to the possibility that some things can be said to communicate in a genus, logically speaking, that is, be made equal in the intention of some common note, which from a physical point of view would not communicate in a genus.[92] This opposition is developed in the commentary on the *Metaphysics* when the different meanings of "genus" are discussed.[93]

Of the four meanings of "genus" distinguished only two have philosophical importance, as St Thomas points out.[94] Genus as the connected generations of things having the same form (as in *genus humanum*), or the closely allied meaning of family or clan, are the less important ones, although they reflect more closely the etymology of the word. The two remaining meanings contribute to our discussion. "Genus" sometimes means subject matter, as surface is the genus or subject of figures.

Genus autem hoc non est quod significat essentiam speciei, sicut animal est genus hominis; sed quod est proprium subiectum specie differentium accidentium. Superficies enim est subiectum omnium figurarum superficialium. Et habet similitudinem cum genere; quia proprium subiectum ponitur in definitione accidentis, sicut genus in definitione speciei. Unde subiectum proprium praedicatur de accidente ad similitudinem generis.[95]

The fourth meaning of "genus," as will have been surmised and as this passage brings out, is that which occupies first place in a definition, "et praedicatur in eo quod quid, et differentiae sunt eius qualitates."[96] *Genus subiectum*, the matter of a composite, is compared to the logical genus in terms of predication; St Thomas goes on to compare them in

---

[91] *In Boethii de trin.*, q. 4, a. 2.
[92] *In VII Physic.*, lect. 7, n. 9: "Est autem considerandum, quod multa quidem secundum abstractam considerationem vel Logici vel Mathematici non sunt aequivoca, quae tamen secundum concretam rationem. Naturalis ad materiam applicantis aequivoce quodammodo dicuntur: quia non secundum eamdem rationem in qualibet materia recipiuntur; sicut quantitatem et unitatem, quae est principium numeri, non secundum eamdem rationem contingit invenire in corporibus caelestibus et in igne et in aere et aqua." On applying mathematics, see *In V Metaphys.*, lect. 7, n. 859.
[93] *In V Metaphys.*, lect. 22, nn. 1119–27.
[94] *Ibid.*, n. 1124.
[95] *Ibid.*, n. 1121.
[96] *Ibid.*, n. 1122. On differences as qualities, cf. *In V Metaphys.*, lect. 16, n. 987.

terms of subject,[97] a comparison we have already examined. What is the significance of the comparison in terms of predication? Earlier, it was the fact that matter could not be predicated of its whole which distinguished it from the logical genus. Indeed, in this very text, the distinction is between the *genus praedicabile* and the *genus subiectum*. In what way is the *genus subiectum* also predicable?

The proper subject enters into the definition of its accident in a way similar to that in which the genus enters into the definition of the species. This puts one in mind of the second mode of predication *per se*, and if we turn to St Thomas' discussion of that doctrine, we find him speaking of two ways in which the subject is put in the definition of its proper accident, directly or obliquely.

Cuius quidem ratio est, quia cum esse accidentis dependeat a subiecto, oportet etiam quod definitio eius significans esse ipsius contineat in se subiectum. Unde secundus modus dicendi per se est quando subiectum ponitur in definitione praedicati, quod est proprium accidens eius.[98]

Direct or oblique positing of the subject in the definition of the property is a question of concrete or abstract signification, e.g. "snub" and "snubness." The first can be defined as "concave nose," the second as "the concavity of the nose." In either case, the proper subject, nose, enters into the definition. Thus, the subject functions as does "animal" in the definition "rational animal." This same example is used in the *Metaphysics* when the question is raised as to whether or not the *copulatum* (of substance and accident) can be defined. If we say it can, we must recognize that it is a definition *ex additione*, i.e. something other than the essence of accident enters into its definition, namely substance. The genus as subject does not express in an indeterminate way the essence of the accident.[99] Indeed, the subject and its accident differ *genere*.[100]

Depending on whether "genus" is taken as the *genus subiectum* or as

---

[97] *In V Metaphys.*, lect. 22, n. 1123: "Hoc enim modo se habet genus ad differentiam, sicut subiectum ad qualitatem. Et ideo patet quod genus praedicabile, et genus subiectum, quasi uno modo comprehenduntur, et utrumque se habet per modum materiae. Licet enim genus praedicabile non sit materia, sumitur tamen a materia, sicut differentia a forma. Dicitur enim aliquid animal ex eo quod habet naturam sensitivam. Rationale vero ex eo quod habet rationale naturam, quae se habet ad sensitivam sicut forma ad materiam."

[98] *In I Post. Analyt.*, lect. 10, n. 4.

[99] Cf. *In VII Metaphys.*, lect. 4, nn. 1343–53.

[100] Just as the compound of subject and accident involves a definition *ex additione*, so too we can say that the property includes its subject in its definition *ex additione* and differs from it *genere* and that substantial form includes its matter in its definition *ex additione* and differs from it *genere*. "Sicut species et materia sunt diversa genere, si secundum suam essentiam considerentur quod nihil est commune utrique." (*In V Metaphys.*, lect. 22, n. 1125) Moreover, the genus and difference are other in essence and cannot be mutually predicated per se. These last two cases are difficult to understand and for somewhat the same reason: the essence of a material thing is composed of matter and form, how then can matter and form be generic-

the *genus praedicabile*, there will be a twofold meaning of "generically different" or "differing in genus." Moreover, things can be one in genus in the second sense and differ in genus in the first.

Patet autem ex dictis quod aliqua continentur sub uno praedicamento, et sunt unum genere hoc modo secundo, quae tamen sunt diversa genere primo modo. Sicut corpora caelestia et elementaria, et colores et sapores. Primus autem modus diversitatis secundum genus consideratur magis a naturali, et etiam a philosopho, quia est magis realis. Secundus autem modus consideratur a logico, quia est rationis.[101]

Things univocal for the *logicus*, and thus equal in their participation in a common notion, can be unequal for the *naturalis* who looks to the *genus subiectum*, the matter. Before continuing our consideration of both

ally different? Likewise, the species or definition is composed of genus and difference, how then can genus and difference be generically different?
The answer to the first difficulty is found in St Thomas' discussion of what he considers the metaphysician's filling of a lack left by natural philosophy, namely the proof (other than from induction) of the existence of prime matter, a proof which proceeds by appeal to modes of predication (Cf. *In VII Metaphys.*, lect .2, nn. 1286–9). Prime matter in itself is neither substance, quantity, quality nor anything else by which something is placed in a determinate genus of being. That there is such a thing is clear from the fact that there must be something of which each of these is predicated and which is other than any of them. What kind of predication is this? It is not ,St Thomas holds (*ibid.*, n. 1288), *praedicatio univoca*, but *praedicatio denominativa*. The first is exemplified by the predication of genus of species: the genus enters into the definition of the species "quia non est aliud per essentiam animal et homo." Denominative predication is exemplified by "Man is white," where the quiddity of the predicate differs from that of the subject. "Unde subiungit, quod alia genera praedicantur hoc modo de substantia, substantia vero praedicatur de materia denominative." (*ibid.*) Although "Man is white" may be true, neither "Man is whiteness" nor "Humanity is whiteness" could be true unless the essence of man and whiteness were the same. So too "Materia est homo" and "Materia est humanitas" are false, but "Hoc materiatum est homo" is true. "Ipsa ergo concretiva, sive denominativa praedicatio ostendit, quod sicut substantia est aliud per essentiam ab accidentibus, ita per essentiam aliud est materia a formis substantialibus." (*ibid.*, n. 1289) "...in definitione formae substantialis oportet quod ponatur illud cuius est forma, et ita definitio eius est per additionem alicuius quod extra eius genus est, sicut et definitio formae accidentalis." (*De ente et essentia*, cap. 7) That is, one integral part of the substantial composite is essentially different from the other. (On denominative predication, see *In IX Metaphys.*, lect. 6, nn. 1839–43.)
So too with the integral parts of the species or definition. The genus and difference are essentially different: "genus non est in differentia sicut pars essentiae eius, sed solum sicut ens extra quidditatem sive essentiam; sicut etiam subiectum est de intellectu passionum: et ideo genus non praedicatur de differentia per se loquendo... nisi forte sicut subiectum praedicatur de passione." (*De ente et essentia*, cap. 3) Thus, the difference is predicated of the genus in the second mode of perseity and of the species in the first mode, although both genus and difference are predicated of the whole of the species. It is because genus is drawn from matter and difference from form that the essential difference of these integral parts of the thing is reflected in the intentions drawn from them, although, again, both genus and difference signify the whole of the species and not parts of it. With respect to the modes of "genus" distinguished in *In V Metaphys.*, lect. 22, "animal" is a genus in the fourth mode with respect to the essence, but a genus in the third mode with respect to the difference. One will appreciate the significance of the notion of *genus subiectum* for the logic of demonstration, since demonstration, properly speaking, consists in showing that the property follows on the subject because of what it is. In conclusion, substantial form, accidents whether contingent or proper, and difference have this in common, that they are essentially different from their subjects and include their respective subjects in their definitions *ex additione*.

[101] *In V Metaphys.*, lect. 22, n. 1127; Cf. *In II de anima*, lect. 22, n. 524.

sides of this option, we would do well to notice that there is another inequality or *per prius et posterius* on the part of things falling under the same *genus praedicabile*, an inequality which does not seem to be at issue in the second division of our text from the *Sentences*.

Things which are equal from the point of view of the common notion which is the genus can be unequal in that one is more perfect than the other. "Si quis enim diligenter consideret, in omnibus speciebus unius generis semper inveniet unum alia perfectiorem, sicut in coloribus albe-dinem et in animalibus hominem."[102] The inequality at issue here is taken from the differences which are related as act and privation. The division of the genus into species which are related as prior and posterior does not mean, of course, that the name signifying the generic notion is predicated analogically of them. Their inequality has to be explained in terms of something else, for in terms of the generic notion and the name signifying it the species are univocals; the name of the genus does not cease to be univocal when the species are discerned. An analogous name, on the contrary, signifies a common notion which is common *per prius et posterius*. That is why the inequality among the species of a genus must not be confused with the inequality of the common notion of an analogous name.

Dicendum quod quando genus univocum dividitur in suas species, tunc partes divisionis ex aequo se habent secundum rationem generis; licet secundum naturam rei una species sit principalior et perfectior alia, sicut homo aliis animalibus. Sed quando est divisio alicuius analogi, quod dicitur de pluribus secundum prius et posterius; tunc nihil prohibet unum esse principalius altero, etiam secundum communem rationem, sicut substantia principaliter dicitur ens quam accidens.[103]

Things which share in the common generic notion can be unequal and related *per prius et posterius* if we look to that which constitutes them specifically, namely the differences which divide the genus and are not expressed by it. Here the inequality is based on what is formal to the species and that is why this type of inequality cannot obtain in the *species specialissima* which is not subject to further formal determination.

---

[102] *In librum de causis*, 4ª.

[103] *IaIIae*, q. 61, a. 1, ad 1. Cf. *In I Periherm*, lect. 8, n. 6: "Sed dicendum quod unum dividentium aliquod commune potest esse prius altero dupliciter: uno modo, secundum proprias rationes, aut naturas dividentium; alio modo, secundum participationem rationis illius communis quod in ea dividitur. Primus autem non tollit univocationem generis, ut manifestum est in numeris, in quibus binarius secundum propriam rationem naturaliter est prior ternario; sed tamen aequaliter participant rationem generis sui, scilicet numeri: ita enim est ternarius multitudo mensurata per unum, sicut et binarius. Sed secundum impedit univocationem generis. Et propter hoc ens non potest esse genus substantiae et accidentis: quia in ipsa ratione entis, substantia, quae est ens per se, prioritatem habet respectu accidentis, quod est ens per aliud et in alio."

"Impossibile est autem naturam speciei communicare ab individuis per prius et posterius, neque esse, neque post secundum intentionem, quamvis hoc sit possibile in natura generis..."[104] Note that St Thomas takes into account here the inequality just mentioned as well as that at issue in our text from the *Sentences*. It is not the inequality which follows on specific differences[105] which is at stake in the division "secundum esse et non secundum intentionem." The source of the inequality envisaged by this phrase is not the differences which divide the genus, but matter. As is pointed out in the commentary on the *De trinitate*,[106] the generic notion is based on a grasp of matter under a common determination. Since the genus is susceptible of further formal determinations productive of less confused notions which more adequately express the essence of material things, the genus is said to be *materiale*. But in that *materiale* there is form and matter and the *logicus* concerns himself only with the form. The *genus praedicabile* expresses a perfection of matter, but the *logicus* does not consider the matter. Thus, the *genus praedicabile* is said to be formal and abstract, and it is this which enables it to embrace things in which the generic notion is saved thanks to different kinds *(genera)* of matter, or even in the absence of all matter.

Sicut patet quod lapis in materia, quae est in potentia ad esse, pertingit ad hoc quod subsistat; ad quod idem pertingit sol secundum materiam quae est in potentia ad ubi et non ad esse, et angelus omni materia carens. Unde logicus inveniens in his omnibus illud ex quo genus sumebat, ponit omnia haec in uno genere substantiae; naturalis vero et metaphysicus, qui considerant principia rerum, omnia non invenientes convenientia in materia, dicunt ea differre genere, secundum hoc quod dicitur in X Metaph., quod corruptibile et incorruptibile differunt genere et quod illa conconveniunt genere quorum est materia una, et generatio ad invicem.[107]

Let us turn now to the physical matter which is the source of unity of genus for the natural philosopher.

From the point of view of the natural philosopher, who considers the *principia rerum*, those things are of one genus which have a common name expressing a *ratio* found in the same kind of matter in each of them.[108] We want now to examine the context of the remark quoted

---

104 *II Sent.*, d. 3, q. 1, a. 4; cf. *Q.D. de ver.*, q. 1, a. 6.
105 *Q.D. de malo*, q. 2, a. 9, ad 16: "...omnia animalia sunt aequaliter animalia, non tamen sunt aequalia animalia, sed unum animal est altero maius et perfectius..."; cf. *Ia*, q. 77, a. 4, ad 1.
106 *In Boethii de trin.*, q. 4, a. 2.
107 *Ibid.*
108 *In X Metaphys.*, lect. 4, nn. 2019-20: "Genere quidem differunt, quorum non est communis materia. Dictum est enim supra in octavo quod licet materia non sit genus, tamen ab eo quod est materiale, sumitur ratio generis. Sicut natura sensibilis est materiale in homine respectu rationis. Et ideo illud quod non communicat in natura sensibili cum homine, est alterius generis. Et quia ea quae non communicant in materia, non generantur adinvicem,

earlier from the commentary on the *Metaphysics*.[109] Having shown that contraries are in the same genus and that they constitute the species of the genus, Aristotle goes on, St Thomas observes, to touch on two exceptions. Some contraries pertain not so much to the species as to the individual and consequently do not constitute specific differences. For example, white and black are contraries, but they do not found the differences of the species of animal.[110] If it is true to say, "Animal is black," this is because a particular animal happens to be black. But black/white is not a contrariety within the genus of animal, since things not falling in this genus can be white or black. Thus, white and black are accidents of the individual, reducible to matter in the same way that individuality itself is. But the contraries which constitute species of a genus pertain to form.

It also happens that contrariety can be constitutive of generic and not merely of specific difference. The example is corruptible/incorruptible. Such contraries are opposed in terms of potency and non-potency, for the corruptible is that which can not-be, whereas the incorruptible lacks this potency. Why should this contrariety found a generic difference? "Et hoc ideo, quia sicut forma et actus pertinet ad speciem, ita materia et potentia pertinent ad genus. Unde sicut contrarietas quae est secundum formas et actus, facit differentiam secundum speciem, ita contrarietas quae est secundum potentiam, facit generis diversitatem."[111] Although this second qualification of the general position also involves appeal to matter, it is important to see how corruptible/incorruptible differs from black/white although both agree in not being the type of contrariety which constitutes specific difference. White and black are accidents of individuals and thus, though we cannot say "Socrates is white and black," we can say, "Man is white and black." The truth of the statement about the universal nature is founded on the different individuals Alcibiades and Othello. But is it possible truly to say of any universal nature that it is corruptible and incorruptible?[112] The reply is negative: corruptible and incorruptible are not predicated *per accidens* as are white and black.

sequitur ea genere esse diversa, quorum non est generatio ad invicem. Quod etiam necesse fuit addere propter ea quae non habent materiam, sicut accidentia sunt. Ut sint genere diversa quaecumque sunt in diversis praedicamentis, ut linea et albedo, quorum unum non fit ex alio."

[109] See above, p. 100.

[110] They are of course productive of different species of color. Cf. *In X Metaphys.*, lect. 12, n. 2144.

[111] *Ibid.*, n. 2137 bis.

[112] *Ibid.*, n. 2138. It may be well to recall that the universal nature, as such, is corruptible only *per accidens*. Cf. *In VII Metaphys.*, lect. 7, nn. 1419–23.

Non enim corruptibile inest secundum accidens alicui eorum de quibus praedicatur; quia quod est secundum accidens contingit non inesse. Corruptibile autem ex necessitate inest his quibus inest. At si hoc non sit verum, sequeretur quod unum et idem sit quandoque corruptibile et quandoque incorruptibile: quod est impossibile secundum naturam.[113]

If it is not predicated accidentally, "corruptible" must express the substance, or something of the substance, of that of which it is predicated. "Est enim unumquodque corruptibile per materiam, quae est de substantia rei. Et similis ratio est de incorruptibili..."[114] Since they express the substance of that of which they are predicated, corruptible and incorruptible cannot be in the same genus: contraries which divide a genus into its species are not of the substance of that genus. But any genus is such that corruptible or incorruptible would pertain to its very notion (de intellectu eius). Such opposites, then, cannot communicate in any genus. "Et hoc rationabiliter accidit. Nam corruptibilium et incorruptibilium non potest esse materia una."[115] It is just at this point that the now familiar distinction is made between the genus physice loquendo, which is the one we have just been discussing and which sumitur a materia, and the genus logice loquendo. What communicates in one common notion can be in the same genus, logically speaking, but if things do not communicate in one matter they will be said, by the natural philosopher, to be generically different.

The natural philosopher is concerned with the principia rei,[116] and physical things are composed of matter and form as of integral parts of their substance. The logical genus expresses the essence of the thing suo modo, but as a whole; it does not express merely a part. The physical genus is based on the matter which is part of illud materiale whence the logical genus is taken, the material notion which is subject to further perfection and imperfection expressed by the contraries which divide it. Things will be said to be in the same physical genus when they are linked by the substratum of absolute change.[117] Contraries of the physical genus will be those things one of which can be the term from which, the other the term to which of a physical change: they thereby have a common subject.[118] To be in the same physical genus is to be one in

---

[113] In X Metaphys., lect. 12, n. 2140. Cf. Q.D. de malo, q. 5, a. 5.
[114] In X Metaphys., lect. 12, n. 2141.
[115] Ibid., n. 2144.
[116] In Boethii de trin., q. 4, a. 2.
[117] Ibid. "...quorum est materia una et generatio adinvicem."
[118] In I de gen. et cor., lect. 19, nn. 5–6: "Dicit ergo quod, quia non quaecumque apta nata sunt agere et pati adinvicem, sed solum illa quae sunt contraria, vel habent contrarietatem, necesse est quod agens et patiens in genere sint idem et similia, et diversa specie et contraria. Et non sumitur hic genus logice: quia hoc modo alia corpora essent eiusdem generis; sed sumitur genus naturaliter: et hoc modo omnia quae communicant in materia, sunt eiusdem

matter[119] – and not merely one in a "material" notion. And, since the
matter from which the physical genus is taken is a component of physical
things, it can be predicated of them as part of whole, i.e. denominatively,
in the way discussed earlier.[120] Thus the common notion, "illud materiale unde sumitur genus," *logice loquendo*, can be considered as a form
which can be found in different kinds of matter or in things which are
in no wise material. "...corporeitas secundum intentionem logicam univoce in omnibus corporibus invenitur; sed secundum esse considerata,
non potest esse unius rationis in re corruptibili et incorruptibili: quia
non similiter se habent in potentia essendi, cum unum sit possibile ad
esse et ad non esse, et alterum non."[121]

Just as *genus logicum* and *genus physicum* differ, so too difference *naturaliter loquendo* is not the same as what satisfies the logician's demands.
For the natural philosopher, differences are the contrary forms which
are terms of change thanks to their common subject matter: there is
generatio ad invicem. The differences dividing the logical genus need not
be contraries in that sense: "...dicendum quod naturaliter loquendo de
genere et differentia, oportet differentias esse contrarias: nam natura,
super quam fundatur natura generis, est susceptiva contrariarum formarum. Secundum autem considerationem logicam sufficit qualiscum-
que oppositio in differentiis, sicut patet in differentiis numerorum, in
quibus non est contrarietas; et similiter est in spiritualibus substantiis."[122]
The species of number are not contrary to one another, nor is there
contrariety, properly speaking, in the genus of number: to maintain
otherwise would imply the absurdity of a greatest number.[123]

(3) Univocal or analogous?

We must now return to the question with which we began: does the
division "secundum esse sed non secundum intentionem" mean that

---

generis (...) Quaecumque agunt et patiuntur adinvicem, sunt contraria; contraria autem
sunt in eodem genere, ut probatur in X Metaphys.; ergo activa et passiva sunt in eodem
genere; et ideo necesse est ipsa *qualiter*, idest quodammodo, esse similia, quia eadem et similia
genere, et *qualiter*, idest quodammodo, altera et dissimilia specie, ut dixerunt antiqui."

[119] *Ibid.*, lect. 20, n. 2: "Subiungit ad horum declarationem quae dicitur materia una
aliquorum. Et dicit quod dicitur esse una materia cuilibet, quae est susceptiva contrariorum:
quae licet sit una subiecto, differt tamen secundum esse: et propter hoc dixit *ut ita dicam*.
Et ipsa materia dicitur ut genus, non quidem praedicabile, sed dicitur genus secundum quod
genus dicitur subiectum primum, quod substat duobus contrariis aut pluribus: contrariorum
autem unum in activo, alterum in passivo: et ideo una materia est activi et passivi."

[120] See note 100.
[121] *II Sent.* d. 12, q. 1, a. 1, ad 1; cf. *In X Metaphys.*, lect. 12, n. 2145.
[122] *Q.D. de anima*, a. 7, ad 18.
[123] Cf. *In V Physic.*, lect. 3, n. 5.

things are named body univocally from the logical point of view and named body analogically from the natural point of view? If this question seems paradoxical, this is because things are said to be named univocally which have a common name which signifies the same *ratio* as said of each of them, whereas things are said to be named analogically which have a common name which does not signify exactly the same *ratio*, but different *rationes* related *per prius et posterius*. How can things, the same things, be named by the same name in both ways? The answer is found in the distinction between the abstract notion which satisfies the *logicus* and the *ratio concreta* of the philosopher. We have seen that the material notion which is the genus contains form and matter and that the logical genus expresses only the form. Thus, logically speaking, "body" means "that in which three dimensions can be designated," saying nothing about the kind of form this is due to, whether that of stone, plant, star or man, and without saying anything about the matter which is actuated by the form. It is thanks to this indifference to matter that "body" can be taken to signify terrestial and celestial bodies univocally. The concrete notion which answers to the philosopher's use of "body" involves a determinate statement about the matter in which the form is found. This gives rise to two different *rationes* of "body" when it is question of terrestial and celestial bodies. The notion of terrestial body expresses a matter which is in potency to another substantial form: thus the body of which such matter is a component can cease to be; on Aristotle's hypothesis, celestial bodies could not *thus* cease to be (i.e. corrupt) and if they are to be said to have matter, this will be in a different sense of the term. Thus, the two concrete *rationes* render the common name equivocal, i.e. analogical. "Et sic non est eadem materia corporis caelestis et elementorum, nisi secundum analogiam, secundum quod conveniunt in ratione potentiae."[124] A similarity of proportions is set up so that celestial bodies are spoken of in terms of what we know to be the case with terrestial bodies. These latter are composed of matter and form (a position arrived at by observation of substantial generation and corruption). Celestial bodies, since long observation has revealed no substantial change (the ground of Aristotle's hypothesis), if they are bodies are not bodies as are terrestial things. And, if we want to speak of matter in celestial bodies, setting up a proportion between their form and their matter, we will manifest the meaning of "matter" in this proportion by appealing to its meaning as applied to terrestial things. And we will negate of it the potency to

[124] *Ia*, q. 66, a. 2.

non-being which follows on prime matter, since it is matter's potentiality to forms other than that presently actuating it which explains the
corruptibility of terrestial bodies. The matter of celestial bodies was
said, consequently, to be the root of the potentiality involved in local
motion. Thus, since "matter" does not mean the same thing and the
ratio concreta of the philosopher expresses the matter determinately,
"body" is not said univocally of terrestial and celestial bodies, but analogically, signifying different bodies *per prius et posterius*. The same thing
can be seen in terms of a *ratio communis* which could be formed with
the aid of "potency."

It is because the genus is, as we saw earlier, one thanks to our mode
of knowing and not because it expresses one essence *in rerum natura*[125]
that Aristotle has warned that "iuxta genera latet multa," i.e. that the
unity of the genus can make us fail to see many equivocations. This
happens, not because of further formal differences expressed by differences, but because a concrete notion takes into account matter as well
as form and reveals the inequality. Before turning to St Thomas' comments on this remark, let us seek some initial clarity from his commentary
on the *Metaphysics*.[126] The text we have in mind is one which will occupy
us again in Chapter VII when we discuss univocal and equivocal causes.
A generation is wholly univocal when the form of what is generated
preexists in the generator "secundum eumdum modum essendi et simili
materia." A generation may be partly equivocal and partly univocal
when the form exists immaterially in the generator and materially in
the generated; e.g. the form of the house in the mind of the artisan and
the form of the house realized in lumber and cement and bricks. It is
this case which interests us, for it seems to answer to the univocity of
the genus *logice loquendo* where the form alone of the genus is considered.
The first type, where both form and matter are considered, seems to
answer to the genus *physice loquendo*. The physical genus reveals the
equivocity concealed by the abstract notion.

St Thomas, commenting on Aristotle's remark that the genus conceals many equivocals, gives a division which is most interesting if
somewhat difficult to understand.[127] To understand it, we must see

---

[125] Cf. *I Sent.*, d. 30, q. 1, a. 3.

[126] *In VII Metaphys.* lect. 8, nn. 1444–6.

[127] *In VII Physic.*, lect. 8, n. 8: "Quia ergo genus *quodammodo* est unum, et non simpliciter,
iuxta genera latent multa: idest, per similitudinem et propinquitatem ad unitatem generis,
multorum aequivocatio latet. Sunt autem *quaedam* aequivocationum multum distantes, in
quibus sola communitas nominum attenditur; sicut si canis dicatur caeleste sidus, et animal
latrabile. *Quaedam* vero sunt quae habent quandam similitudinem; sicut si hoc nomen homo
dicatur de vero homine et de homine picto, inquantum habet similitudinem quandam veri

that he is not enumerating the equivocations which can be hidden by the logical genus (this is one member of the division), but the way in which equivocations can be hidden because a genus, i.e. a physical genus, seems to be involved. Thus, even pure equivocations enter into his division, although all they have in common with the genus is that one name is applied to many things; pure equivocation, however, has only the unity of the word: inquiry into what that word means in its various uses reveals totally different meanings.

It is difficult to know whether the remainder of the text contains two or three members. St Thomas ends by noting that either the unity of the logical genus or similarity can conceal the equivocation. And yet there are two types or, if not, two examples of equivocals concealed because of similarity. "Man" is said of Socrates and a painting of him because the latter is like the former. We have encountered this example before, and we saw how it can be said to involve an analogous name although sometimes spoken of as *omnino aequivoce*. It is analogous because the notion signified by the term as applied to the painting includes the notion signified by it as applied to Socrates. The second similarity, "master" as applied to the head of a household and the teacher in school, is based on a similarity of proportions or functions. Though both are directors *(rectores)*, the one is in the home, the other in school. Is there any univocity involved here as there is in the case of "body"? That is, could we find at least a logical genus? Or is *magister* thought of as transferred from the majordomo to the teacher? The last possibility could render the name analogical and seems the preferable interpretation, for it explains the twofold similarity with physical genus with which St Thomas ends, namely that of the logical genus and similarity. We might add that "being" too has a similarity with the genus, something which can conceal its equivocation.[128]

---

hominis. *Quaedam* vero aequivocationes sunt proximae: aut propter convenientiam in genere (sicut si corpus dicatur de corpore caelesti et de corpore corruptibili, aequivoce dicitur, naturaliter loquendo, quia eorum non est materia una. Conveniunt tamen in genere logico: et propter hanc generis convenientiam videntur omnino non aequivoca esse): aut etiam sunt propinquae secundum aliquam similitudinem; sicut ille qui docet in scholis dicitur magister, et similiter ille qui praeest domui dicitur magister domus, aequivoce, et tamen propinqua aequivocatione propter similitudinem; uterque enim est rector, hic quidem scholarum, ille vero domus. Unde propter hanc propinquitatem vel generis vel similitudinis, non videntur esse aequivocationes, cum tamen sint."

[128] Cf. e.g. *In IV Metaphys.*, lect. 4, n. 583.

(4) Who is the 'logicus'?

There remains an important question. We have seen that the genus *logice loquendo* is distinguished from the genus *physice loquendo*, that some things are named equivocally from the point of view of the natural philosopher which are named univocally so far as the *logicus* is concerned. Just who is this *logicus?* The question gains importance from the fact that univocation and equivocation are logical intentions. If this is the case, what is the point of speaking of logical univocals and physical univocals? What has been called the abstract *ratio* which constitutes the genus, *logice loquendo*, brings to mind a discussion from the commentary on *On the Soul*.

Si quis ergo assignet definitionem, per quam non deveniatur in cognitionem accidentium rei definitae, illa definitio non est realis, sed remota et dialectica. Sed illa definitio per quam deveniatur in cognitionem accidentium est realis et ex propriis et essentialibus rei.[129]

St Thomas manifests the difference between a logical or dialectical definition and a natural definition by the example of anger. One might define anger as desire for revenge or, on the other hand, as the "churning of the blood around the heart." The former is the logical or dialectical definition; the latter, or better, both together, would be the natural definition.

Quod autem definitio prima sit insufficiens manifeste apparet. Nam omnis forma quae est in materia determinata, nisi in sua definitione ponatur materia, illa definitio est insufficiens: sed haec forma, scilicet *appetitus vindictae* est forma in materia determinata: unde cum non ponatur in eius definitione materia, constat quod ipsa definitio est insufficiens. Et ideo necesse est ad definitionem, quod in definitione ponatur hoc, scilicet forma, esse in materia huiusmodi, scilicet determinata.[130]

The definition which does not take into account the determinate matter in which the form is found is said to be logical as opposed to natural: "illa quae considerat formam tantum, non est naturalis, sed logica."[131]

To encounter a logical as opposed to a natural or real definition is puzzling since there is a logical doctrine on definition which presumably has application in any of the sciences. What is the relationship between the logical definition and the logic of definition? Every science is such because it satisfies the canons of logic. What then is the meaning, within the science of nature, of the distinction between logical and natural definitions, between logical and natural arguments?[132]

---

[129] *In I de anima*, lect. 1, n. 15.
[130] *Ibid.*, lect. 2, n. 25; cf. *In VIII Metaphys.*, lect. 2, n. 1700.
[131] *In I de anima*, lect. 2, n. 27.
[132] Cf. *In III Physic.*, lect. 8, n. 1.

Consider the distinction, within the logic of argumentation, between reasoning which concludes necessarily (demonstration), reasoning which concludes with probability (dialectics), and reasoning which is only apparently conclusive (sophistics). The logical doctrine of each of these types puts us in possession of scientific knowledge of how they proceed.[133] That is, the logic of sophistical reasoning *(sophistica docens)* is a science; the logic of dialectics *(dialectica docens)* is not probable, but necessary, a science. So too is the logic of demonstration. To use dialectics, however, is to argue in such a fashion that only probable knowledge is attained. To use sophistics is to appear to reason validly. This use is spoken of by St Thomas as if it constituted only a modality characterizing arguments about reality *(modo adiuncto)*.[134] That more than this is involved is clear from his rejection of any distinction between *demonstrativa docens* and *demonstrativa utens*.

Sed in parte logicae quae dicitur demonstrativa, solum doctrina pertinet ad logicam, usus vero ad philosophiam et ad alias particulares scientias quae sunt de rebus naturae. Et hoc ideo, quia usus demonstrativae consistit in utendo principiis rerum, de quibus fit demonstratio, quae ad scientias reales pertinet, non utendo intentionibus logicis. Et sic apparet, quod quaedam partes logicae habent ipsam scientiam et doctrinam et usum, sicut dialectica tentativa et sophistica; quaedam autem doctrinam et non usum, sicut demonstrativa.[135]

To argue demonstratively is not to make use of the logical intentions considered in the logic of demonstration, but to argue from the *principia rerum:* the result is philosophy of nature, mathematics or metaphysics, not a *logica utens. Logica utens*, then, consists of the use of logical intentions in arguing and he who does this will be called the *logicus* as opposed to the *philosophus*. The *demonstrator*, on the other hand, is always the philosopher of nature, the mathematician or the metaphysician – and, of course, the logician setting forth *logica docens*.

The *logicus* or dialectician who reasons about things by making use of logical intentions is not the *logicus* who expounds logical doctrine; if he were, the result would be science. But the result of the efforts of

---

[133] *In IV Metaphys.*, lect. 4, n. 576: "Licet autem dicatur, quod Philosophia est scientia, non autem dialectica et sophistica, non tamen per hoc removetur quin dialectica et sophistica sint scientiae. Dialectica enim potest considerari secundum quod est docens, et secundum quod est utens. Secundum quidem quod est docens habet considerationem de ipsis intentionibus, instituens modum, quo per eas procedi possit ad conclusiones in singulis scientiis probabiliter ostendendas; et hoc demonstrative facit, et secundum hoc est scientia. Utens vero est secundum quod modo adiuncto utitur ad concludendum aliquid probabiliter in singulis scientiis; et sic recedit a modo scientiae. – Et similiter dicendum est de sophistica; quia prout est docens tradit per necessarias et demonstrativas rationes modum arguendi apparenter. Secundum vero quod est utens, deficit a processu verae argumentationis."
[134] *Ibid.*
[135] *Ibid.*, n. 577.

the *logicus* or dialectician is only probability. The dialectician can be considered as a kind of rival of the metaphysician because of the equal scope, so to speak, of logic and metaphysics. Since all being is the object of reason and logic is concerned with the relations reason sets up among things as known, logical entities comprise as much as the object of reason itself.[136] It is just this that permits the dialectician to operate. "Dialecticus autem procedit ad ea (i.e. communia accidentia entis) consideranda ex intentionibus rationis, quae sunt extranea a natura rerum. Et ideo dicitur, quod dialectica est tentativa, quia tentare proprium est ex principiis extraneis procedere."[137]

In commenting on the *De trinitate* of Boethius, St Thomas distinguishes two modes of *logica utens* when he is discussing three ways in which we can be said to proceed *rationabiliter*. "Rational process" can be denominated from logic, the *scientia rationalis*, in two ways.[138] First, because of the principles from which it proceeds, as if someone were to try to prove something about reality from the intentions of genus, species, opposites, analogy, etc. This is to make use of logical propositions in arguing about things. Say we know that love is a passion of the sense appetite and argue that since love and hate are opposites, and opposites are in the same genus, hate must be a passion of the sense appetite. We are using a logical truth to argue about non-logical entities. "Sed hic modus procedendi non potest competere proprie alicui particulari scientiae, in quibus peccatum accidit, nisi ex propriis procedatur."[139]

Secondly, reasoning can be called a rational process from the point of view of the end or term. Science is had when we are able so to resolve a conclusion into its principles that we see its necessity. When reason does not achieve this term and is not determined to one of contradictory propositions, opinion or faith is the result, and the argument leading to it only probable. Such a dialectical procedure is legitimate in any

[136] "Dialecticus autem circa omnia praedicta procedit ex probabilibus; unde non facit scientiam, sed quamdam opinionem. Et hoc ideo est, quia ens est duplex: ens scilicet rationis et ens naturae. Ens autem rationis dicitur proprie de illis intentionibus quas ratio adinvenit in rebus consideratis; sicut intentio generis, speciei et similium, quae quidem non inveniuntur in rerum natura, sed considerationem rationis consequuntur. Et huiusmodi, scilicet ens rationis, est proprie subiectum logicae. Huiusmodi autem intentiones intelligibiles, entibus aequiparantur, eo quod omnia entia naturae sub consideratione rationis cadunt. Et ideo subiectum logicae ad omnia se extendit, de quibus ens naturae praedicatur. Unde concludit, quod subiectum logicae aequiparatur subiecto philosophiae, quod est naturae." – *In IV Metaphys.*, lect. 4, n. 574; cf. *In VII Metaphys.*, lect. 2, n. 1287; *ibid.*, lect. 3, n. 1308; *In Boethii de trin.*, q. 6, a. 1.

[137] *In IV Metaphys.*, lect. 4, n. 574.

[138] "Et his duobus modis denominatur processus rationalis a scientia rationali; his enim modis utitur logica, quae rationis dicitur scientia, in scientiis demonstrativis..." – *In Boethii de trin.*, q. 6, a. 1, *ad primam quaestionem.* Cf. Sheilah O' Flynn, *op cit.*

[139] *In Boethii de trin.*, q. 6, a. 1, *ad primam quaestionem.*

science as a preparation for necessary conclusions. It is this second type
St Thomas seems to have in mind in commenting on the *Physics*. "Dicuntur autem primae rationes logicae, non quia ex terminis logicis logice
procedant, sed quia modo logico procedunt, scilicet ex communibus et
probabilibus quod est proprium syllogismo dialectici."[140] The arguments in question proceed from what is common in the sense of what
is commonly held or believed.[141]

It would seem to be the first type of rational process which answers
most closely to the use of the adjective "logical" in speaking of definitions.
To group terrestial and celestial bodies under a common notion which
ignores the *principia rerum* is to depend on a unity which results from our
mode of knowing. The definition and genus are logical not as pertaining
to logical doctrine, but as using logical entities to speak of real entities.
Logica docens will mention real things by way of examples, it is dependent
on a psychology which teaches how our knowledge attains real entities,[142]
but as such *logica docens* is not about things as they exist and would have
nothing to say about terrestial and celestial bodies. The logic of definition
cannot decide what is a proper mode of defining in any science, anymore than the logic of demonstration decides what is the proper mode
of this science or that. For this there is required a proper methodology
which applies the common mode of logic to the degree this can be done
given the subject matter of the science in question.[143] By the same token,
the logic of analogical signification does not decide what in a given
science will be considered to be named analogically, any more than
logic can decide what in a particular science will be said to be named
univocally. This does not mean that the common logical doctrine is
altered by a consideration of what is a good definition or *ratio* in a
given science. And, if one settles for a common or abstract notion in
speaking of univocity in a determinate area, he will be proceeding
logically in the sense of dialectically. To note the inadequacy of this
approach is not to call *logica docens* into question, nor to demand further
development of the properly logical doctrine.[144]

By way of conclusion to this lengthy analysis of the way in which things
are named analogically "secundum esse sed non secundum intentio-

---

[140] *In III Physic.*, lect. 8, n. 1.
[141] *Ibid.*, n. 4: "Attendendum est autem quod istae rationes sunt probabiles et procedentes
ex iis quae communiter dicuntur."
[142] *On Interpretation*, 16a9.
[143] Cf. *In II Metaphys.*, lect. 5, nn. 335–7.
[144] For criticism of arguments which proceed *ex intentionibus*, see *II Sent.*, d. 17, q. 1, a. 1;
In I Physic., lectiones 2 – 6.

nem," let us state briefly what we have found. Faced with a situation where things have a common name, we can say they are named both univocally and analogically. They are named univocally insofar as the term signifies an abstract, formal, common *ratio* which owes its unity only to our mode of knowing. *Logice loquendo*, they are in the same genus and are named univocally, where *logice* means "dialectically." If the common name takes into account both the form and the matter of "illud materiale unde sumitur genus," several concrete notions can result, as in the case of "body," and then the name is no longer common univocally but analogically, *secundum prius et posterius*, insofar as the matter of celestial bodies is made known from what we know of the matter of terrestial bodies and denominated from the latter. All terrestial bodies will be named such univocally insofar as the term "body" signifies the appropriate concrete notion; the common doctrine of univocation is saved, just as the common doctrine of analogical signification is saved when "body" signifies the diverse concrete notions appropriate to terrestial and celestial bodies, or a *ratio communis* formed in terms of potency. By identifying the *logicus* as the dialectician, we are enabled to avoid the erroneous conclusion that a different logical doctrine of univocation and of the analogy of names is required when it is a question of concrete notions. Rather what we see is a particular science determining, thanks to its proper subject, what will and what will not satisfy the canons of univocity and the analogy of names.

(c) *Secundum intentionem, secundum esse*

Vel secundum intentionem et secundum esse; et hoc est quando neque parificatur in intentioni communi, neque in esse; sicut ens dicitur de substantia et accidente; et de talibus oportet quod natura communis habet aliquod esse in unoquoque eorum de quibus dicitur, sed differens secundum rationem majoris et minoris perfectionis. Et similiter dico, quod veritas, et bonitas et omnia hujusmodi dicuntur analogice de Deo et creaturis. Unde oportet quod secundum suum esse omnia haec in Deo sint, et in creaturis secundum rationem majoris perfectionis et minoris; ex quo sequitur, cum non possint esse secundum unum esse utrobique, quod sint diversae veritates.

We are reading the present text as presenting, not a division of the analogy of names, but as pointing out that the foundation of analogous names is not always the same. In such an example as "healthy," that from which the name is imposed has existence in only one of the things named by it. Various references or proportions to that in which *sanitas* exists are the foundation for the extension of the word *sanum*. In the second division, we were apprised of a remote and proper way of looking at things. These different vantage points can give rise to univocity and

analogy with respect to the same name and the same things named by
it. In the third division, we are told of analogous names which are so
founded that that from which the name is imposed exists in each of the
things named analogically, but "secundum rationem majoris et minoris
perfectionis." Although the text makes its point with particular reference to the divine names, the names common to God and creature, we
are not presently concerned with those. But we do want to say a word or
two now about the phrase just quoted, a phrase which could be rendered
as "unequal participation in a common perfection." This inequality
must not be confused with the manner in which species participate in a
genus, a contextually important point, since St Thomas teaches that
God and creature cannot communicate in a genus, even *logice loquendo*.

Greater and lesser possession of a common perfection can be understood in such a way that it is not productive of even specific diversity,
or in such a way that it does result in different species, or in such a
way that it is productive of generic diversity and excludes all univocation.
In the first place, then, we can speak of things as more and less white, but,
since it is the same form that is possessed, such a "magis et minus non di-
versificant speciem."[145] The term "white" applied to the more and less
white signifies the same *ratio*; nevertheless, their similarity is imperfect.[146]

The more and less which diversifies species is read in terms of that
which is primary in a given genus. "Diversi enim colores specie sunt
secundum magis et minus propinque se habent ad lucem..."[147] The
measure in the genus of color is white, defined as *disgregativa visus*.[148]
Notice that this *magis et minus* does not destroy the univocity of the
genus, since the *per prius et posterius* involved is that read in terms of
specific differences, something we discussed above; the differences assigned are taken from the effect on our sight because the real differences
are unknown.[149]

Greater and lesser possession of the form in terms of which things
can be called similar sometimes gives rise to generic diversity. St Thomas,
following Aristotle, uses the example of the sun as cause of the heat of
terrestrial things. "Sicut sol est causa caloris in istis inferioribus; non
tamen inferiora corpora possunt recipere impressionem solis aut aliorum
caelestium corporum secundum eamdem rationem speciei, cum non
communicent in materia. Et propter hoc non dicimus solem esse calidis-

---

[145] *Q.D. de anima*, a. 7, ad 6; *Q.D. de spirit. creat.*, a. 8, ad 8.
[146] *Ia*, q. 4, a. 3.
[147] *Q.D. de anima*, a. 7, ad 6.
[148] *In X Metaphys.*, lect. 9, n. 2107; *De ente et essentia*, cap. 7; *I Sent.*, d. 8, q. 4, a. 3, ad 3.
[149] *In X Metaphys.*, lect. 9, n. 2107.

simum sicut ignem, sed dicimus solem esse aliquid amplius quam calidissimum."[150] Fire is first in the genus of hot terrestial things; the sun
is outside this genus entirely. The reason St Thomas gives takes us back
to the second member of the tripartite division of the *Sentences*, something
productive of a problem. He sometimes uses this example to show how
creatures can be similar to God and yet, as we have seen, between
celestial and terrestial bodies there can be similarity *secundum genus logicum*. Taking this into account, St Thomas writes: "Si igitur sit aliquod
agens, quod non in genere contineatur, effectus eius adhuc magis acce-
dent remote ad similitudinem formae agentis: non tamen ita quod partici-
pent similitudinem formae agentis secundum eandem rationem speciei
aut generis, sed secundum aliqualem analogiam, sicut ipsum esse est
commune omnibus."[151] While allowing that a logical genus can contain
angels and material things, St Thomas will always deny that God can
be included in a genus – at least a *genus univocum*.[152]

It will be appreciated that a full commentary on the member "secundum intentionem et secundum esse" at this point would not be in
keeping with the order of our discussion. Subsequent chapters will return
to the points just mentioned, particularly those concerned with analogical cause and with the divine names.

5. SUMMARY

Noting that both "healthy" and "true" are admitted to be analogous
names, the objector moves from the fact that things named healthy are
such that the form *sanitas* from which the name is imposed to signify
exists in only one of them, to the conclusion that the same must be true
of the things called true. St Thomas has set out to show that you cannot
argue from identity of mode of signifying to identity in the remote
foundation of this mode, since things named analogically may found
this mode of signifying in utterly different ways. The names common
to God and creature, like "being" said of what falls into the various
genera, happen to be such that the perfection from which the name is
imposed to signify is in each of the things, but according to a scale of
greater and lesser perfection, a *magis et minus* which will be revealed in
the various *rationes* of the common name. Thus there will be a participation *per prius et posterius* or, in the case of the divine names, God will
have the perfection *essentialiter*, be one in substance with truth, for ex-

---

[150] *In II Metaphys.*, lect. 2, n. 293.
[151] *Ia*, q. 4, a. 3; cf. *Q.D. de pot.*, q. 7, a. 7, ad 3.
[152] *In Boethii de trin.*, q. 6, a. 3.

ample, and creatures will be true *per participationem*. That is, "illud invenitur secundum propriam rationem in uno eorum tantum." Thus it is clear that this is not a division of that mode of signifying which is the analogy of names, but the pointing out of a difference among kinds of things which can be the remote foundation of this mode of signifying. "To be named analogically" is always an extrinsic denomination of things, not something which belongs to them as they exist *in rerum natura*. This is something which attaches to things as known, and on this level, the reason is always the same: many things receive a common name insofar as they are denominated from what the name principally signifies. The remote foundation for this can be of various kinds. However, it is not the case that there is no foundation in the secondary analogates of "healthy" thanks to which they receive the common name; it is not in this that they differ from the things which are named "being" and "true" secondarily, but in the kind of foundation. But the mode of signifying which is founded in any instance of an analogous name will be explained by the logical doctrine insofar as we are talking of things named analogically. It is just here that the similarity between things named healthy and God and creature as receptive of a common name lies, not in the remote foundations, the things as such. If the analogy of names were to be distinguished on the basis of real differences among the things so named, where would we draw the line? There would be as many kinds of analogous name as there are instances of it, and those who have tended to go in this direction are not doing anything essentially different from what Cajetan did. For it is not the same foundation *in re* which underlies "good" and "true," at least in the case of creatures.

We know that Cajetan equates this third division with what he calls proper proportionality. Later, when we have seen that "proper proportionality" is not a mode of analogous name, the significance of this third member and of the division in which it occurs will be seen to be what we now take it to be: a warning that though things may be alike in this that one group is named analogically just as is another group, the first group is not thereby like the second apart from the way a name is common to it. We cannot argue from what they have in common, a mode of being named, to what is in no way decided by the way in which they have a common name. "Dicendum quod non oportet secundum diversas rationes vel intentiones logicas, quae consequuntur modum intelligendi, diversitatem (or similarity) in rebus naturalibus accipere..."[153]

[153] *Ia*, q. 76, a. 3, ad 4.

CHAPTER VII

THE ANALOGICAL CAUSE

We often read, in the writings of St Thomas, of univocal as well as of non-univocal causes. Such an application of properties of signification to causes must be correctly understood, for predication implies universality and causes can be said to be universal in two widely different senses.[1] For example, when assigning the efficient cause of a pair of shoes, we might say the shoemaker made them or that an artisan did. By proceeding in the direction of greater predicable universality (for candlestick makers are also artisans), we can be said to assign prior or more universal causes of the effect. It is the same man who is designated shoemaker and artisan in the example of the shoes, and to say that "artisan" is a prior or more universal cause means only that the cause is being denominated in a more universal, common and vague way. Causes, however, are sometimes said to be universal in quite another sense, this time with respect to a community of causality and not a community of predicability. In this second sense, unlike the first, the more universal cause is numerically different from the less universal cause. For example, the farmer is the less universal, the sun the more universal, cause of the crop.[2]

What is meant by a univocal or non-univocal cause? Such designations imply predication, and yet it is not likely that what is meant is that the cause is predicated univocally or non-univocally of its effect. Causes are never predicated of their effects.[3] Rather such qualifications of causes indicate the way in which the cause and its effect can be denominated. The univocal cause is that which has in common with its effect a name signifying exactly the same *ratio* or definition. In non-univocal causes, this is not the case.[4] Of course, it is not because an

---

[1] *In II Physic.*, lect. 6, n. 3: "Advertendum est autem quod causa universalis et propria, vel prior et posterior, potest accipi aut secundum *communitatem praedicationis*, secundum exempla hic posita de medico et artifice; vel secundum *communitatem causalitatis*, ut si dicamus solem esse causam universalem calefactionis, ignem vero causam propriam: et haec duo sibi invicem correspondent."

[2] Cf. *In V Metaphys.*, lect. 3, n. 785.

[3] *In X Metaphys.*, lect. 3, n. 1964.

[4] *In VIII Physic.*, lect. 10, n. 4: "Et similiter est in omnibus aliis, in quibus movens est *univocum*, idest conveniens in nomine et ratione cum moto; sicut cum calidum facit calidum, et homo generat hominem. Et hic ideo dicit, quia sunt quaedam agentia non univoca, quae

agent is temporally prior to its effect that univocity is impeded. Thus, to speak of a cause as univocal or non-univocal is to say something of it in terms of signification, in terms of predicable universality, but there is no question of the cause being predicated of its effect, nor is the cause being looked at as in the first way of speaking of prior or universal cause mentioned above. We are not concerned with how the cause alone can be denominated, but how the cause and effect can receive a common name. And, as having a name in common, cause and effect will be named either univocally or non-univocally, something to be determined by appeal to the *ratio* signified by the name. Univocal names do not as such imply a cause/effect relationship between what is named, but cause and effect can have a name which is common to them either univocally or non-univocally.

1. *DIVERSUS MODUS EXISTENDI IMPEDIT UNIVOCATIONEM*

Presupposed by the discussion of this chapter is the view that the agent and its effect are in some way similar, a view expressed in the dictum: *omne agens agit sibi simile.* To speak of univocal and non-univocal causes therefore, is to say something about the kind of similitude that exists between effect and cause. A perfect similarity enables us to name them univocally;[5] when perfect similarity is absent, a univocal name is impossible. It is in this connection that St Thomas will say that a diverse mode of existing on the part of that in which cause and effect are similar impedes univocation.[6] In order to arrive at an understanding of that phrase, which has sometimes been interpreted as meaning that *esse* or existence is the source of analogy (rendering analogy fundamentally metaphysical, it is thought), we shall first examine statements on the gradation of similarity between effect and cause, a gradation at issue in designating causes as univocal or non-univocal.

Although different statements of this hierarchy can be found, we

---

scilicet non conveniunt in nomine et ratione cum suis effectibus, sicut sol generat hominem. In quibus tamen agentibus, etsi non sit species effectus secundum eandem rationem, est tamen quodammodo altiori et universaliori." Cf. *In II Physic.*, lect. 11, n. 2.

  [5] *In II Metaphys.*, lect. 2, n. 293: "Facit autem mentionem de univocatione, quia quandoque contingit quod effectus non pervenit ad similitudinem causae secundum eamdem rationem speciei, propter excellentiam ipsius causae. Sicut sol est causa caloris in istis inferioribus: non tamen inferiora corpora possunt recipere impressionem solis aut aliorum caelestium corporum secundum eamdem rationem speciei, cum non communicant in materia. Et propter hoc non dicimus solem esse calidissimum sicut ignem, sed dicimus solem esse aliquid amplius quam calidissimum."

  [6] *Q.D. de pot.*, q. 7, a. 7.

shall take as basic a text referred to in a previous chapter.[7] The context
of the passage to be considered is this: why is it that some things can
be products both of art and nature while others are products of art
alone? For example, health can be brought about either by natural
causes or by the art of medicine, whereas houses are produced by art
alone.[8] In either case, the argument runs, there must be similitude of
cause to effect. Only per se causality implies this similitude, of course;
the agent to which an accidental effect is attributed is not such that its
effect is similar to it. But that which generates or causes per se is cause
of its effect as such and there must be some kind of similitude of agent
with effect.

Sed hoc contingit tripliciter: (a) *Uno modo* quando forma generati praecedit in generante secundum eumdem modum essendi et simili materia. Sicut cum ignis generat
ignem, vel homo generat hominem. Et haec est generatio *totaliter univoca*. (b) *Alio
modo*, quando forma generati praecedit in generante, non quidem secundum eumdem
modum essendi, nec in substantia eiusdem rationis; sicut forma domus praecedit in
artifice, non secundum esse materiale, sed secundum esse immateriale, quod habet
in mente artificis, non in lapidibus et lignis. Et haec generatio est *partim ex univoco*,
quantum ad formam, *partim ex aequivoco* quantum ad esse formae in subiecto. (c)
Tertio modo quando ipsa tota forma generati non praecedit in generante, sed aliqua
pars eius, aut aliqua pars partis; sicut in medicina calida praecedit calor qui est
pars sanitatis, aut aliquid ducens ad partem sanitatis. Et haec generatio *nullo modo
est univoca*.[9]

As we have seen in the previous chapter, (a) and (b) here differ as do
the *ratio concreta* and the *ratio abstracta*. If we do not take into account
the fact that the form is realized in different matter, or in one case in
matter and in the other not in matter, we can achieve a remote, abstract or logical univocity. A determinate statement of the mode of
realization, the mode of existing, results in equivocity. Thus the sun
and the terrestial bodies it warms will not be called hot univocally, i.e.
"secundum eamdem rationem speciei, cum non communicent in materia."[10] In both cases, however, the form has *esse naturale*.[11] And just as
a logical genus common to material things and angels can be formed
if we ignore that the *ratio substantiae* is founded with matter in the former
and without matter in the latter,[12] so the artisan who conjures up in
his mind what he will effect in matter can be called a univocal agent

---

[7] *In VII Metaphys.*, lect. 8, nn. 1443–6; cf. *Q.D. de ver.*, q. 27, a. 7; *I Sent.*, d. 8, q. 1, a. 2.
[8] Another example: although men have a natural ability to move themselves about, they
need an art to be able to dance. Cf. *In VII Metaphys.*, lect. 8, n. 1439.
[9] *Ibid.*, nn. 1444–6.
[10] *In II Metaphys.*, lect. 2, n. 293.
[11] *Q.D. de ver.*, q. 27, a. 7; cf. *In II de anima*, lect. 5, nn. 282–6.
[12] *In Boethii de trin.*, q. 4, a. 2; *ibid.*, q. 6, a. 3.

insofar as the form in his mind and the form he effects are the same.[13] When we consider their different modes of existence, however, we can deny univocity; the form of the house in the carpenter's mind and as realized in bricks and lumber are not house in the same sense.[14] Such an agent, however, is not wholly equivocal. Let us look more closely at the second member of this division.

St Thomas has exemplified the agent which is partly univocal and partly equivocal by the house in the mind of the artisan and the completed house. He uses this example in another text when he makes the remark which heads this section.

> Item patet quod, etsi una sit ratio formae existentis in agente et in effectu, diversus tamen modus existendi impedit univocam praedicationem; licet enim eadem sit ratio domus quae sit in materia et domus quae est in mente artificis – quia unum est ratio alterius – non tamen domus univoce de utraque praedicatur, propter hoc quod species domus in materia habet esse materiale, in mente vero artificis immateriale.[15]

It will be noticed that *ratio* is used in two ways in this text: as what the term means and, in the parenthetical remark that the artisan's idea is the *ratio* of the house, as cause. What is meant here by *diversus modus existendi*: is *esse* or existence being assigned the role of that which bases or causes analogy? In the first place, we must realize that the reference is not simply to the numerical diversity of acts of existence since this, far from impeding univocation, is a requisite for it. Unless Peter and Paul are diverse in existence, they would not be several things for what-it-is-to-be-a-man to be common to. "Hujus ratio est quia cum in re duo sit considerari: scilicet naturam vel quidditatem rei, et esse suum, oportet quod in omnibus univocis sit communitas secundum rationem naturae, et non secundum esse, quia unum esse non est nisi in una re..."[16] Since numerical diversity of existents (and consequently of acts of existence)[17] does not destroy univocation, the meaning of the phrase in question must be sought elsewhere. That is, the meaning must be sought, not in existence, but in what diversifies existence. For the form to be is, in the one case, for it to be in the mind, in the other to be in matter, and this is a difference which is expressed in the concrete notion of each.

---

[13] *In VII Metaphys.*, lect. 8, n. 1447: "Potest enim dici quod generatio fit vel ex forma, sive parte formae, vel ex habente formam, vel partem formae. Sed ex habente quidem sicut ex generante; ex forma sive parte formae, sicut ex quo generans generat. Nam forma non generat nec agit, sed habens formam per eam."

[14] Cf. *Q.D. de ver.*, q. 27, a. 7, "tertio modo." Man, in reproducing himself, is not acting as artisan, but as *agens naturale*. Cf. *Ia*, q. 15, a. 1; *Q.D. de pot.*, q. 7, a. 1, ad 8. For a discussion of father and semen as causes of the child, cf. *In VII Metaphys.*, lect. 8, nn. 1451–3.

[15] *Q.D. de pot.*, q. 7, a. 7.

[16] *I Sent.*, d. 35, q. 1, a. 4; cf. *ibid.*, d. 8, q. 4, a. 2; *Q.D. de ver.*, q. 2, a. 11.

[17] Cf. *Q.D. de pot.*, q. 7, a. 2, ad 5.

Existence of itself causes no difference, since this is what all things have in common. There is, then, no basis for an "existential" interpretation of the phrase, "diversus modus existendi impedit univocam preadica-tionem," as if existence were the cause of non-univocal signification. Diversity must be sought in something other than existence.[18]

It may be well to point out here that the diverse mode of existence of the form in the mind and in matter which impedes univocity is not the diversity of the concept and that of which it is the concept. If this is what were meant, we might think that the very notion of univocity is called into question by the example. That is, we might ask how "man" can univocally signify the concept of man and such individuals as Peter and Paul. But of course the concept is that through which Peter and Paul are named man univocally. The form in the mind that St Thomas is speaking of is not the concept, but the *idea*.[19]

We have spoken thus far only of equivocal causes which are in some way univocal. What then of causes which are in no wise univocal? God is called an analogous cause of creatures.[20] "...non dicitur esse similitudo creaturae ad Deum propter communicantiam in forma secundum ean-dem rationem generis et speciei: sed secundum analogiam tantum; prout scilicet Deus est ens per essentiam, et alia per participationem."[21] St Thomas points out that even if, *per impossibile*, a form had the same *ratio* in God and creature, the name signifying the form would not be univocally common to them because of diverse modes of existence.[22] But of course the form cannot be of the same *ratio*, for then there would be some univocity between God and creature.

2. PREDICATION AND CAUSALITY

The designation of causes as univocal or non-univocal seems to involve little more than the application to cause and effect of what we have already seen of univocation and analogy. Nevertheless, because it is to causes that types of predication are here applied, we must notice the difference between reduction of causes and reduction of predicates.

---

[18] *Q.D. de pot.*, q. 7, a. 7: "Et praeterea ens non dicitur univoce de substantia et accidente, propter hoc quod substantia est tamquam per se habens esse, accidens vero tamquam cuius esse est inesse. Ex quo patet quod diversa habitudo ad esse impedit univocam praedicationem entis." The difference between *esse substantiale* and *esse accidentale* is founded, not in *esse*, but in essence. It is difficult to see what it would mean "to put the accent on *esse*" in this matter.

[19] *Q.D. de ver.*, q. 3, a. 1.

[20] *I Sent.*, d. 8, q. 1, a. 2.

[21] *Ia*, q. 4, a. 3, ad 3.

[22] *Q.D. de pot.*, q. 7, a. 7. On the problem of the creature's similarity to God and to God's ideas, cf. *ibid.*, q. 7, a. 1, ad 8.

Dicendum quod licet *in praedicationibus* oporteat aequivoca ad univoca reduci, tamen *in actionibus* agens non univocum ex necessitate praecedit agens univocum. Agens enim non univocum est causa universalis totius speciei, ut sol est causa generationis omnium hominum. Agens vero univocum non est causa agens universalis totius speciei, alioquin esset causa sui ipsius, cum sub specie contineatur, sed est causa particularis huius individui, quod in participatione speciei constituit. Causa autem universalis totius speciei non est agens univocum. Causa autem universalis est prior particulari. – Hoc autem agens universale, licet non sit univocum, non tamen est omnino aequivocum, quia sic non faceret sibi simile; sed potest dici agens analogicum; sicut in praedicationibus omnia univoca reducuntur ad unum primum, non univocum, sed analogicum, quod est ens.[23]

When the analogical cause is called universal, its community is not one of predication. The sun is not predicated of all generable things, although its causality extends to them all. It is on the basis of the difference between these two kinds of community that St Thomas argues for a different reduction of causes and predicates. Causes are such that univocal agents are reducible to a first equivocal or analogical cause; things said equivocally, on the other hand, are reduced to the univocal. Or are they? In the passage quoted, St Thomas seems to contradict himself: at the outset, he says the equivocal is reduced to the univocal predicate; at the end, he says that the univocal predicate is reduced to an analogical one. There are two ways of explaining this shift.

First, we can understand the reduction to univocity to apply to analogous names. The analogous name is first of all univocal, having like any name its *ratio propria*. So long as its proper notion is all it has, it can only be used metaphorically of things which do not save the proper notion.[24] It is only when its signification is extended, when it receives a *ratio communis*, that it becomes analogous. For example, "healthy" first of all signifies what has a proper proportion among its humors, and only animals save this notion; anything else is called healthy metaphorically. However, when usage sanctions the extension of the meaning of the term, urine, food and medicine can be called healthy properly, if less so than animal. The extension of meaning whereby a univocal term becomes analogous does not eradicate its *ratio propria*, however; as we have seen, its extended meanings involve a reference to what saves the *ratio propria*. In any absolute reduction of names, St Thomas suggests, we are going to get back to "being" which is analogically common. Moreover, insofar as the first cause is named being, we are faced with a name common to God and creature which is incorrigibly analogous. Though creatures are named analogically, it is always possi-

---

[23] *Ia*, q. 13, a. 5, ad 1. Cf. *In Boethii de trin.*, (ed. Calcaterra), proemium, q. 1, a. 4, ad 4.
[24] See Chapter VIII, section 4.

ble to have a name which is univocally common to them, if only in terms of a logical genus. Between God and creature, however, no univocal name is possible and, since God must always be named from creatures, any name applied to him will be, if proper, analogous – even the name "God."[25]

A second way of resolving the seeming contradiction is suggested by the fact that the objection is stated in terms of pure equivocation.[26] A name which, when applied to different things signifies unrelated *rationes*, can be reduced to univocation by restricting it to one *ratio*. Thus, while a star and barking animals are called dog equivocally, barking animals are so named univocally.

In another text as well, St Thomas contrasts what is most common in predication and what is most common in causality. After setting down the difference between these two kinds of community, he writes:

Omnium autem entium sunt principia communia non solum secundum primum modum, quod appellat Philosophus in XI Metaphysicorum, omnia habere eadem principia secundum analogiam, sed etiam secundum modum secundum, ut sint quaedam res eaedem numero existentes omnium rerum principia, prout scilicet principia accidentium reducuntur in principia substantiae, et principia substantiarum corruptibilium reducuntur in substantias incorruptibiles, et sic quodam gradu et ordine in quaedam principia omnia entia reducuntur.[27]

The analogical cause is not the reification of a more common predicate; rather this cause is *unum numero* and is designated universal from the multitude and diversity of its effects. And, having a name in common with its effects, a name which is in no wise univocal, the cause is designated analogical. But what is first in the order of causality need not be first in the order of the signification of the name. To use the familiar example, although from the point of view of the community of the name, animal is first denominated healthy, from the point of view of causality, medicine is prior. When medicine is said to be an analogical cause, the order of the signification is not thereby changed: we have seen that medicine may be able to cause health because it is has part, or a part of a part, of what health consists in.[28]

---

[25] *Ia*, q. 13, a. 10.

[26] *Ia*, q. 13, a. 5, obj. 1: "Omne enim aequivocum reducitur ad univocum, sicut multa ad unum. Nam si hoc nomen canis aequivoce dicitur de latrabile et marino, oportet quod de aliquibus univoce dicatur, scilicet de omnibus latrabilibus; aliter enim esset procedere in infinitum. Inveniuntur autem quaedam agentia univoca, quae conveniunt cum suis effectibus in nomine et definitione, ut homo generat hominem; quaedam vero agentia aequivoca, sicut sol causat calidum, cum tamen ipse non sit calidus nisi aequivoce. Videtur igitur quod primum agens, ad quod omnia agentia reducuntur sit agens univocum. Et ita quae de Deo et creaturis dicuntur, univoce praedicantur."

[27] *In Boethii de trin.*, q. 5, a. 4.

[28] *In VII Metaphys.*, lect. 8, n. 1446.

At this point, it may occur to one that the examples St Thomas gives when he is speaking of the analogy of names usually involve a cause/effect relationship and it may appear that it is impossible to speak of the former without appeal to the latter.[29] In such texts, St Thomas speaks of the primary analogate, the *per prius* of the name, in terms of the various kinds of cause. That the analogy of names is not inextricably linked with causality is a point which bears repetition.

A diligent perusal of the texts in question indicates two things. First, that the doctrine of the analogy of names does not require any explicit mention of a cause/effect relation between what is named analogically; second, the foundation in things for analogical signification is often, but not necessarily, such a relation. The proximate foundation of a logical intention is things as known and when the things named analogically are related as cause and effect, the order of the signification of the name need not reflect the real order of prior and posterior.[30] Moreover, when things are said to be proportioned to a cause, this is not necessarily *their* cause. This is obvious in the example usually given of an efficient cause as the *per prius* of an analogous name.[31] The things which are said to receive a common name with reference to a cause are not necessarily its effects.

What is relevant to the analogy of names is that there be an order among the things as known. Whatever be the foundation in reality for their similarity – and it need not be cause/effect – it is unimportant for the statement of what it means for things to be named analogically. Indeed, we would be hard pressed in the case of many analogous names – e.g. "virtue"[32] – to find a relation of cause and effect between the things named analogically. One reason for believing that things named analogically must be such that one is cause, the other effect, is that St Thomas' most explicit statements on analogy are found in treatments of the divine names. And yet, St Thomas will insist that God is not named good, wise, etc. only *causaliter*[33] – as we shall see in Chapter IX.

3. *PRIMUM IN ALIQUO GENERE*

In speaking of God as cause, St Thomas calls him an analogical cause. Moreover, he is in every way an analogical cause so that in no way

---

[29] Cf. *De principiis naturae*, cap. 6; *In IV Metaphys.*, lect. 1, nn. 537–9.
[30] *I Contra Gentiles*, cap. 34; *Q.D. de ver.*, q. 1, a. 2.
[31] *In IV Metaphys.*, lect. 1, n. 538.
[32] Cf. *Q.D. de virt. in com.*, a. 7.
[33] *Ia* q. 13, a. 2.

can a name signify God and creature univocally. Not even a logical genus can comprise God and creature. Despite the unequivocal nature of such statements, St Thomas sometimes speaks as if God were in the same genus as the creature. The most striking instance of this is found in the *quarta via*, a proof of God's existence drawn from the hierarchy in reality. Things are more and less good, true, noble; but "more and less" implies an approximation to the "most," as the warmer approaches the warmest. Thus there must be something which is truest, best and most noble and, consequently, *maxime ens*.

> Quod autem dicitur maxime tale in aliquo genere, est causa omnium quae sunt illius generis; sicut ignis, qui est maxime calidus, est causa omnium calidorum (...) Ergo est aliquod quod omnibus entibus est causa esse, et bonitatis et cuiuslibet perfectionis: et hoc dicimus Deum.[34]

God is here spoken of as the maximum in the genus of being, something which seemingly involves two things elsewhere emphatically rejected by St Thomas: that God is in a genus and that being is a genus. That which is the maximum in any genus is the measure of everything else in that genus. This recalls the discussion from the *Metaphysics* where white is said to be first in the genus of color.[35] White is the chief color and its opposite, black, is its privation, that which is at the furthest remove from it. All other colors are spoken of as approaching more or less to white as to their measure.[36] Of the many things that could be said of this, let us single out the following: the genus in question is a physical genus.[37] The same thing must be said of the example of fire in the genus of warm things: the univocity involved is based on a physical genus.[38] But of the genus of warm things we can assign a maximum which is outside it, namely the sun which is accordingly said to be something more than the hottest thing.[39] The sun and terrestial hot things, though not in the same genus because of the supposed difference in their matter, are in the same genus *logice loquendo*. How can St Thomas apply such considerations to God's causality? Since the sun is considered to be a maximum outside the physical genus and cause of heat in the

---

[34] *Ia*, q. 2, a. 3.
[35] *In X Metaphys.*, lect. 5, n. 2023, 2027–9. St Thomas explicitly recalls this discussion. Cf. *I Sent.*, d. 8, q. 4, a. 2, ad 3: "Exinde transumptum est nomen mensurae ad omnia genera, ut illud quod est primum in quolibet genere et simplicissimum et perfectissimum dicatur mensura omnium quae sunt in genere illo eo quod unumquodque cognoscitur habere de veritate generis plus et minus, secundum quod magis accedit ad ipsum vel recedit, ut album in genere colorum." Cf. *I Sent.*, d. 24, q. 1, a. 1.
[36] *In X Metaphys.*, lect. 5, n. 2025.
[37] *Ibid.*, n. 2024.
[38] *In II Metaphys.*, lect. 2, n. 292.
[39] *Ibid.*, n. 293.

genus, the example provides St Thomas with a stepping stone to the view that God is a maximum outside the genera of his effects, whether genus be understood *logice* or *physice*: if God is first in the genus of being, "genus" must be understood *largo modo*.

Ita etiam in genere substantiae, illud quod habet esse perfectissimum et simplicissimum dicitur mensura omnium substantiarum, sicut Deus. Unde non oportet quod sit in genere substantiae sicut contentum, sed solum sicut principium, habens in se omnem perfectionem generis sicut unitas in numeris, sed tamen diversimode quia unitate non mensurantur nisi numeri, sed Deus est mensura non tantum substantialium perfectionum, sed omnium quae sunt in omnibus generibus, sicut sapientiae, virtutis et hujusmodi. Et ideo quamvis unitas contineatur in uno genere determinato sicut principium, non tamen Deus.[40]

God is not in a genus as the principle of one determinate genus. He can, however, be said to be in a genus *largo modo*.[41] What is this genus in a wide sense? It is precisely the *commune analogicum* which is opposed to the *genus univocum*.[42] Thus, God and creature are not in any genus which could give rise to univocity, any more than being can be a *genus univocum*. Nevertheless, St Thomas will sometimes say that being is a genus.[43] "Genus" must then be taken in an extended sense, i.e. analogously, and so long as we do not think "being" fulfills the *ratio propria* of "genus," we are not likely to attribute to St Thomas contradictory views. So too when God is said to be *maximum in genere entis*: this in no way suggests that God is a univocal cause of creatures.

---

[40] *I Sent.*, d. 8, q. 4, a. 2, ad 3; cf. *Q.D. de pot.*, q. 7, a. 7, ad 4.

[41] "Vel dicendum quod veritas prima est quodammodo de genere animae largo modo accipiendo genus, secundum quod omnia intelligibilia vel incorporalia unius generis esse dicuntur." – *Q.D. de ver.*, q. 1, a. 4, ad 8 in contr.

[42] *Q.D. de malo*, q. 7, a. 1, ad 1.

[43] *Q.D. de malo*, q. 1, a. 1, ad 11: "...prout genus dici potest id quod genera transcendit, sicut ens et unum." *De ente et essentia*, cap. 7: "...substantia, quae est principium in genere entis..." *In IV Metaphys.*, lect. 4, n. 583: "...inducunt in unum et ens tamquam in genera; sed ratione suae communitatis quamdam similitudinem generum habent." *In IV Metaphys.*, lect. 2, n. 563: "...omnes partes habent pro genere unum et ens." *In X Metaphys.*, lect. 8, n. 2092: "Sed est quasi genus, quia habet aliquid de ratione generis, inquantum est communis."

CHAPTER VIII

KNOWLEDGE AND ANALOGY

Since we name as we know, there is always a priority of knowledge with respect to that mode of signification called the analogy of names. Moreover, in the realm of knowledge, there is a use of the term "analogy" which must be distinguished from its use as signifying a type of name. Thus, we speak of reasoning from analogy, coming to know something by an analogy with something else. Such knowledge sometimes occasions an analogous name, at others does not; consequently it must be distinguished from the analogy of names. In drawing this distinction, we shall be calling into question Cajetan's interpretation of the role that proportionality plays in the analogy of names. As a sign of the difficulties inherent in his interpretation, we can recall his subdividing of proportionality, which for him is analogy *par excellence*, into proper and improper. The former is an analogous name, the latter, curiously enough, is not, although he seems to feel that it has as much claim to the title as what he calls attribution. This suggests that the proportionality is not itself constitutive of the analogous name. Given the difficulty involved in ascertaining the status of metaphor in Cajetan's interpretation, we believe that one of the merits of this chapter is that it provides a clear-cut distinction between metaphor and analogous names. Moreover, knowledge from analogy will be seen as that which can occasion either a metaphor or an analogous name.

1. JUSTICE AND ANALOGY

In the fifth book of the *Nicomachean Ethics*, Aristotle argues that the just mean is determined by a proportionality. In the course of his argument, he has some things to say about proportionality itself before he applies it to the problem before him. We want to look at St Thomas' comments on this with a view to obtaining some general information on what it means to come to know something by a proportionality or by analogy.

Aristotle first establishes that the mean of distributive justice is discovered in a proportionality. This entails holding that the mean is an equality. The unjust is the unequal, consisting in either too much or too little, but where there can be too much or too little, there can also be equal amounts. "Aequale enim est medium inter plus et minus."[1] Equality implies a mean, therefore, and the just is the equal and it is a mean. Further, this mean is had according to a proportionality. "Cum ergo iustum sit et medium et aequale, oportet quidem quod inquantum est iustum, sit ad aliquid, idest per respectum ad alterum (...), inquantum autem est aequale, sit in quibusdam rebus, secundum quas scilicet attenditur aequalitas inter duas personas."[2] The just can be considered from three points of view: as a mean it is between two things; namely the more and the less; as equal it implies two things; as just it implies a relation to another. The just, consequently, involves four terms: "duo enim sunt homines, quibus observatur iustitia: duae sunt res in quibus eis iustitia fit."[3] At least two persons, at least two portions or things, and the just will consist in establishing the same proportion or equality in the things as there is between the two persons. Person: person :: thing : thing. Thus the mean which is equal is established in a proportionality.

It is at this point that Aristotle says some things about the nature of proportionality as such. What is proportionality?

...proportionalitas nihil aliud est quam aequalitas proportionis; cum scilicet aequalem proportionem habet hoc ad hoc, et illud ad illud. Proportio autem nihil est aliud quam habitudo unius quantitatis ad aliam. Quantitas autem habet rationem mensurae: quae primo quidem invenitur in unitate numerali, et exinde derivatur ad omne genus quantitatis, ut patet decimo Metaphysicorum.[4]

Since a proportionality consists in an equality of proportions, it involves four terms. "Four" need not be taken too rigidly, however, for a proportionality can involve only three different members: e.g. 12:6 :: 6:3. Such a proportionality is called continuous as opposed to the disjunctive proportionality exemplified by 8:4 :: 6:3.[5] Both are species of geometrical proportionality: whatever numbers figure as terms in the proportionality, the equality sought is "double," "triple," etc., and not a fixed numerical distance, such as "greater by two." When the latter is the case, we have what is called an arithmetical proportionality: e.g. 9:7 :: 5:3.[6] Aristotle employs arithmetical proportionality in speaking of commutative justice. Two properties of proportionalities are pointed out:

[1] *In V Ethic.*, lect. 4, n. 933.
[2] *Ibid.*, n. 934.
[3] *Ibid.*
[4] *Ibid.*, lect. 5, n. 939.
[5] *Ibid.*, n. 940.
[6] *Ibid.*, lect. 6, n. 950.

first, that they are commutative. Thus $8:4 :: 6:3 = 8:6 :: 4:3$.[7] Secondly, "in his quae sic sunt proportionalia, quod quae est proportio unius ad alterum, eadem est proportio totius ad totum."[8] Thus, $8:4 :: 6:3 = 8 + 6 : 4 + 3$.

In applying all this to distributive justice, we notice that the proportionality will be geometrical and disjunctive. It cannot be continuous because distributive justice involves two persons and two portions.[9] And, since common goods are not distributed with quantitative equality, but according to merit, the proportionality will not be arithmetical but geometrical. Thus, if Plato works two hours and receives two dollars, Socrates who has worked one hour should receive one dollar, *ceteris paribus*. This indicates that proportionality is a device whereby we come to knowledge of something. Say we wonder how much Socrates is owed. The proportionality provides knowledge of this unknown. Two hours labor : one hour of labor :: two dollars : X = two hours, two dollars :: one hour : one dollar. In commutative justice, where equal quantity is the mean, Aristotle uses the example of lines. Thus if Socrates has 1 and Plato 3, we add the quantities and divide by two to get our measure. Then Plato is seen to have in excess of the mean the same quantity whereby Socrates is short of it. When this amount is taken from Plato and given to Socrates, justice is done.

Obviously the nature of our interest dictates that we run the risk of distorting the context from which we are drawing what is relevant to our discussion. We must, however, raise one question which will do something towards drawing attention to the context. In presenting the above doctrine, we might have given the impression that the search for what is just is a thoroughly objective calculus, as impersonal and as independent of the character of the calculator as mathematics itself. Yet we know that the judgments of the virtuous man, prudential judgments, are certain in a different way than are scientific judgments. "Sed virtus est certior omni arte, et etiam melior, sicut et natura."[10] The prudential judgment is connatural and its truth consists not in conformity with reality, but in conformity with rectified appetite.[11] The nature of moral decisions makes the apparent mathematizing of the just mean difficult to understand, and yet even in other areas we may wonder what permits the invocation of the mathematics of proportionality.

---

[7] *Ibid.*, lect. 5, n. 941.
[8] *Ibid.*, n. 942.
[9] *Ibid.*, n. 945.
[10] *In II Ethic.*, lect. 6, n. 315.
[11] *In VI Ethic.*, lect. 4, nn. 1172–3.

2. PROPORTION AND QUANTITY

We have seen that one of the properties of proportionality is that it is commutative or alternating (A:B :: C:D = A:C :: B:D) and we have seen St Thomas make use of this property in discussing distributive justice. Sometimes, however, he will disagree with an argument based on alternating proportionals, not because of its basis, but because it is wrongly understood. In discussing whether two bodies can be in the same place, he is faced with an objection that just as one body is to one place, so are two bodies to two places. But one body can't be in two places, so two bodies can't be in one place.

> Ad primum ergo dicendum, quod proportione commutata sic est utendum: sicut se habet primum ad secundum, ut duo ad tria, ita se habet tertium ad quartum; ergo commutatim, sicut se habet primum ad tertium, ita et secundum ad quartum, idest tria ad sex. Et secundum hoc ratio sic deberet procedere. Sicut se habet unum corpus ad unum locum, ita duo corpora ad duo loca; ergo sicut unum ad duo corpora, ita unus locus ad duo loca; et sic non sequitur quod si unum corpus non possit esse in duobus locis, duo corpora non possint esse in uno loco.[12]

Here it is the failure to argue correctly from alternating proportionals and not the appeal to mathematical properties which is criticized. At other times, however, St Thomas will reject its applicability to the matter under discussion.[13] "...cum gratia sit perfectio naturae, non sic se habet gratia ad naturam sicut e converso. Commutata autem proportio non in omnibus tenet, sed in mensuris continuis vel discretis."[14] Now something of the same sort was suggested in the commentary on the *Ethics*. In discussing the mean of moral virtue in terms of the more, the less and the equal, St Thomas observes, "Ad cuius evidentiam oportet praeaccipere quod tria quaedam, idest plus et minus et aequale, tam in contingentibus continuis, quam etiam in quolibet alio divisibili, contingit accipere, sive per accidens, puta per intensionem et remissionem qualitatis in subiecto."[15] So too in discussing proportionality with respect to justice, St Thomas writes, "Et ideo numerus primo quidem invenitur in numero unitatum: et exinde derivatur ad omne aliud quantitatis genus quod secundum rationem numeri mensuratur."[16] Wherever number can be found, proportionality can be found. By asking now what is meant by the *genera quantitatis*, we will see how the notion of proportionality can be saved wherever there is quantity. Then we will

---

[12] *Quodl. I*, q. 10, q. 2, ad 1.
[13] *Q.D. de ver.*, q. 27, a. 7, obj. 4 et ad 4; q. 29, a. 8, ad 7.
[14] *Q.D. de ver.*, q. 29, a. 8, ad 7.
[15] *In II Ethic.*, lect. 6, n. 310.
[16] *In V Ethic.*, lect. 5, n. 939.

want to reexamine what was said earlier about the extension of the notions of proportion and proportionality beyond quantity however taken.

The quantified is divisible by those things which are in it, parts which, unlike essential parts, are of the same nature as the whole.[17] A multitude is divisible into non-continuous parts, magnitude into parts which are *continua*.[18] The quantity of a thing is revealed by a measure; that of multitude by one, that of magnitude by a minimum magnitude. What can be meant by a minimum magnitude? Surely there is no shortest possible line in the mathematical sense. St Thomas has spoken of the priority of the one as measure: first of all, it is the measure of discrete quantity, of number, and then it is extended to the other genera of quantity. This is what happens in the case of proportionality in continuous quantity. Lines, for example, have to be numbered. E.g. two inches: one inch :: six inches : three inches. In this order we take the inch as indivisible, as measure, in the way in which one, the principle of number, is indivisible. But in continuous quantity, the measure is established only by convention, since the line we call an inch is infinitely divisible.[19] Two inches, three inches, etc., are not so much numbers as what is numbered,[20] and the one is not one but something one. "Nam unum in aliis speciebus quantitatis non est ipsum unum, sed aliquid cui accidit unum; sicut dicimus unam manum, aut unam magnitudinem."[21] In this way, there is a measure in weights and motions as well as magnitudes.[22] Some things are modes of quantity only accidentally, insofar as they are accidents of *quanta*. For example, color is quantified only accidentally, thanks to surface.[23] This white is greater than that insofar as the first is the color of a surface four feet square, the other of a surface two feet square.

What has this to do with proportionality? "Quia vero proportio est quaedam habitudo quantitatum adinvicem; ubicumque dicitur quantum aliquo modo, ibi potest dici proportio. Et primo quidem in numeris; quia omnes in prima mensura, quae est unitas, sunt ad invicem commensurabiles."[24] And where there can be proportion, there can be

---

[17] *In V Metaphys.*, lect. 15, n. 977.

[18] *Ibid.*, n. 978.

[19] *In X Metaphys.*, lect. 2, n. 1953.

[20] *In IV Physic.*, lect. 17, n. 11: "...numerus dicitur dupliciter. Uno modo id quod numeratur actu, vel quod est numerabile, ut puta cum dicimus decem homines aut decem equos; qui dicitur numerus *numeratus*, quia est numerus applicatus rebus numeratis. Alio modo dicitur numerus *quo numeramus*, idest ipse numerus absolute acceptus, ut duo, tria, quatuor."

[21] *In X Metaphys.*, lect. 2, n. 1939.

[22] *Ibid.*, nn. 1944–1952.

[23] Cf. *In V Metaphys.*, lect. 15, n. 984.

[24] *In de sensu et sensato*, lect. 7, n. 98.

proportionality. Thus, with respect to quantity, proportion is verified first in discrete quantity, then in continuous quantity insofar as it is numerable; then it is verified in those things which are called quantity *per posterius*, such as motion, time, weights;[25] finally, in those things like colors which are quantities only accidentally. We are also told of a proportion among continuous quantities which is not numerical; namely, the incommensurability of the diagonal of the square with its sides. There is a proportion between diagonal and sides, but it cannot be expressed numerically whether the numerical proportion be stated vaguely (greater than) or determinately (double, half again as much, etc.), since, however stated, the numerical proportion implies a measure, i.e. commensurability.[26] Thus the notion of proportion is quite complex even in its proper domain, quantity. Proportionality as derived from the properties of numbers will always involve expressing a determinate distance, that is, a determinate relation of one quantity to another. It is only in virtue of an extension of meaning, the formation of a *ratio communis* ("quaelibet habitudo unius ad alterum,") that we can speak of proportion outside the realm of quantity. According to its proper notion *(ratio propria)* proportionality, like one and measure, applies only to quantity. So too the law of alternating proportionals is applicable only where the proper notion of proportionality is verified.[27] Where we do not have continuous or discrete measures, proportionals do not alternate.[28]

It seems that knowledge from analogy, i.e. from proportionality, although its use in the discussion of justice relies on its origin in quantitative relations, can be had even when no type of quantity is involved. We want now to examine such a case of coming to know by analogy.

3. OUR KNOWLEDGE OF PRIME MATTER

When in the first book of the *Physics* Aristotle gives his own account of the principles of the coming to be and being of those things which

[25] *In V Metaphys.*, lect. 15, n. 985.

[26] *Ibid.*, lect. 17, nn. 1020–1.

[27] *In I Post. Analyt.*, lect. 12, n. 8: "Dicit ergo quod esse proportionale commutabiliter convenit numeris, et lineis, et firmis, idest corporibus, et temporibus. Sicut autem de singulis determinatum est aliquando seorsum, de numeris quidem in arithmetica, de lineis et firmis in geometria, de temporibus in naturali philosophia vel astrologia, ita contingens est, quod de omnibus praedictis commutatim proportionari una demonstratione demonstretur. Sed ideo commutatim proportionari, de singulis horum seorsum demonstratur, quia non est nominatum illud commune, in quo omnia ista sunt unum. Etsi enim quantitas omnibus his communis est, tamen sub se et alia praeter haec, comprehendit, sicut orationem et quaedam quae sunt quantitates per accidens."

[28] *Q.D. de ver.*, q. 29, a. 8, ad 7.

are as a result of a change, he begins by noting that when we speak of a change, we sometimes use simple, sometimes complex terms. Consider the following statements. (1) Man becomes musical. (2) The nonmusical becomes musical. (3) The non-musical man becomes a musical man. In (1) and (2), that to which the change is attributed and the term of the change are expressed simply. In (3) both are complex or composite. Various other differences between these expressions of a change are pointed out. In the case of (2) and (3), besides the mode of expression given, we could use the form, From X, Y comes to be. For example, From non-musical, musical comes to be; From the non-musical man, musical man comes to be. In the case of (1), however, we would not so readily say, From man, musical comes to be. Our way of speaking suggests this difference between our three original expressions: the grammatical subjects of (2) and (3) are non-permanent terms of the change. Non-musical ceases to be when musical has come to be. The subject of (1) is permanent; man does not cease to be when the change has reached its term.[29] On this basis, Aristotle asks us to notice that any change involves a subject which persists throughout the change and is that to which the change is attributed. Moreover, although the subject of (1) is simple and permanent, it must be understood in a dual manner. For it is at once the subject of the change and lacking that which will be its as the result of the change.[30]

Aristotle wants now to show that any natural change involves a subject which persists throughout the change. How will he do this? His method, St Thomas points out, is induction.[31] It is up to the metaphysician to prove that there is a subject of unqualified becoming;[32] the natural philosopher arrives at the generality by an induction from the various kinds of change. The fact that the induction is made is sufficient indication that the previous analysis is not thought to have arrived at the general truth. It is important to bear this in mind: *fieri* applies to changes in different categories and cannot, therefore, be a univocal term. The previous analysis has shown that a permanent subject is involved in such changes as a man's becoming musical. Moreover, this suggests something about other things which are said to come to be, even though they are patently different changes from the acquisition of an accident. We say of Socrates that he has come to be; that before he came to be he simply speaking was not. Only here is absolute

[29] *In I Physic.*, lect. 12, nn. 4–5.
[30] Cf. *ibid.*, nn. 7–9.
[31] *Ibid.*, n. 10.
[32] Cf. Chapter VI, note 100.

change attributed to Socrates, for Socrates comes to be only in a certain respect when he grows, blushes, learns to play the violin and moves from place to place. Is there a subject of such absolute or unqualified change as that whereby Socrates comes to be? "Sed etiam in substantiis, si quis considerat, manifestum fit quod fiunt ex subiecto: videlicet enim quod plantae et animalia fiunt ex semine."[33] "Seed" here is not the permanent subject, but rather a sign that such a subject is involved. The question remains, how do we know that such a subject is involved?

Et dicit quod natura quae primo subiicitur mutationi, idest materia prima, non potest sciri per seipsam, cum omne quod cognoscitur, cognoscatur per suam formam; materia autem prima consideratur subiecta omni formae. Sed scitur *per analogiam*, idest secundum proportionem. Sic enim cognoscimus quod lignum est aliquid praeter formam scamni et lecti, quia quandoque est sub una forma, quandoque sub alia. Cum igitur videamus hoc quod est aer quandoque fieri aquam, oportet dicere quod aliquid existens sub forma aeris, quandoque sit sub forma aquae: et sic illud est aliquid praeter formam aeris, sicut lignum est aliquid praeter formam scamni et praeter formam lecti. Quod igitur sic se habet ad substantias naturales, sicut se habet aes ad statuam et lignum ad lectum, et quodlibet materiale et informe ad formam, hoc dicimus esse materiam primam.[34]

This procedure implies that we accept the fact that such substantial units as Socrates come to be and cease to be. As well, we accept the fact that such changes as Socrates becoming tan or musical take place. By analysis of this last kind of change, we have seen that it involves a subject which persists throughout the change. To make the notion of persistent subject more obvious, we appeal to changes due to human art. The carpenter takes wood and fashions it into a table. Since he might as easily have used it to make a chair, we are able to distinguish the shape or determination which makes wood to be a table or chair from the wood itself. We return now to the observation that from air, water comes to be; from seed, plant comes to be. The assumption is that these are recognized as being more drastic changes than that whereby a plant changes color or a man becomes musical. The flower comes to be on the condition that the seed ceases to be and yet it is to seed that the change is attributed in "The seed becomes a plant." This suggests what has already been said about the qualified change, "Man becomes musical." St Thomas says, accordingly, that it is by a comparison[35] or analogy with other changes that we come to know the subject of absolute or unqualified becoming. For just as shape is other than the wood and musical is other than man, so it would seem that when one substantial

---

[33] *In I Physic.*, lect. 12, n. 10.
[34] *Ibid.*, lect. 13, n. 9.
[35] *In Boethii de trin.*, q. 4, a. 2.

unit is said to come from another, there is a subject which is other than
that determination whereby we denominate the substantial units seed
and plant. Now the wood can be known through its natural properties
without appeal to the shapes imposed upon it by man; Socrates can
be known as to what he is, and his definition will not include musical.
But if the subject of absolute becoming is something other than substantial determinations, it cannot be known in itself.[36] It must be known,
if it is to be known, by means of something other than itself, by an
analogy or comparison with something else. And yet the question arises,
how can it be known by comparison with the subject of artifical change
or the subject of natural but accidental or qualified change, since it is
so utterly different from them? The *similitudo proportionum* does[37] not
imply that all these are subjects in the same sense; as a matter of fact,
the only description we have of prime matter is a series of negations.[38]
What we set out to know remains unknown in itself; whatever we know
of it is by reference to something else: to the forms which determine it
or to the subjects of other changes.[39] Let us turn now to the kind of
naming which can be based on this kind of knowing.

4. PROPORTIONALITY, METAPHOR, ANALOGOUS NAMES

It is extremely important to realize that knowledge by analogy, so called
because it involves a *similitudo proportionum*, is quite distinct from the
analogy of names. To be sure, when we come to know X by analogy
with Y, this leads to calling X a Y. The point is, this can amount to
nothing more than a metaphorical use of Y's name. And, as it happens,
when St Thomas speaks of names applied metaphorically to God, he
will say that they are based on a proportionality, or on a *similitudo
proportionalitatis*.[40] As for names said properly of God, he will say that
they are based on a *similitudo analogiae* as opposed to a *similitudo propor-*

---

[36] *Ibid.*

[37] *In Metaphys.*, lect. 2, n. 1277: "Exemplificat autem hic membra in artificialibus, in quibus
aes est ut materia, figura ut 'forma speciei,' idest dans speciem, statua compositum ex his.
Quae quidem exemplificatio non est accipienda secundum veritatem, sed secundum similitudinem proportionis. Figura enim et aliae formae artificiales non sunt substantiae, sed
accidentia quaedam. Sed quia hoc modo se habet figura ad aes in artificialibus, sicut forma
substantialis ad materiam in naturalibus, pro tanto utitur hoc exemplo, ut demonstret ignotum
per manifestum."

[38] *Ibid.*, n. 1289.

[39] Cf. *In Boethii de trin.*, q. 4, a. 2; *Q.D. de ver.*, q. 10, a. 4.

[40] *Summa theologiae*, Suppl., q. 69, a. 1, ad 2; *I Sent.*, d. 34, q. 3, a. 1, ad 2; *ibid.*, d. 45, q. 1,
a. 4; *II Sent.*, d. 16, q. 1, a. 2; *III Sent.*, d. 2, q. 1, a. 1, sol. 1, ad 3; *IV Sent.*, d. 1, q. 1, a. 1,
sol. 5, ad 3.

tionalitatis.[41] A fairly common example of a name applied metaphorically to God is "fire." What leads to the predication of such a name to God? Precisely a proportionality. As fire destroys fuel, so God destroys impurity.[42] Or, God is called "Sun" because he is the principle of spiritual life just as the sun is of corporeal life.[43] An examination of discussions of such metaphorical predicates reveals that they are based on a similarity of effects. Thus, "living waters" are so called because their activity is like that which follows on soul; the name of the principle of the latter effects is transferred to water as if it had the same cause of movement.[44] St Thomas points this out as the basis of names applied metaphorically to God; e.g. names of passions are predicated of God "secundum similitudinem effectus."[45] When we are angry, we punish those who cause our passion; but God punishes the sinner, so we say that God is angry with the transgressor. So too we speak of the eye of God, or attribute the names of other parts of the body to him, "ratione suorum actuum secundum quamdam similitudinem."[46] Generally speaking, things which are said metaphorically of God "dicuntur de eo per similitudinem proportionabilitatis ad effectum aliquem."[47]

Should this terminology cause us to become confused about the difference between predicating a term metaphorically and predicating it analogically? Cajetan and Sylvester, we remember, were not a little vacillating on this score. They tend to refer metaphor to what they call "analogy of attribution." On that basis, "healthy," St Thomas' favorite example of an analogous name, would seemingly be a metaphor. Indeed, the difficulty could be pointed up with texts of St Thomas. He writes that names said metaphorically of God are said *per prius* of creatures and of God only because of a similarity of proportions.[48] But if said *per prius* of creatures, aren't they said *per posterius* of God and with reference to creatures? And isn't that what we mean by an analogous name? Or consider this text.

[41] *II Sent.*, d. 16, q. 1, a. 2, ad 5.
[42] *III Sent.*, d. 2, q. 1, a. 1, sol. 1, ad 3.
[43] *Suppl.*, q. 69, a. 1, ad 2.
[44] *Ia*, q. 18, a. 1, ad 3.
[45] *Ia*, q. 19, a. 11; *ibid.*, a. 7, ad 1; *ibid.*, q. 3, a. 2, ad 2.
[46] *Ia*, q. 3, a. 1, ad 3.
[47] *I Sent.*, d. 45, q. 1, a. 4; *Ia*, q. 3, a. 1, ad 3.
[48] *Ia*, q. 13, a. 6: "Sic ergo omnia nomina quae metaphorice de Deo dicuntur, per prius de creaturis dicuntur quam de Deo, quia dicta de Deo nihil aliud significant quam similitudines ad tales creaturas. Sicut enim ridere dictum de prato nihil aliud significat quam quod pratum similiter se habet in decore cum floret sicut homo cum ridet, secundum similitudinem proportionis; sic nomen leonis dictum de Deo nihil aliud significat quam quod Deus similiter se habet ut fortiter operetur in suis operibus, sicut leo in suis. Et sic patet quod secundum quod

Respondeo dicendum quod per prius dicitur nomen de illo in quo salvatur tota ratio nominis perfecte, quam de illo in quo salvatur secundum aliquid; de hoc enim dicitur quasi per similitudinem ad id in quo perfecte salvatur, quia omnia imperfecta sumuntur a perfectis. Et inde est quod hoc nomen *leo* per prius dicitur de animali in quo tota ratio leonis salvatur, quod proprie dicitur leo, quam de aliquo homine in quo invenitur aliquid de ratione leonis, ut puta audacia vel fortitudo, vel aliquid huiusmodi: de hoc enim per similitudinem dicitur.[49]

Does this mean that, because in analogous names the *ratio propria* is saved in only one, that it is said metaphorically of everything else? If this were what St Thomas meant, names common to God and creature would be said only metaphorically of creatures, since in such names what the name signifies is found perfectly only in God. Clearly, unless we can distinguish metaphor from the analogous name, we shall have arrived at confusion compounded.

Metaphors are said to be based on a similitude of proportions thanks to which a name is transferred. Thus, Christ is called the lion of the tribe of Juda. Why? Well, because just as lions act bravely, so too does Christ. The metaphor is based on the similarity of effects, but notice that it is not the name of the effect which is transferred, but "lion." What does "lion" mean? Such and such an irrational animal. But Christ does not fall under that signification; in other words, the term "lion" cannot properly suppose for Christ. Metaphor, John of St Thomas has wisely said, is a matter of improper supposition. What does that mean? Simply that a word is predicated of something which does not fall under what the word signifies. If all the things which are lions were brought together Christ would not be among them. "Lion" does not signify something thanks to which it can suppose for Christ; if it is predicated of him this is because he acts in a way similar to the things for which the term does properly suppose. When St Thomas says that metaphors are based on not just any kind of similarity, "sed secundum convenientiam in illo quod est de propria ratione rei cuius nomen transfertur,"[50] he does not mean that bravery is part of the definition of lion; otherwise he would not speak of a similarity of effects. What he seems rather to mean is that bravery is associated with lion in a particular way, as if it were a property.[51]

A name is used metaphorically when that to which it is transferred

---

dicuntur de Deo, eorum significatio definiri non potest, nisi per illud quod de creaturis dicitur."

[49] *Ia*, q. 33, a. 3.

[50] *Q.D. de ver.*, q. 7, a. 2.

[51] It is of interest to note that the lion is called brave metaphorically. Cf. *In VII Ethic.*, lect. 6, n. 1399.

does not fall under the *ratio propria* of the name. Does this enable us to distinguish metaphor from analogous names? Seemingly not, since only one of the things of which the analogous name is said saves its *ratio propria*. What distinguishes the analogous name from metaphor is this: those things which do not verify the proper notion of the common name are nonetheless properly, if less so, signified by it and consequently it can properly suppose for them. This is just what St Thomas suggests when he opposes the *similitudo analogiae* and the *similitudo proportionalitatis* which is metaphor.[52]

Dicendum quod proprietates divinae ostenduntur in creaturis dupliciter: vel secundum similitudinem analogiae, sicut vita, sapientia et hujusmodi, quae analogice de Deo et creaturis conveniunt, et sic divinae proprietates praecipue ostenduntur in rationali natura :vel secundum similitudinem proportionalitatis, secundum quod spirituales proprietates corporalibus metaphorice designantur, et hoc modo in igne ostenduntur proprietates divinae.[53]

It might be thought that this text means that in names said analogically of God and creature no similitude of proportionality is involved. Yet we are told that we come to knowledge of what God is by an analogy with creatures, something which would seeming imply – creature : wisdom :: God : wisdom, just as – fire : purifies :: God : purifies. We have arrived at the point where our dissatisfaction with the view that "life" said of God means "as life is to the creature so is life to God – only proportionally" can be explained. To do this we appeal to a beautiful text.

This text, which has not been given the attention it deserves in discussions of the analogy of names, is in function of the question, "Utrum lux proprie invenitur in spiritualibus?"[54] The word discussed is parti-

[52] *Suppl.* q. 69, a. 1, ad 2; *I Sent.*, d. 34, q. 3, a. 1, ad 2.
[53] *II Sent.*, d. 16, q. 1, a. 2, ad 5.
[54] *II Sent.*, d. 13, q. 1, a. 2: "Respondeo quod in hoc videtur esse quaedam diversitas inter sanctos. Augustinus enim videtur velle quod lux in spiritualibus verius inveniatur quam in corporalibus. Sed Ambrosius et Dionysius videntur innuere quod in spiritualibus non nisi metaphorice inveniatur. Et hoc quidem videtur magis verum: quia nihil per se sensibile spiritualibus convenit nisi metaphorice, quia quamvis aliquid commune possit inveniri analogice in spiritualibus et corporalibus, non tamen aliquid per se sensibile determinat, ut patet in ente et calore; ens enim non est per se sensibile, quod utrique commune est; calor autem, quod per se sensibile est in spiritualibus proprie non invenitur. Unde cum lux sit qualitas per se visibilis, et species quaedam determinata in sensibilibus, non potest dici in spiritualibus nisi vel aequivoce vel metaphorice.
Sciendum tamen quod transferuntur corporalia in spiritualia per quamdam similitudinem, quae quidem est similitudo proportionabilitatis; et hanc similitudinem oportet reducere in aliquam communitatem univocationis vel analogiae; et sic est in proposito: dicitur enim lux in spiritualibus illud quod ita se habet ad manifestationem intellectivam sicut se habet lux corporalis ad manifestationem sensitivam. Manifestatio enim verius est in spiritualibus; et quantum ad hoc, verum est dictum Augustini, ubi supra, quod lux verius est in spiritualibus quam in corporalibus, non secundum propriam rationem lucis, sed secundum rationem

cularly fortunate for our purposes, as will appear. Is "light" said properly, that is non-metaphorically, of spiritual things? For instance, is "In
the light of new evidence, I understand..." a metaphorical use of "light"?
St Thomas begins by noting that theologians are divided on the matter.
St Augustine holds that "light" not only properly signifies spiritual
things, but does so more properly than it signifies corporeal things.
St Ambrose and Denis, on the other hand, feel that "light" is said only
metaphorically of spiritual things. Surely the latter view is correct, St
Thomas suggests, for nothing which is per se sensible, which involves
matter in its very definition, can belong to spiritual things save metaphorically. To be sure, something can be analogically common to the
corporeal and spiritual, but nothing per se sensible can be common to
both. Take "being" and "heat." "Being" is not per se sensible and can
therefore be common to corporeal and spiritual things, but "heat" cannot be thus common precisely because its signification restricts it to
the sensible. Elsewhere[55] St Thomas uses "cognitio" and "sensus" to
make the same point. Now surely "light" is like "heat," not "being,"
and St Ambrose and Denis hold the correct view.

Having rendered the obvious position its due, St Thomas proceeds
to examine that of St Augustine more closely. This is not surprising,
nor is the final acceptance of St Augustine's view as the best. Especially
where the Hexameron is concerned, St Thomas prefers St Augustine,
and he has earlier said that to interpret "light" and "day" as signifying
spiritual things properly "subtilis et congrua est."[56]

We must remember, St Thomas says, that corporeal things are transferred to the spiritual by a similitude of proportionality. His next remark
is of the utmost importance: *et hanc similitudinem oportet reducere in aliquam
communitatem univocationis vel analogiae.* This is the question raised by the
diversity of opinion among the theologians mentioned. There is a proportional similitude: light is to spiritual things as light is to corporeal
things. Both Augustine and Ambrose presuppose this similitude: they
differ in their interpretation of the signification of "light." Ambrose
insists on the fact that "light" properly signifies that whereby things can
be seen with bodily eyes; thus its proper meaning involves the material,

manifestationis, prout dicitur in canonica Joannis, quod 'omne quod manifestatur, lux est';
per quem modum omne quod manifestum est, clarum dicitur, et omne occultum obscurum."
Cf. *Ia*, q. 67, a. 1. Hayen (*op. cit.*, p. 84) is one of the few to allude to the passage just quoted
from the *Sentences*, but he takes the transition from metaphor to analogy to be based on a
real relation. "Mais, il importe de le remarquer, ce n'est pas la *proportionalitas* comme telle
qui assure la réalité de la relation entre les deux termes rapportés l'un à l'autre."
   [55] *I Sent.*, d. 22, q. 1, a. 2.
   [56] *II Sent.*, d. 12, q. 1, a. 3.

sensible order. As said of spiritual things, it cannot properly suppose for them; it is a metaphor based on similar effects – just as God is called Sun. How then can Augustine be right? His view recognizes that the first and most proper meaning of "light" (its *ratio propria*) involves matter, for it refers to the external sense. However, there is also a common notion *(ratio communis)* signified by the term, namely "principle of manifestation." Taken as signifying this common notion, which contains no reference to matter, spiritual things can be properly signified by the term and it can properly suppose for them in a proposition. What is more, the term which then signifies spiritual things, does so more properly than it does corporeal things. This requires explanation.

We have just traced the order of imposition of the term "light." It is first assigned to signify a notion expressing something in the sensible order, that which makes bodies visible, and this is its *ratio propria*. Given this meaning, only those things are signified by the term which save this *ratio propria*. Used of anything else, it is used metaphorically and supposes improperly. However, if usage indicates that the meaning of the name has been extended, we can recognize a *ratio communis* of the name. This is what Augustine feels has happened with "light." If we consider the things which fall under the common signification of the term, the spiritual principle of manifestation, e.g. the agent intellect, is really or ontologically more perfect than the sun. This scale of priority and posteriority is *secundum ordinem rerum*, of course; according to the order of the imposition of the name, the sun is most properly signified by the term.[57] That is, it is still true that the "ratio propria nominis non invenitur nisi in uno tantum."[58] As St Thomas says, "Lux verius est in spiritualibus quam in corporalibus, non secundum propriam rationem lucis, sed secundum rationem manifestationis." This has nothing to do with intrinsic possession of a quality. Notice too that if we have in mind the proper notion of the name, spiritual things are not signified by the name and it is used only metaphorically of them; if we have in mind the common notion, they are signified by it, and *secundum rem* that notion is verified most perfectly of them.[59] This is reminiscent of the way we can deny and then admit that accidents have an essence.[60]

What distinguishes the analogy of names from metaphorical usage is this: the former have been given an extended meaning and are no longer univocal terms having only a *ratio propria*. Thanks to their *ratio*

---

[57] *I Contra Gentiles*, cap. 34; cf. *infra* Chapter IX, section 4.
[58] *Ia*, q. 16, a. 6.
[59] Cf. *Q.D. de ver.*, q. 1, a. 8.
[60] *In VII Metaphys.*, lect. 4.

communis they have become analogous. The metaphor, on the other hand, is a univocal term used in a proposition to suppose for something which does not fall under its signification. Thus the term is used improperly. Since it is precisely the *ratio communis* which distinguishes the analogous name from metaphorical usage, it is easy to see why Cajetan has difficulty with metaphor and why, finally, his "analogy of attribution" becomes indistinguishable from metaphorical usage. Speaking of the example of "healthy," he argues[61] that there is no *ratio communis* of the term. Animal, urine, medicine, etc. all agree in this that the *id a quo* of the word *sanum* applied to each of them is *sanitas*. However, no common reference to *sanitas* can be abstracted from all these special relations, that is, there is no *ratio communis* of the term. He gives two reasons for this alleged impossibility. First, it is false to say that the term "healthy" means "pertaining or related in some way to health." Secondly, if such a *ratio communis* were possible, "healthy" would be a univocal term. These are particularly useful objections, since they are bound to occur to one when he reads the text on "light" we have just seen. If you have a *ratio communis lucis*, why doesn't the term thereby become univocal?

First of all, the example of "healthy." There is a *ratio communis* of the term insofar as it is analogous. "Respectus ad sanitatem" or "proportio ad sanitatem" is that common notion thanks to which animal is called healthy as subject of health, urine as sign, medicine as cause. This is clear from chapter thirty-four of the first book of *Contra Gentiles*, the third lesson (n. 2197) of the commentary on the eleventh book of the *Metaphysics* and many other texts. When Cajetan says that it is not true that "healthy" signifies this, we can agree only if we restrict the name to its proper notion, when "healthy" means what has a quality whereby there is a proper proportion among its humors.

Does a *ratio communis* entail univocity? Does the common notion "principle of manifestation" make "light" univocally common to spiritual and corporeal things? Well, does the *ratio communis entis* make "being" univocally common to substance and accident? Cajetan has referred us to the definition of univocal terms. Things are named univocally which have a common name signifying exactly the same notion as said of each of them. It is true that both the univocal and analogous name have a *ratio communis ;* the difference lies in the way the notion is common. The analogous name has a proper notion as well as a common notion which is why, if the meaning of the name is sought, the answer will most likely

[61] Cajetan, *op. cit.*, n. 51.

be the proper notion. Moreover, if the word is used, it is going to be taken to mean only the proper notion unless some indication to the contrary is given.[62] In the univocal name, there is no such distinction between a proper and common notion: the two are identical because it is not predicated *per prius et posterius*. That is why the proper notion is said to be saved by each of the things of which the univocal name is said. However, although the analogous name has a common as well as a proper notion, the latter is saved in only one of the things of which the name is said. The other things save the *ratio communis* in such a way that when we explain what the term means, the proper notion enters into their notion. Thus, the proper notion is "that which has health" and this is verified only in the animal. When urine is called healthy, it is denominated from health, not directly, but with reference to the animal. This is what is meant when it is said that the analogous name is divided by diverse modes and not by formal differences.[63]

A final word on metaphor. The metaphor consists of speaking of one thing in terms of another and applying the name of the latter to the former although it does not fall under what is signified by the name. Such a procedure is called for when what we want to talk about is obscure and unintelligible to us and the best we can do is refer it to something less obscure on the basis of a similarity. The similarity of proportionality does not argue for any substantial similarity in the lion and Christ, but for a similarity of mode of action. On this basis, the term "lion" is transferred ($\mu\varepsilon\tau\alpha\varphi\varepsilon\varrho\varepsilon\tilde{\iota}\nu$) to Christ and by a quick shuttle the mind goes through the proportionality and there is surprise and delight. Poetical knowledge is characterized by metaphor, St Thomas feels, and it has this character because of the obscurity of its subject matter. Perhaps it would not be far wrong to call that subject human existence, man's involvement in the world. Just as the mythos of tragedy is a principle of intelligibility, imposing an intelligible pattern on action (action which, in ordinary life is obscure, anything but intelligible in its ultimate purport, in a word, for the most part absurd), so the linguistic device of metaphor casts a slanting and delightful light. Whether it is nature which is personified or non-human terms which are applied to man, poetic knowledge is fundamentally anthropocentric. For a somewhat similar reason, Scripture makes use of metaphor – that of which it would speak is remote from and unintelligible to us.[64] Does the

---

[62] *In I Periherm.*, lect. 5, n. 19.
[63] *I Sent.*, d. 22, q. 1, a. 3, ad 2.
[64] *I Sent.*, prolog., q. 1, a. 5, ad 3; *IaIIae*, q. 101, a. 2, ad 2.

poet lie by means of his delightful abuse of terms? No deception is intended and "aliquis loquens per metaphoricas locutiones non mentitur; non enim intendit sua locutione ducere in res quae per nomina significantur, sed magis in illas quarum illae res, significatae per nomina, similitudinem habent."[65] As Cajetan points out, metaphors are not verified of the things of which they are said according to their proper signification, but rather according to a similarity to what is properly signified by the term.[66] Since we first know sensible things, the transfer of their names to non-sensible things must first involve a metaphor. Then, with the sanction of usage and the recognition of a common notion, these names becomes analogous. Thus, while some metaphors become but tired clichés, banalities incapable any longer of eliciting the delight and wonder which was their original justification, others become analogous names thanks to an extension of their meaning. Philosophical terms are always open to the charge of being metaphors, at least philosophical terms in the Aristotelian tradition. How quaint and metaphorical to call white a $\mu o \varrho \varphi \acute{\eta}$, to call man a $\H{\upsilon} \lambda \eta$ in "Man becomes white."[67] Precisely, if usage had not sanctioned the extended meaning whereby these terms are there used properly. That is why St Thomas can say that the subject of absolute becoming is not called matter metaphorically. "Nec etiam utitur hic figurata locutione, sed exemplari."[68] As the example of "light" makes clear, we can always say that an analogous name is used metaphorically of what doesn't fall under its proper notion if we ignore the common notion.

---

[65] *I Sent.*, d. 16, q. 1, a. 3, ad 3.

[66] "...uti metaphoris est uti locutionibus quae non verificantur de his de quibus dicuntur, secundum propriam significationem, sed secundum aliquam similitudinem ad proprie significata." – *In Iam*, q. 1, a. 9, n. 1.

[67] Cf. Margaret Macdonald, "The Philosopher's Use of Analogy," *Essays* on Logic and Language, ed. Flew, (New York, 1951).

[68] *In I Physic.*, lect. 15, n. 10.

CHAPTER IX

THE DIVINE NAMES

Our concern has been to present the doctrine of the analogy of names, a doctrine we have seen to belong to the logic of signification. If we now examine some particular analogous names, those common to God and creature, it is because so much of what St Thomas has to say of analogical signification occurs in discussions of such names; moreover, the uniqueness of the thing we are trying to name in this case has led to some of the misapprehension concerning analogy which we have sought to correct. To say that God and creature have a name analogously in common is manifested by appeal to the examples of "healthy" and "being" for the indisputable reason that the divine names involve the same mode of signification. On the level of the *res* named, however, there is all the difference in the world (and out of it), but it is important to realize that that is where the difference lies. The divine names are not a subdivision of the analogy of names, but instances of it. The present chapter has for its purpose to make that one point; consequently it should not be read as an essay on St Thomas' doctrine on the names of God, a subject which would demand a study at least as lengthy as this on the logic of analogy.

1. CAN GOD BE NAMED BY US?

We name things as we know them so that our names signify things through the mediation of what we know of them. Thus a thing can be named by us to the degree that we can know it. The kind of being we are, a corporeal thing among corporeal things, has a decided effect on that mode of being which is our knowing, a mode which enables us to transcend the limitations of our individuality.[1] Physical contact with things is a prerequisite for sense knowledge whereby we are the forms of other things, their color, temperature, taste, shape, etc., possessing these forms, not as they are possessed by bodies, but intentionally, to some degree without the"conditions of matter"; that is, in seeing red, we are or possess that form differently from the way it is had by the surface

[1] *Q.D. de ver.*, q. 2, a. 2.

of the apple. It is from such sensible effects that we denominate that
which has these sensible forms, their substance which is called sensible
not because it is a per se object of sense, but because it is known through
what is sensed. The quiddity of sensible things is said to be the connatural object of our mind because it is such that it is cognitively accessible
by us in terms of our natural way of coming to know, through what can
be sensed.[2] St Thomas holds that the sensible effects of such substances
adequately manifest to us what those substances are; consequently, the
ratio of the name of such a substance is said to declare sufficiently its
essence.[3] The concept or species is that in which the sensible substance
is known: it is not however something *(quod)* which is first known and
from which we infer the thing; rather it is that by which *(quo)* something
is known.[4] The sensible thing is known in itself through a concept which
adequately expresses what it is.

It is obvious that God cannot be considered the connatural object of
our intellect, obvious in the sense that the discussion on which we are
relying[5] follows on proofs that God exists and that he is not a body.[6]
If God is to be known, he cannot be known through his sensible qualities
since he has none. However, he can be known through the sensible
things which are the connatural objects of our intellect, known as their
cause. Thus knowledge of God follows on knowing something else as
a *quod* and then arguing to God's existence: this is discursive knowledge
and it is radically imperfect. For discursive knowledge may mean either
now thinking of this thing, now of that; there is priority and posteriority
here, but knowledge of the first thing is not cause of knowledge of the
second.[7] Sometimes, however, knowledge of one thing is cause of our
knowledge of another, but in either case there is imperfection. In the
first, successive but not causative priority and posteriority, the imperfection of discursive knowledge is revealed because it indicates that we
must know each nature by a concept proper to it and cannot form a
concept which would distinctly represent diverse things.[8] The second
type of discourse indicates that our knowledge of principles is not sufficient of itself to give us actual knowledge of what flows from them.[9]

[2] *Ia,* q. 85, a. 1.
[3] *Ia,* q. 13, a. 1.
[4] *Q.D. de anima,* a. 7, ad 8; *Ia,* q. 84, a. 5; *ibid.,* q. 85, a. 2.
[5] *Ia,* q. 13.
[6] *Ia,* q. 2, a. 3; *ibid.,* q. 3, a. 1.
[7] *Ia,* q. 14, a. 7.
[8] Cf. Charles De Koninck, "Concept, Process and Reality," *Philosophy and Phenomenological Research,* (1949), pp. 440–7.
[9] *Ia,* q. 58, a. 4.

Discursive knowledge involves a passage "ex uno cognito in aliud cognitum,"[10] but of course there are degrees of discursive knowledge. What is called *propter quid* demonstration consists in coming to know that a property follows on the essential principles of its subject, and this is to know perfectly what a property is.[11] When we come to know a cause from its effects, we can attain perfect knowledge of the cause if the effects are proportionate to it. The discourse whereby we attain knowledge of God through creatures as his effects provides us with most imperfect knowledge of God, since God is an analogical cause. Since God can be known only through created effects, he can be named only from them.[12] "Sic igitur potest nominari a nobis ex creaturis: non tamen ita quod nomen significans ipsum exprimat essentiam secundum quod est, sicut hoc nomen *homo* exprimit sua significatione essentiam hominis secundum quod est..."[13]

2. WHY MANY DIVINE NAMES?

Prior to raising the question of the divine names, St Thomas has argued that God is utterly simple by denying of him all the sources of multiplicity and complexity.[14] Since God is simple, it would seem either that one name should suffice for him or, if we allow many names, that they are synonyms, all signifying one, simple reality. The resolution of both these doubts is based on the same point, the way in which names signify. If we apply many names to God, these names signify either one notion or many notions. Only if they all signified the same notion would they be synonyms, but "good," "wise," "being" and "true," though they are all used to name the one utterly simple thing which is God, have different significations and therefore are not synonyms.[15] God is known and named from creatures in whom wisdom and justice are different perfections and found different *rationes*. If these names are applied to God, they will signify him by way of the conceptions which answer to these names and, since no one of these conceptions alone adequately represents

---

[10] *Ibid.*, a. 3.
[11] *In I Post. Analyt.*, lect. 2, n. 5.
[12] This is as true of revealed knowledge as it is of natural knowledge. "Unde de substantiis illis immaterialibus secundum statum viae nullo modo possumus scire *quid est*, non solum per viam naturalis cognitionis, sed nec etiam per viam revelationis, quia divinae revelationis radius ad nos pervenit secundum modum nostrum, ut Dionysius dicit. Unde quamvis per revelationem elevemur ad aliquid cognoscendum, quod alias esset nobis ignotum, non tamen ad hoc quod alio modo cognoscamus nisi per sensibilia." – *In Boethii de trin.*, q. 6, a. 3.
[13] *Ia*, q. 13, a. 1.
[14] *Ia*, q. 3.
[15] *Ia*, q. 13, a. 4; *Q.D. de pot.*, q. 7, a. 6.

God (nor all taken together), there is a kind of foundation for their diversity in God, even though he is perfectly simple.[16] Indeed, St Thomas maintains that if the intellect, seeing God in his essence, should name what it understands, it would need a multiplicity of names. This is true of every created intellect, angelic or human: "...sed conceptio perfecte repraesentans eum est verbum increatum; et ideo unum tantum."[17]

3. *OMNE NOMEN CUM DEFECTU EST*

We have already discussed the difference between the metaphorical use of a term and analogical signification. If a term involves in its principal signification corporeal conditions, it cannot properly signify God. The name "light," since its proper notion includes sensible matter, cannot signify spiritual things except in virtue of a common notion. But not all names attributed to God are like "light." What of those names in whose definition "non clauditur defectus, nec dependent a materia secundum esse, ut ens, bonum, et alia huiusmodi?"[18] If God is called being, wise, etc., are these names devoid of corporeal conditions? It hardly seems so, since we must say of God either that he is good or goodness, living or life, being or existence, i.e. make use of either concrete or abstract terms, and such modes of signifying are intimately tied up with what is the connatural object of our mind. For, while the concrete term signifies something as subsisting, it implies composition: that which is good, wise, etc., whereas if we use abstract terms, we achieve simplicity at the expense of the connotation of subsistence, for life, goodness and existence are not subsistent things.[19] On this showing, all our words seem to involve corporeal conditions and, while we might agree that something is named good from what it is, it is rather difficult to see how "wise" can denominate except from an accident. Why then does St Thomas suggest that "living," "being," etc., do not signify defectively, whereas "lion," "angry" and other names used metaphorically of God do?

---

[16] "Et sic patet quartum, quod pluralitas istorum nominum non tantum est ex parte intellectus nostri formantis diversas conceptiones de Deo, quae dicuntur diversae ratione, ut ex dictis patet, sed ex parte ipsius Dei, inquantum scilicet est aliquid in Deo correspondens omnibus istis conceptionibus, scilicet plena et omnimoda ipsius perfectio, secundum quam contingit quod quodlibet nominum significantium istas conceptiones, de Deo vere et proprie dicitur; non autem ita quod aliqua diversitas vel multiplicitas ponatur in re, quae Deus est, ratione istorum attributorum." – *I Sent.*, d. 2, q. 1, a. 3; *ibid.*, d. 22, q. 1, a. 3.

[17] *I Sent.*, d. 2, q. 1, a. 3.

[18] *Q.D. de ver.*, q. 2, a. 11.

[19] *Ia*, q. 13, a. 1, ad 2; *I Contra Gentiles*, cap. 30.

Let us look first at such names as "wise" and "just" which are used to name God. When we say of Socrates that he is wise or just, we are not denominating him from what he is, but from an accident. A man is a man before acquiring wisdom and justice and if he should lose these virtues he does not for all that cease to be a man. They are, then, accidental predicates. How can they be said of God? When St Thomas takes into account a statement of St John Damascene to the effect that such names predicate an accident of God, he says this: "Damascenus loquitur de istis nominibus non quantum ad id *quod* praedicant de Deo, sed quantum ad id a *quo* imponuntur ad significandum. Imponuntur enim a nobis ad significandum ex formis accidentalibus quibusdam in creaturis repertis."[20] And yet, shortly thereafter, he says, "hoc nomen sapientia verificatur de Deo quantum ad illud a quo imponitur nomen."[21] We have seen that *id a quo* can mean two different things, either the etymology or the form from which the term in imposed to signify, but it is difficult to apply that distinction here. In the first text, the *quod* is distinguished from the *a quo* which seems to be precisely the form from which the name is imposed to signify. In the second text, the *id a quo* is expressly distinguished from the etymology. What is St Thomas getting at here?

The clue is to be found in yet another answer to an objection in the same article.[22] Such a term as "just" signifies something in the genus of quality; that genus, therefore, will enter into its definition. As well there will be a difference, that from which the term is imposed to signify. "Sapientia autem et iustitia non ex hoc nominantur, sed magis ex aliqua perfectione vel ex aliquo actu; unde talia veniunt in divinam praedicationem secundum rationem differentiae et non secundum rationem generis."[23] "Wisdom" signifies "qualitas per quam sapientialia intellectualiter habentur": this is the *ratio propria* of the term and as such it was imposed to signify from an accidental form, something however which is clear from the complete notion and not from that which is formal in the definition. It is according to the whole notion that a man is called wise, but God is not so named according to the proper notion of the term. What is involved is the formation of a *ratio communis* by dropping the genus and retaining the difference, the *id a quo*. It is always in this fashion that St Thomas explains the extension of words to signify divine perfections. "Et ideo dicendum est quod

[20] *Q.D. de pot.*, q. 7, a. 4, ad 1.
[21] *Ibid.*, ad. 9
[22] *Ibid.*, ad 2.
[23] *Ibid.*

omnia hujusmodi proprie dicuntur de Deo quantum ad rem significatum, licet non quantum ad modum significandi; et quantum ad id
quod est proprium de ratione cujuslibet horum, licet non quantum ad
rationem generis..."[24]

Dicitur autem nomen imponi ab eo quod est quasi differentia constitutiva et non ex
ratione generis; et ideo quandocumque aliquid secundum suum genus dicit imperfec-
tionem, et secundum differentiam perfectionem, illud invenitur in Deo quantum ad
rationem differentiae, et non quantum ad rationem generis: sicut scientia non est in
Deo quantum ad rationem habitus vel qualitatis, quia sic habet rationem accidentis;
sed solum secundum id quod complet rationem scientiae, scilicet cognoscitivum certi-
tudinaliter aliquorum.[25]

These names do not signify the same notion as applied to God and
creature; that is, they are rendered analogous.

We can see now why it is that a term can be said to involve corporeal
conditions in two ways, either with respect to what is principally signified by it, the *id a quo*, or with respect to the mode of signifying. The
latter "proprie dicuntur de Deo, quamvis non perfecte ipsum repraesentet."[26] Such words as "lion," "angry," "fire" etc. involve corporeal
conditions in that which they principally signify; such words as "wise"
and "just" do not. "Dico autem aliqua praedictorum nominum perfectionem absque defectu importare, quantum ad illud ad quod significandum nomen fuit impositum: quantum enim ad modum significandi, omne nomen cum defectu est."[27] No difficulty to our exposition
is presented by the fact that St Thomas sometimes says that both the
specific and generic names can be said of God. For instance, both
"science" and "knowledge" are said of God. Clearly this does not mean
that the genus which would enter into the proper notion of each, quality,
is part of the *ratio* signified by the name when it is applied to God;
rather it means that the *id a quo* of both the generic and specific names
does not involve corporeal conditions.[28]

How can a name whose proper signification includes genus and difference be used to signify God in whom only one of these is verified?
To the objection that such names are falsely attributed to God, St Thomas replies that he could agree only if they were intended to signify
God and creature univocally.[29] Since this is not case, it is hardly surprising that the names signify different notions as said of God and

[24] *I Sent.*, d. 35, q. 1, a. 1, ad 2.
[25] *Ibid.*, d. 4, q. 1, a. 1; cf. *ibid.*, 22, q. 1, a. 2.
[26] *I Sent.*, d. 8, q. 2, a. 2, ad 2.
[27] *I Contra Gentiles*, cap. 30.
[28] *I Sent.*, d. 19, q. 4, a. 2, ad 4.
[29] *Q.D. de pot.*, q. 7, a. 4, ad 3.

creature. And, of course, these names are said less properly of God,

cum in nomine duo sunt, modus significandi et res ipsa significata, semper secundum alterum potest removeri a Deo vel secundum utrumque; sed non potest dici de Deo nisi secundum alterum tantum. *Et quia ad veritatem et proprietatem affirmationis requiritur quod totum affirmatur*, ad proprietatem negationis sufficit si alterum tantum desit, ideo dicit Dionysius quod negationes sunt absolutae verae, sed affirmationes non nisi secundum quid: quia quantum ad significatum tantum, et non quantum ad modum significandi.[30]

This enables us to appreciate the three steps in naming God which St Thomas borrows from Denis. First, we affirm a name of God, saying, God is good. Secondly, since the name is verified of God only because of the *id a quo*, we deny it of him, saying God is not good. Finally, we once more affirm it of him, intending to say that goodness is found in God supereminently and beyond all possibility of our grasping what the divine goodness is.[31] What we finally know, therefore, is that we do not know what God is.[32] These names remain the names of creatures and do not become names of God in any full sense: "sic hoc nomen quamvis ei aliquo modo conveniat, non tamen convenit ei ut nomen eius, quia id quod nomen significat est definitio; causato vero convenit ut nomen eius."[33]

But is this always true? Isn't there one name, *Qui est*, which is God's proper name? Of all the names which can be attributed to God, "being" is the most proper: *qui est* substitutes another gender for the *quod* in *quod est* and both are equivalent to *ens*.[34] The reason this name is most properly applied to God is this: "Non enim significat forma aliquam, sed ipsum esse."[35] God's essence is his existence and thus "being" or "He who is" properly names God; "unumquodque enim denominatur a sua forma."[36] Any other name adds some determination of existence, but "being" is the most indeterminate of all words, not signifying any determinate mode of being, but indeterminate with respect to any mode whatsoever. "Ens autem non dicit quidditatem, sed solum actum essendi..."[37] How can *ens*, which means *quod est* or *id quod habet esse*, be said to signify only existence? Doesn't the notion signified by the word include *quod* as well? Certainly, but St Thomas' point is that the subject

---

[30] *I Sent.*, d. 22, q. 1, a. 2, ad 1.
[31] *Q.D. de pot.*, q. 7, a. 4, ad 2.
[32] *Ibid.*, ad 14.
[33] *Ibid.*, ad 5; *Q.D. de ver.*, q. 2, a. 1, ad 11.
[34] Cf. *I Sent.*, d. 8, q. 1, a. 1: "...hoc nomen 'qui est' vel 'ens' imponitur ab actu essendi." The present discussion is substantially the same as that to be found in our, "Being and Predication," *Laval théologique et philosophique*, xv, (1959), 2, pp. 236–274.
[35] *Ia*, q. 13, a. 11.
[36] *Ibid.*
[37] *I Sent.*, d. 8, q. 4, a. 2, ad 2.

is left wholly undetermined as to what it is; the word is imposed solely from the formality of actuality, which is existence, and the mode of reception or possession of that act is left wholly undetermined. Thus, although the *quod* is primarily substance, substance is not expressed determinately by *ens*. The *ratio entis* is composite, but one component is formal with respect to the other, that component namely which is the *id a quo nomen imponitur ad significandum*. Every name principally signifies the *id a quo;* that is why "being" primarily signifies existence and is the most proper name of God. Here, just as in the names discussed above, it is not the whole notion signified by "being" which is meant when God is called by that name. Rather, we drop the subject and retain only the form, the difference, the *id a quo* which is existence. To take only this as the signification of the term is to understand it less properly, since proper signification involves both *res* and *modus*.

The thought will occur that by taking *esse* instead of *ens*, we can escape the impropriety just mentioned. St Thomas suggests this in reply to an objection which cites the Boethius of the *De hebdomadibus* to the effect that *ens* is that which participates *esse*. But God is *ens*, ergo etc. St Thomas writes, "dicendum quod dictum Boetii intelligitur de illis quibus esse competit per participationem, non per essentiam; quod enim per essentiam est, si vim locutionis attendamus, magis debet dici quod est ipsum esse quam sit id quod est."[38] What is preferred here is the abstract term, *esse*, but abstract terms too involve a mode of signifying which will have to be denied when they are said of God. What does *esse* mean, properly speaking? Like any form, it must be defined *ex additione*, i.e. with reference to that of which it is the form. "Unde patet quod hoc quod dico esse est actualitas omnium actuum, et propter hoc est perfectio omnium perfectionum."[39]

Intellectus autem noster hoc modo intelligit esse quo modo invenitur in rebus inferioribus a quibus scientiam capit, in quibus esse non est subsistens, sed inhaerens. Ratio autem invenit quod aliquod esse subsistens sit: et ideo licet hoc quod dicunt esse significetur per modum concretionis, tamen intellectus attribuens esse Deo transcendit modum significandi, attribuens Deo id quod significatur, non autem modum significandi.[40]

Whether we call God *ens* or *esse*, these words will not signify the same *ratio* as when they apply to creatures. That is why we need not fall into the error of those who maintain that God's existence is the existence of

[38] *Q.D. de pot.*, q. 7, a. 2, ad 8.
[39] *Ibid.*, ad 9.
[40] *Ibid.*, ad 7.

creatures, even though we say God *is* existence.[41] *Omne nomen cum defectu est*, and "cum esse creaturae imperfecte repraesentet divinum esse, et hoc nomen qui est imperfecte significat ipsum, quia significat per modum cujusdam concretionis et compositionis; sed adhuc imperfectius significatur per alia nomina."[42] As Cajetan remarks,[43] it is the most proper name of God only in the sense that it is the least improper. That is why "being" and "existence" are sometimes denied of God. "Ad ultimum autem etiam hoc ipsum esse, secundum quod est in creaturis, ab ipso removeamus; et tunc remanet in quadam tenebra ignorantiae."[44]

4. *ORDO NOMINIS* : *ORDO RERUM*

In names common to God and creature, the creature is always the *per prius* of the name, in him only is the *ratio propria* of the name saved, a *ratio* which involves the subject as well as the act from which the name is imposed to signify. These names apply secondarily to God and, although the denial of the imperfection of the mode eliminates created perfection, the common notion is understandable only by reference to the proper notion. God is in no way *comprehended* or defined by such words, but insofar as we know that his infinite perfection founds the *ratio* of the name, they are truly affirmed of him. Thus, in these names as in any analogous name, the "ratio propria non invenitur nisi in uno tantum" and the meaning of the word as extended is dependent for its intelligibility on the *ratio propria* of the word. As is always the case with analogous names, the names common to God and creature must be discussed in terms of *rationes:* the creature is the *per prius* precisely *secundum rationem nominis.*[45] The order of the notions signified by a name reflects the order of our knowledge, since we name as we know. Moreover, since what is first known by us is not thereby what is most knowable in reality, we cannot argue from the *ordo nominis* to the *ordo rerum.*

---

[41] *De ente et essentia*, cap. 6 : "Nec oportet, si dicimus quod Deus est esse tantum, ut in errorem corum incidamus, qui Deum dixerunt esse illud esse universale quo quaelibet res formaliter est. Hoc enim esse quod Deus est, huius conditionis est ut nulla sibi additio fieri possit; unde per ipsam suam puritatem est esse distinctum ab omni esse (...) Esse autem commune, sicut in intellectu suo non includit aliquam additionem, ita nec includit in intellectu suo aliquam praecisionem additionis; quia si hoc esset, nihil posset intelligi esse in quo super esse aliquid adderetur." Cf. *Q.D. de pot.*, q. 7, a. 2, ad 6; *I Sent.*, d. 8, q. 4, a. 1, ad 1. One can see why St Thomas denies that God enters into the subject of metaphysics, though that subject is designated *ens commune*. See the proemium of his commentary on the *Metaphysics*.
[42] *I Sent.*, d. 8, q. 1, a. 1, ad 3.
[43] *In Iam*, q. 13, a. 11, n. V.
[44] *I Sent.*, d. 8, q. 1, a. 1, ad 4; *ibid.*, d. 3, q. 1, a. 1, ad 1.
[45] *In V Metaphys.*, lect. 5, n. 824; *I Contra Gentiles*, cap. 34; *Q.D. de malo*, q. 1, a. 5, ad 19.

Sometimes these are the same, sometimes they are different (indicating that this order is accidental to the discussion of analogical signification) and in the case of names common to God and creature, the *ordo rerum* is quite the opposite of the *ordo nominum*, a fact certain to be stressed by the metaphysician and theologian.

What is intended when names are attributed to God? As St Thomas points out, there are divine names and divine names; some of them signify negatively (e.g. incorporeal), some relatively (e.g. Lord), some substantially.[46] We are presently concerned only with the third type. Now some names of this kind are accidental predicates of creatures, e.g. "wise" and "just," but, as we have seen, are essential or substantial predicates as said of God since he is utterly simple. Besides God's simplicity, the treatise on the divine names presupposes that God is first cause and that all created perfections preexist in him unified and eminently.[47] Although the *via causalitatis* is but one of the ways St Thomas mentions whereby we come to knowledge of God,[48] the fact that creatures are effects and God their cause underlies any attribution of names to God. Nevertheless, it is not our intention, when we say that God is good, simply to say that God is the cause of the goodness of creatures. If this were all we meant, we could say that God is a stone, since he is cause of the stone.[49] It is precisely the purpose of imposing such names which makes it hazardous to compare them with other analogous names on the basis of their foundation in reality. When we say that medicine is healthy, we don't intend this to be a substantial or essential predicate anymore than when we call the animal healthy. Moreover, if we want to talk about quinine or aspirin apart from their salutary effects on ailing animals, we have other more direct recourses, other names. But in the case of God, when we want to say something about what he is, we have no choice but to name him from creatures. And even when we name him from what in creatures is an accident, the name is imposed to signify what God is. Since the *id a quo* of names common to God and creature exists eminently in God, we can say that *secundum rem nominis*, God is the *per prius* of these names.[50] This is strikingly exemplified by the word "being" which, we have seen, is least improperly attributed

---

[46] *Ia*, q. 13, a. 2.

[47] *Ibid.*

[48] "Via remotionis, via causalitatis, via eminentiae." Cf. I Sent., d. 35, q. 1, a. 1, ad 2; *ibid.*, d. 3, q. 1, a. 3.

[49] "Cum igitur dicitur 'Deus est bonus,' non est sensus, 'Deus est causa bonitatis,' vel 'Deus non est malus': sed est sensus, 'id quod bonitatem dicimus in creaturis, praeexistit in deo,' et hoc quidem secundum modum altiorem." – *Ia*, q. 13, a. 2; cf. *Q.D. de pot.*, q. 7, a. 5.

[50] *Ia*, q. 13, a. 6.

to God. With respect to that from which the word is imposed to signify, *esse*, we can say that only God is being *essentialiter* and that creatures are beings *per participationem*.

...ens praedicatur de solo Deo *essentialiter*, eo quod esse divinum est esse subsistens et absolutum; de qualibet autem creatura praedicatur *per participationem*: nulla enim creatura est suum esse, sed est habens esse. Sic et Deus dicitur bonus essentialiter, quia *est* ipsa bonitas; creaturae autem dicuntur bona per participationem, quia habent bonitatem.[51]

At this point, it is useful to recall the difficulties of Cajetan and Sylvester with respect to the *per prius secundum ordinem rerum*. Medicine, since it is the cause of the health of the animal, is said to be prior in the real order although it receives the designation "healthy" by reference to its effect. But in names common to God and creature, God is prior in the real order. And yet there is a great deal of difference between the really prior in these two cases. Medicine is denominated healthy *causaliter*, something which involves, of course, a similarity between medicine and the quality in the animal. This similarity, however, is only partial: medicine possesses only part, or a part of a part, of what constitutes the quality healthy; for example, the medicine may be warm and warmth be considered as part of health.[52] That is why medicine is not denominated from this quality as if it possessed health, but only because it causes the health of the animal. And neither animal nor medicine is called healthy *per essentiam*. Now, if God were designated being or good only *causaliter*, an analogous name would be involved just as an analogous name is involved in "healthy." But we intend more than this when we call God good (a sign of this being that we don't call God a stone); because that from which names like "being" and "good" are imposed need not connote created perfections, we can say that God is good and being *essentialiter*.[53] *Essentialiter* here is not opposed to *accidentaliter*, but to *participative*.[54] This does not mean, as Cajetan and Sylvester thought, that in names common to God and creature, the *ratio propria* of the name is found in each. Creature and God are not called good or being *secundum easdem rationes*: according to the imposition of these names, *secundum rationem nominis*, in terms of the familiar and usual meaning attached to these words, these names are said properly of creatures and of God in only an extended sense. But God is *essentialiter* the perfection which functions as the *id a quo* of these words: God and

---

[51] *Quodl. II*, q. 2, a. 1.
[52] *In VII Metaphys.*, lect. 8, n. 1449.
[53] *Ia*, q. 13, a. 2.
[54] Cf. *In Boethii de hebdomadibus*, lect. 2, for modes of participation.

goodness are one, God and existence are one. God is being; creatures have it. The perfection from which these names are imposed exists in God, not partially, but in a manner which wholly transcends the manner in which it is found in creatures. Thus God is prior not only *secundum ordinem rerum*, but *secundum rem nominis:* "haec in eo eminentius praeexistunt."[55] These perfections now appear to be merely nominally or verbally verified of creatures.[56] Thus the order of the things named is exactly the reverse of the order of the imposition of the name: God is named from creature with regard to the *ratio nominis;* creatures can be said to be named from God in the sense that that from which the name is imposed to signify is an effect of God who is this perfection eminently and *essentialiter.* Thus God is the *per prius* of these names and that precisely from the point of view of that from which the name is imposed to signify. Once a *ratio communis* is formed by dropping the mode of signifying, God *is* what the name signifies whereas creatures *have* or participate it. These metaphysical and theological considerations underlying the application of the intention of analogy do not alter the doctrine of analogous names. It is important to remember that God and creature could be named good analogically even if God were named such only *causaliter;* furthermore, it is a great mistake to identify "predicated *causaliter*" and "said metaphorically," although it is true that many things could be predicated of God *causaliter* which do not signify him *proprie.*[57]

On the basis of our analysis, we can see why Sylvester disitnguished three steps in the imposition of a name like "being." It is first imposed from a perfection which creatures have and substances are not called good with reference to God. Secondly, God is said to be insofar as he is the cause of creatures; thus God is denominated from creatures and

---

[55] *Ia,* q. 13, a. 6.

[56] Cf. *In Ephesios,* cap. 3, lect. 4: "Utrum autem paternitas quae est in coelis et in terra derivetur a paternitate quae est in divinis, dubitatur. Et videtur quod non, quia nomina sic imponimus secundum quod res nominatas cognoscimus; quidquid autem cognoscimus, est per creaturas; ergo nomina imposita a nobis rebus ipsis, plus et prius conveniunt creaturis quam ipsi Deo. Respondeo et dico quod nomen alicuius rei nominatae a nobis, dupliciter potest accipi, quia vel est expressivum aut significativum conceptus intellectus (quia voces sunt notae vel signa passionum vel conceptuum qui sunt in anima), et sic nomen prius est in creaturis quam in Deo; aut inquantum est manifestativum quidditatis rei nominatae exterius, et sic est prius in Deo. Unde hoc nomen *paternitas* secundum quod significat conceptionem intellectus nominantis rem, sic per prius invenitur in creaturis quam in Deo, quia per prius creatura innotescit nobis quam Deus; secundum autem quod significat ipsam rem nominatam, sic per prius est in Deo quam in nobis, quia certe omnis virtus generativa in nobis, est a Deo; et ideo dicit, 'Ex quo omnis Paternitas quae est in coelo et in terra nominatur,' quasi dicat: Paternitas quae est in ipsis creaturis, est quasi nominalis vel vocalis, sed illa paternitas divina qua Pater dat totam naturam Filio absque omni imperfectione, est vera paternitas."

[57] *Ia,* q. 13, a. 6.

the term may be taken *causaliter*. Thirdly, thanks to an analysis like our own above, God is said to be the perfection *essentialiter* and creatures can be said to be denominated from God.

God is known and named from creatures; some names are analogically common to God and creature. To know what analogical signification is is to know what to expect here with regard to the notions signified by the common name, but analogical signification does not decide what order will obtain *secundum ordinem rerum*, nor does it decide differences between the kinds of *per prius secundum ordinem rerum*. Substance and accident are named being analogically; the animal and medicine are named healthy analogically; God and creature are named being analogically. The logical doctrine concerning things named analogically applies to each of these instances, and applies equally. Yet there are great differences between these examples. The question then arises as to whether we want to erect into differences of what it means to be named analogically these ontological diversities. To do so is somewhat like making rational a difference of the intention of species because the human species is rational. Logic, as St Thomas envisages it, is dependent upon reality, but not directly; it is immediately dependent on being as known. Concepts may be of real things, but insofar as concepts are named they take on the intention of *ratio*; a determinate kind of relation among the *rationes* signified by a common name is involved when things are said to be named analogically. The determinate content of these concepts may involve all kinds of differences which, from the viewpoint of analogical signification, are irrelevant. It is for this reason that we suggest that the real differences among things named analogically cannot be divisive of the intention of analogical signification.

CHAPTER X

CONCLUDING

"Extra chorum canens."[1]

The logic of analogical signification, once it is separated from the many contexts of its application, is a simple if important doctrine. Things are said to be named analogically which have a common name which does not signify totally different notions as said of each of them, but according to priority and posteriority. One of these things is primarily named by the term and the others are named by it because of their proportion to what is chiefly named. There is a twofold division of this mode of being named: either several things are named with reference to what is primarily named by the term, or one thing is named with reference to another which is again what is primarily named by the term. Contrary to Cajetan, it makes no difference to the logical doctrine whether the analogical extension of a term is based on a proportionality or whether the perfection from which the name is imposed to signify belongs essentially or intrinsically to the things named. Once the irrelevancy of such considerations is recognized, the validity of any distinction between "analogy of attribution" and "analogy of proportionality" is immediately called into question. We have tried to show that the texts of St Thomas do nothing towards supporting Cajetan's division of the analogy of names. As for the alleged metaphysical character of analogy, it is clear that while analogical signification is extremely important for metaphysics, it is also important for the philosophy of nature as well as for the naming of logical entities (e.g. "genus," "universal" and "demonstration.") It is easy enough to agree that the analogy of names has special importance for the metaphysician, just as logic generally does, but this hardly makes a logical doctrine a metaphysical one.

Needless to say, to insist that the analogy of names is a logical intention is not to say that the things named analogically are logical entities, although this is sometimes the case. But whatever the things involved, when we say of them that they are named analogically, we are referring

---

[1] "Sic, ut iam unum alterumve testimonium afferamus, 'esset extra chorum canere,' aiebat Banez ex propriis solius Logicae de analogia disserere." – Fr. Alvarez-Menendez, O.P., Introduction to Cajetan, *De nominum analogia, ed. cit.,* p. xi.

to a relation they take on as known by us and not to some property they enjoy *in rerum natura*. That is why it is necessarily nonsense to speak of metaphysical analogy in the context of the analogy of names. Unless we want to equivocate hopelessly, there is nothing metaphysical about the intentions things take as known and named by us. As the foregoing makes clear, this is in no wise to attribute to St Thomas a logic which has no roots in reality. It is *things* as known which are named and sometimes named analogically. But "to be named analogically" is a *nomen intentionis*, like "genus," "species" and "syllogism," not a *nomen rei* like "effect," "wise" and "substance."

The reader may hesitate to agree that the analogy of being is simply the analogy of "being." For a long time, the analogy of being has been taken to mean the ontological dependence of accident on substance and of all created substance on God. Even if one is willing to admit that the analogy of "being" is a logical question, he may wish to insist that the dependence in being of creatures on God, or of accident on substance, etc. is the ultimate basis of that mode of signification and that these real relations can also be called analogies. Since our purpose has been to determine the thought of St Thomas, let us look at a discussion of his which seems relevant to the objection.

In discussing metaphysics, St Thomas asks whether it is concerned with things separate from matter and motion.[2] He begins by observing that any science considers a *genus subiectum* and that it achieves its end or perfection in knowing the principles of that genus. Principles, however, are of two kinds. Some principles are complete entities in themselves and can be considered not only as causes of other things but in themselves. For example, heavenly bodies are considered both as principles of terrestial things and in themselves. Other principles are not complete entities and therefore can be considered only in the science concerned with their effects, e.g. unity as principle of number, the point as principle of the line, matter and form as principles of physical body.

Sicut autem uniuscuiusque generis determinati sunt quaedam communia principia, quae se extendunt ad omnia principia illius generis, ita et omnia entia secundum quod in ente communicant, habent quaedam principia, quae sunt principia omnium entium; quae quidem principia possunt dici communia dupliciter secundum Avicennam in sua *Sufficientia* (I,2). Uno modo, *per praedicationem* sicut cum dico "forma est commune ad omnes formas," quia de qualibet praedicatur. Alio modo *per causalitatem*, sicut dicimus solem unum numero esse principium ad omnia generabilia. Omnium autem entium sunt communia principia non solum secundum primum modum, quod appellat Philosophus in *Metaph.*, omnia entia habere eadem principia *secundum analogiam*, sed etiam secundum modum secundum, ut sint quaedam res

2 *In Boethii de trin.*, q. 5, a. 4.

eaedem numero existentes omnium rerum principia, prout scilicet principia accidentium reducuntur in principia substantiae et principia substantiarum corruptibilium
in substantias incorruptibiles, et sic quodam gradu et ordine in quaedam principia
omnia reducuntur.[3]

We notice that the reduction in the order of predication is here called
analogy whereas that in the order of causality is not. Analogy, and this
is surely no surprise, designates the way certain things can be said of
many. With respect to the order of causality, we will remember from
Chapter VII that the first cause can be called an analogical one, but
this is to speak of the cause in terms of the way something can be predicated of it and its effect. This can entail, we recall, a reversal of the real
order, for the cause may be named from its effect. The analogy of names
always means a proportion or relation of one thing to another in terms
of the notions signified by a name common to both. It will be quite
accidental if what is the primary signification of the name is also primary in reality, since the order of the name is dependent on knowability
for us and not on the degree of perfection in reality. That is why the
sciences concerned with the *principia rerum* do not settle their proper
task by distinguishing the intentions of a common name; they must go
beyond the relations among *rationes* to the things themselves. Nothing
in the mode of signifying, as logical doctrine, can foretell what the
ontological situation will be, nor do the varieties of ontological situation
introduce differences into the logical doctrine.

But is it not legitimate to designate the real relation or proportion
of creature to God as an analogy and thereby to speak of an analogy
in the being of things? The question comes down to asking whether
or not "analogy" is an analogous name and, in agreeing that it is,
we become aware of how easy it is to think that the analogy of names
is a direct commentary on things as they exist. We have seen that the
ratio propria of "proportion" or "analogy" has nothing to do with modes
of signification, but with determinate quantitative relations. Thanks
to an extension of its meaning, it comes to signify any relation of one
thing to another, and the most frequent and familiar use of the term
in St Thomas concerns the proportion or relation of one thing to another
as they receive a common name. It is perfectly true that "analogy" may
mean the proportion or relation of effect to cause; however, it is extremely important to notice that in this way we can speak of the analogy or
proportion of an effect to a univocal cause. Indeed, "proportionate
effect" usually means the effect of a univocal cause. Notice furthermore

[3] *Ibid.*

that when we say that "analogy" is an analogous name, one of its analogates (the analogy of names) explains the mode of signification of the common term "analogy." "Analogy" is an analogous name, not according to the *ratio propria* of "analogy" (determinate quantitative relations), but according to an extended meaning having to do with modes of signification. Thus not every use of "analogy" involves the analogy of names, but most texts in St Thomas which figure in discussions of analogy have to do with the analogy of names and this, as is amply clear, is purely and simply a logical intention. Thus, just as an analogy or proportionality which may or may not give rise to an analogous name is involved in a certain kind of argument, so too we can speak of real relations as proportions, but such proportions do not entail that the things thus related are named analogically. Most importantly, if we call a real relation among things named analogically an analogy, we must not confuse the two orders of predication and causality. The text we quoted a moment ago shows how careful St Thomas is to distinguish them.

This then is our interpretation: the analogy of names is, for St Thomas, a logical intention and in speaking of it we must observe the general rule that the logical and real orders must not be confused. It is our hope that the interpretation has been so presented that its fundamental accuracy is clear and that criticism and development of it will be facilitated.

TABLE OF TEXTS CITED

The purpose of this appendix is to facilitate the reader's checking to see which texts have been cited in the study and where a comment on their contents *may* be found. No attempt has been made to distinguish between texts which are merely cited and those which are the object of long or short commentary. The nature of the appendix is dictated by the nature of the preceding study. While our purpose has been to attempt a textual analysis of St Thomas, we have not adopted the methodology of first setting forth every text in which *analogia* or some derivitive of it is found in St Thomas and then seeking divisions. A number of approaches to the problem of the analogy of names in the texts of St Thomas underlie the interpretation we have presented, but we have thought it better to spare the reader the vagaries of our personal history. Having become convinced that "to be named analogically" is on the same level as "to be named equivocally" or "to be named univocally," we have tried to arrange our material in such a way that the proper location of the problem of the analogy of names should be made clear and, with that clear, how the various divisions of analogy which have been proposed – many of them with a seeming basis in the texts of St Thomas – amount to a hybrid consideration. The construction of the following table was of interest to the author, for it enabled him to see which texts he had actually made use of in presenting his interpretation. He was struck by the fact that many texts which might have been mentioned do not occur in his references and considered adding other texts to his notes. However, since the texts which might thus have been added are, for the most part, parallels to those actually cited, and since the works to which reference are made list these parallels, such additions were not made. But of course many things which occurred at the time the following table could be made, possibilities of tightening the argument by a more rigorous mode of speech, of bolstering it by the inclusion of discussions of texts which seemingly threaten the interpretation, the addition of a section devoted to the *ratio communis* of the analogous name against the background of Scotus* – all these had to be set aside. Perhaps only the author can be fully aware of the imperfections of a book. Nevertheless, since the fundamental argument of the book, that the analogy of names is a logical intention, with all the consequences of that truth, seems unassailable on the basis of the texts, those cited and those not cited, it seems permissable to hope that the inadequacies of this study can be removed in the future either by the author or those wiser than he.

The appendix is divided into two parts. First a list of the editions of the works of St Thomas which have been used is given, a list which follows the same order as the table itself. That order is not the possible chronological order in which St Thomas wrote the works in question, nor is it based on a division between philosophical and theological works. Rather it moves from works which were occasioned directly by the works of others, commentaries, expositions, etc., to those which may be called independent works. No particular significance is intended by the choice of this order. These then are the editions of the works of St Thomas which we have used in our study.

---

* cf. "The *ratio communis* of the Analogous Name," to appear in *Laval théologique et philosophique*.

1. THE EDITIONS USED

(a) P. F. Angeli M. Pirotta, O.P., *In Aristotelis Librum DE ANIMA Commentarium*, Taurini: Marietti, 1948. (References to this work are made in the following way. *In I de anima*, lect. 1, n. 13 refers to paragraph thirteen of the first lesson of the commentary on the first book of Aristotle's work.)

(b) R. M. Spiazzi, O.P., *In Aristotelis libros PERI HERMENEIAS et POSTERIORUM ANALYTICORUM Expositio*, Cum textu ex recensione leonina, Taurini: Marietti, 1955. (The scholastics divided *On Interpretation* into two books; consequently a typical reference to the first of these is: *In I Periherm.*, lect. 5, n. 15. A typical reference to the commentary on the *Posterior Analytics* is: *In I Post. Analyt.*, lect. 12, n. 8.)

(c) R. M. Spiazzi, O.P., *In Aristotelis libros DE COELO ET MUNDO, DE GENERATIONE ET CORRUPTIONE, METEOROLOGICORUM Expositio*, Cum textu ex recensione leonina. Taurini: Marietti, 1952. (Use was made only of the first two of these, and typical references are: *In I de coelo*, lect. 7, n. 6; *In I de gen. et cor.*, lect. 20, n. 2.)

(d) R. M. Spiazzi, O.P., *In Aristotelis libros De sensu et sensato, De memoria et reminiscentia Commentarium*. Taurini: Marietti, 1949. (References only to the first of these; e.g. *In de sensu et sensato*, lect. 7, n. 98.)

(e) *In Octo Libros Physicorum Aristotelis Commentarium*, in *Opera Omnia S. Thomae De Aquino*, iussu impensaque Leonis XIII, P.M. edita, Romae, Vol. II. (References made in the following manner: *In II Physic.*, lect. 11, n. 2.)

(f) R. M. Spiazzi, O.P., *In Decem Libros ETHICORUM ARISTOTELIS AD NICOMACHUM Expositio*. Taurini: Marietti, 1949. (A typical reference is: *In I Ethic.*, lect. 7, n. 96.)

(g) M. R. Cathala, O.P. et R. M. Spiazzi, O.P., *In Duodecim Libros METAPHYSICORUM ARISTOTELIS Expositio*. Taurini: Marietti, 1950. (References are either to the *proemium* of the commentary or in the following fashion: *In IV Metaphys.*, lect. 4, n. 576.)

(h) M. Calcaterra, O.P., *In Boetium De Trinitate et De Hebdomadibus Expositio* in *Opuscula Theologica S. Thomae Aquinatis*, Vol. II. Taurini: Marietti, 1954. (With respect to the first work, we cite it according to the older division also given by Calcaterra: e.g. *In Boethii de trin.*, q. 4, a. 2. *Unless otherwise indicated, all such references are to the body of the article*: this warning is to be applied wherever a work of St Thomas is divided into articles where the *corpus articuli* is preceded by objections and followed by replies to those objections. For questions five and six of the exposition of the *De trinitate*, Calcaterra has made use of Paul Wyser, O.P., *Thomas von Aquin In librum Boethii de Trinitate, Quaestiones quinta et sexta*. Friburg-Louvain, 1948. References to the second exposition of Boethius are made thus: *In Boethii de hebdomadibus*, lect. 2.)

(i) C. Pera, O.P., *In librum beati Dionysii de divinis nominibus*, cum introductione historica Petri Caramello et synthesi doctrinali Caroli Mazzantini. Taurini: Marietti, 1950. (References are made in this way: *In de divinis nominibus*, lect. 5, n. 735.)

(j) R. Cai, O.P., *Super Epistolas Sancti Pauli Lectura*. Taurini: Marietti, 1953. 2 vols. (The only reference is: *In Ephesios*, cap. 3, lect. 4.)

(k) H. D. Saffrey, O.P., *Super librum de causis expositio*. Friburg, 1954. (References either to *proemium* or to comments on various propositions in this way: *In librum de causis*, 4a.)

(l) Mandonnet et Moos, *Scriptum Super Libros Sententiarum Magistri Petri Lombardi*. 4 vols. Parisiis, 1929. (References to this work tend to become quite complex. *In I Sent.*, d. 19, q. 5, a. 2, ad 1, refers to the commentary on the first book, distinction nineteen, question five, article two, the answer to the first objection. Sometimes articles are further divided into *quaestiunculae*. References may also be made to the *divisio textus* and the *expositio textus* which precede and follow St Thomas' division into questions and articles.)

(m) *Sancti Thomae Aquinatis Summa Theologiae*, cura Fratrum Ordinis Praedicatorum. Matriti: Biblioteca de Autores Cristianos, 1955. (This edition includes the Leonine text. Sample reference: *IaIIae*, q. 61, a. 1. The *Summa* is divided into three parts, the second part into a first and second subpart; there is as well *Supplementum* devised to complete the work's original plan by bringing together other writings of St Thomas.)

(n) *Summa Contra Gentiles, Editio Leonina Manualis*. Romae: Apud Sedem Commisionis Leoninae, 1934. (Typical reference: *I Contra Gentiles*, cap. 34, refers to thirty-fourth chapter of first book.)

(o) *Compendium Theologiae ad Fratrem Reginaldum*, cura et studio R. Verardo, O.P., in Vol. I, *Opuscula Theologica*. Taurini: Marietti, 1954.

(p) R. M. Spiazzi, O.P., *Quaestiones Quodlibetales*. Taurini: Marietii, 1949. (*Quodl. II*, q. 2, a. 1 refers to the body of the first article of question two, of the second quodlibetal question.)

(q) I. Sestili, *Opusculum De ente et essentia*. Taurini: Marietti, 1948. (References are to the chapter divisions of this edition.)

(r) *Opusculum De principiis naturae*, in *Opuscula Philosophica*. Taurini: Marietti, 1954.

(s) *Quaestiones Disputatae*. 2 vols. Taurini: Marietti, 1949. The following are contained in the second volume:
    (1) R. P. Pession, O.P., *De potentia Dei*. (Reference is made in this way: *Q.D. de pot.*, q. 7, a. 7. Remember the caution made in item (h) above.)
    (2) Calcaterra et Centi, O.P., *De anima*. (Since there is but one question here, references cite only article and, when the *corpus articuli* is not meant, the answer to a numbered objection.)
    (3) Calcaterra et Centi, O.P., *De spiritualibus creaturis*. (Again, there is but one question.)
    (4) Calcaterra et Centi, O.P., *De unione verbi incarnati*. (Again, but one question.)
    (5) Bazzi et Pession, O.P., *De malo*. (E.g. *Q.D. de malo*, q. 5, a. 5.)
    (6) P. A. Odetto, *De virtutibus in communi*. (One question.)
    R. M. Spiazzi, O.P., *De veritate*. (This work fills the entire first volume of the edition cited. A sample reference is this: *Q.D. de ver.*, q. 24, a. 6.)

2. TABLE OF TEXTS CITED

INDEX RERUM ET NOMINUM

(1)

DATE DUE

DEC 31 '81			